THE PARADOX OF INTENTION

Reaching the Goal by Giving Up the Attempt to Reach It

AAR

American Academy of Religion
Studies in Religion

Number 48
THE PARADOX OF INTENTION
Reaching the Goal by Giving Up
the Attempt to Reach It
by
Marvin C. Shaw

THE PARADOX OF INTENTION
Reaching the Goal by Giving Up the Attempt to Reach It

by
Marvin C. Shaw

Scholars Press
Atlanta, Georgia

THE PARADOX OF INTENTION
Reaching the Goal by Giving Up the Attempt to Reach It

by
Marvin C. Shaw

Library of Congress Cataloging in Publication Data

Shaw, Marvin C.
The paradox of intention : reaching the goal by giving up the attempt to reach it / by Marvin C. Shaw.
p. cm. -- (Studies in religion / American Academy of Religion ; no. 48)
ISBN 1-555-40109-0 (alk. paper). ISBN 1-555-30110-4 (pbk. : alk. paper)
1. Goal (Philosophy) 2. Renunciation (Philosophy) 3. Intentionality (Philosophy) 4. Paradox. I. Title. II. Series: Studies in religion (American Academy of Religion) ; no. 48.
B105.G63S48 1987
128--dc19 87-29488

Printed in the United States of America

CONTENTS

ACKNOWLEDGMENTS

For help in the completion of this study, I am thankful to the late Professor Horace Leland Friess of Columbia University; Rev. Frederick Carl Kuether of the American Foundation of Religion and Psychiatry; my wife Jeanne Paul Shaw; and Caroline M. Zimmerman, Nanci N. Brug, Joseph J. DeSalvo, and Joseph Mangiantini of Montana State University.

Chapter 1

INTRODUCTION: THE ETHIC OF CONSOLATION AND ITS PARADOX: REACHING THE GOAL BY GIVING UP THE ATTEMPT TO REACH IT

If any man cannot grasp the matter, let him be idle and the matter will grasp him.

—Heinrich Suso
The Exemplar

One does not discover the absurd without being tempted to write a manual of happiness.

—Albert Camus
The Myth of Sisyphus

This book is a study of a single, simple idea, that of reaching a goal by giving up the attempt to reach it. The difficulty which some readers may have in understanding this is not caused by any complexity or abstractness in the concept, but by the fact that it seems contrary to common sense and everyday practice. Normally, we assume that goals are reached through the expenditure of mental and physical effort, and the so-called paradox of intention strikes us as perhaps intriguing, as some sort of mental puzzle, but finally as illogical and unavailing. Now if this or any other difficulty arises, and the point of what you are reading escapes you, you have an opportunity to put into practice this paradoxical method we are attempting to understand. Simply take the advice of the medieval Christian mystic Suso quoted above, let go of the effort to grasp the meaning, read on, and the meaning which evades you may well arise on its own.

Presenting the idea in this way may remove some of the foreignness which at first attaches to anything paradoxical, and it may now occur to you that, without much self-consciousness about it, you have already experienced its validity and power. The everydayness of the paradox of intention is shown in these lines of the great American psychologist William James (1842-1910) in which he is discussing some observations of his fellow psychologist Edwin D. Starbuck.

You know how it is when you try to recollect a forgotten name. Usually

> you help the recall by working for it, by mentally running over the places, persons, and things with which the word was connected. But sometimes this effort fails; you feel then as if the harder you tried the less hope there would be, as though the name were *jammed*, and pressure in its direction only kept it all the more from rising. And then the opposite expedient often succeeds. Give up the effort entirely; think of something altogether different, and in half an hour the lost name comes sauntering into your mind, as Emerson says, as carelessly as if it had never been invited. A certain music teacher, says Dr. Starbuck, says to her pupils after the thing to be done has been clearly pointed out, and unsuccessfully attempted: "Stop trying and it will do itself!"[1]

We have had just this experience of finding that effort blocked our success while relaxation of effort succeeded, without of course complicating matters by calling it a manifestation of the paradox of intention.

In fact, when our action is at its best and we have achieved real proficiency and expertness in something, it has the character of being flowing or self-moving. When we are doing our best, in a sense, we act without acting. Starbuck gives the examples of athletic and artistic performance.

> An athlete . . . sometimes awakens suddenly to an understanding of the fine points of the game and to a real enjoyment of it, just as the convert awakens to an appreciation of religion. If he keeps on engaging in the sport, there may come a day when all at once the game plays itself through him — when he loses himself in some great contest. In the same way, a musician may suddenly reach a point at which pleasure in the technique of the art entirely falls away, and in some moment of inspiration he becomes the instrument through which music flows.[2]

When we are adroit and skillful, we find that we have let go of the intensity of effort. Relating this to religious conversion introduces a new and intriguing element to which we must return.

At this point, however, there is a possibility of misunderstanding. The danger is that getting the goal by giving up the attempt to get it may be taken as itself a technique, and a book devoted to a study of this idea then will appear as yet another self-help book. If the principle is rightly understood, it is a criticism and rejection of the idea that life is fulfilled through technique. Therefore, this is an "anti-self-help book," a book which maintains our problem is precisely that we approach ourselves as projects to be completed. The hunger and need manifest in the present rush hour of the manuals of happiness comes from an excess of concern about how life is managed and happiness

[1] William James, *The Varieties of Religious Experience* (New York: Random House, [1902]), 202.

[2] Edwin D. Starbuck, *Psychology of Religion*, 385, quoted in James, *Varieties*, 203.

contrived, and not merely from the fact that we haven't yet found the recipe suited to our temperament. Thus the words of Camus quoted at the beginning of this chapter are to be taken ironically, as he intended them. As we shall see, a manual of happiness is just what we do not need and, in fact, cannot have, for the claim we will be exploring is that the very idea of getting the goal through efforts renders those efforts counter-productive.

You will notice that the focus of our talk about the paradox of intention has been shifting. At first we were merely to recall that often a forgotten name returns to awareness when we give up the effort to dig it out of our memory by force. Now we find ourselves talking about the fulfillment of life as a whole; James and Starbuck were, in fact, most interested in the way in which the paradox of intention played a part in religious conversions of the evangelical Christian type. For many, the context in which the paradox of intention is most familiar is religion. We have no doubt heard that Buddhist sages make much of the fact that the desire-filled quest for enlightenment renders its achievement impossible. "As long as you seek Buddhahood, specifically exercising yourself for it," they say, "there is no attainment for you."[3] The corollary would then seem to be that the desired release arises of its own accord when efforts to grasp it are relaxed. Mystics, both Eastern and Western, are known for indulging in dark and paradoxical sayings of the sort that is our subject. For example, Johannes Eckhart (1260-1327), the medieval German Dominican, embodies the paradox of intention in many of his sermons. In a sermon titled "God Laughs and Plays," Eckhart quotes a fellow monk as saying in prayer:

> Sometimes I feel such a sweetness in my soul that I forget everything else — and myself too — and dissolve in thee. But when I try to catch it perfectly, O Lord, thou takest it away.[4]

That experience of God that comes when received as a gift flees when sought as an attainment and possession. The Buddhist and the Christian seem to agree at least regarding the paradox that effort blocks the religious quest and the abandonment of effort fulfills it.

But then one expects mystics and oriental wise men to say inscrutable things. What is sometimes not noticed is that the sayings of Jesus in the Gospels are full of paradoxes. Those who anxiously seek security and the satisfaction of their everyday needs are advised to be as thoughtless about these matters as are the lilies of the field.

[3] Yung-chia Ta-shih, *Cheng-tao Ke*, in Daisetz Teitaro Suzuki, *Manual of Zen Buddhism* (New York: Grove Press, 1960), 90.

[4] Johannes Eckhart, in *Meister Eckhart, a Modern Translation*, trans. Raymond B. Blakney (New York: Harper and Row, 1941), 145.

> But if God so clothes the grass which is alive in the field today and tomorrow is thrown into the oven, how much more will he clothe you, O men of little faith? And do not seek what you are to eat and what you are to drink, nor be of anxious mind. For all the nations of the world seek these things; and your Father knows that you need them. Instead, seek his kingdom, and these things shall be yours as well. (Luke 12.28-31, *R.S.V.*[5])

That carelessness about everyday matters that cannot be achieved by the energetic quest for security is received as a gift when participation in God's kingdom becomes foremost. Participation in God's kingdom seems to mean letting go of self-concern, the willingness to be expendable. "Whoever exalts himself will be humbled, and whoever humbles himself will be exalted." (Matt. 23.12, *R.S.V.*) The rule of God's kingdom is the reverse of what the world calls common sense.

> And they came to Capernaum; and when he was in the house he asked them, "What were you discussing on the way?" But they were silent; for on the way they had discussed with one another who was the greatest. And he sat down and called the twelve; and he said to them, "If any one would be first, he must be last of all and servant of all." (Mark 9.33-35, *R.S.V.*)

It thus becomes clear that the paradox of intention in the teaching of Jesus involves risk-taking and self-denial.

> And he called to him the multitude with his disciples, and said to them, "If any man would come after me, let him deny himself and take up his cross and follow me. For whoever would save his life will lose it; and whoever loses his life for my sake and the gospel's will save it. For what does it profit a man, to gain the whole world and forfeit his life?" (Mark 8.34-36, *R.S.V.*)

A kind of security arises when we abandon concern for security, and our lives are saved when we are willing to lose them. It remains to be seen whether we are to understand this as meaning we will be taken care of if we are careless of ourselves, or if it means we are, in fact, carefree when we accept our vulnerability and insecurity as inescapable in this life.

The paradox of intention, meaning a goal which could not be reached through effort comes to us when we let go of effort, has been discovered in everyday experience; further, in religion and philosophy it has been raised to the level of a precept about the fulfilling of life as a whole. We could then say, there are two general views of the role of

[5] *Holy Bible, Revised Standard Version* (Copyright, Division of Christian Education of the National Council of the Churches of Christ in the U.S.A., 1946, 1971).

human effort in the attainment of the good of human life, one corresponding to the common sense notion that goals are reached through effort, and the other embodying the paradox of intention. We can call the first "the ethic of attainment" because it sees the good of human life as, like any other goal, the outcome of human striving. Opposed to this is what we may call "the ethic of consolation," which begins with the despair of all human attempts to achieve the good. It insists that the good of human life is not an attainment at all, but is received, so to speak, as a gift when all attempts to achieve it are abandoned.

The paradoxically indirect approach to fulfillment contained within the ethic of consolation we may call "the law of the reversal of effort." This is the doctrine that the good of human life occurs not through the direct and active attempt to achieve it, but rather by giving up the attempt to achieve it. This term for the paradox of intention comes from Alan Watts, the popular interpreter of Buddhist thought.

> I have always been fascinated by the law of reversed effort. Sometimes I call it the "backwards law." When you try to stay on the surface of the water, you sink; but when you try to sink you float. When you hold your breath you lose it — which immediately calls to mind an ancient and much neglected saying, "Whosoever would save his soul shall lose it."[6]

According to the ethic of consolation in all of its philosophical and religious forms, fulfillment cannot be found through the successful attainment of the usual goals of wealth, power, acclaim, and control over our lives; but we are to take consolation for this failure and impossibility in finding a peace and fulfillment, which could not otherwise be found, by simply giving up self-effort. This state of acceptance, trust, openness, this sense of being at home in the universe, cannot by its very nature be the outcome of efforts; the pond cannot be forced to be still, but becomes still of its own accord when efforts cease. The goal then is not a matter of doing, but of being. Contrary to the logic of common sense, with its endless flow of "how-to manuals," *this* one goal is not an attainment, but a gift. However the condition in which gifts are received is one in which efforts to earn and attain are replaced by receptivity.

* * * * *

The present is a time of heightening of human self-consciousness, the culmination of a centuries-long process in which self-awareness has been intensified through the uniquely modern forms of autobiography, drama, and the novel, through the introspectiveness of idealist philosophy, and now in the "human sciences" of anthropology, sociology, and

[6] Alan W. Watts, *The Wisdom of Insecurity* (New York: Pantheon Books, 1951), 9.

psychology. We would therefore expect that if the reversal of effort idea is a universal theme, a recurrent discovery, it would come to explicit awareness in a time such as ours.

In the early years of this century, a number of the new empirical psychologists turned their attention to the psychology of religion, and working within an American religious context they became interested in the psychology of dramatic religious conversion as it occurs in evangelistic meetings. Most important among these early psychologists of religion were Edwin D. Starbuck, William James, George A. Coe, and James H. Leuba. Starbuck's *Psychology of Religion* (1899) made clear the association of religious conversion with the paradox of intention, and James' *The Varieties of Religious Experience* (1902) developed this theme and drew together the insights of the new inquiry and thus may be taken as representative.

James' personal life is very relevant to understanding his study of religious psychology. As a medical student and physiologist in the 1860s James absorbed the world view of "mechanistic materialism." In this perspective, nature is a self-sustaining system of matter and energy in which the growth of order is due to the workings of chance; but in the process of the evolution of ever higher order, there is a great waste of individuals. The world is thus depicted as devoid of any care for human hopes and aspirations, and as only accidentally and grudgingly supportive of human physical needs. This world-view also implied to James that mind is simply an epiphenomenal by-product of the material process, just as the foam is an insignificant side effect of the waves. The mind is wholly conditioned and determined by its material basis in this way of seeing things and is no more able to affect consequences within the world than is the foam able to influence the waves. James shared the dilemma of many late nineteenth century intellectuals in that he was intellectually convinced of this view, but emotionally discontented with it. The problem is, how can one accept and affirm such a universe?

James liked to tell this story.

> "I accept the universe" is reported to have been a favorite utterance of our New England transcendentalist, Margaret Fuller; and when some one repeated this phrase to Thomas Carlyle, his sardonic comment is said to have been: "Gad! She'd better!"[7]

But James went on to point out there is a difference in accepting the universe grudgingly and unforgivingly, making a virtue out of a necessity, and accepting it enthusiastically and with serenity. For James, the

[7] James, *Varieties*, 41.

problem would be to find a way of belief that would make this latter kind of affirmation possible.

James' movement toward a different form of belief is related to a personal crisis. In a letter to Tom Ward in October, 1868, James described himself as poisoned by his philosophical outlook and as contemplating suicide; he states he admires Ward's healthy minded sense of a purpose in living.[8] In a moment of crisis, the sense of aimlessness in James' life and his powerlessness to effect a change rose to the level of panic.

> Whilst in this state of philosophic pessimism and general depression of spirits about my prospects, I went one evening into a dressing-room in the twilight to procure some article that was there; when suddenly there fell upon me without any warning, just as if it came out of the darkness, a horrible fear of my own existence. Simultaneously there arose in my mind the image of an epileptic patient whom I had seen in the asylum, a black-haired youth with greenish skin, entirely idiotic, who used to sit all day on one of the benches, or rather shelves against the wall, with his knees drawn up against his chin, and the coarse gray undershirt, which was his only garment, drawn over them enclosing his entire figure. He sat there like a sort of sculptured Egyptian cat or Peruvian mummy, moving nothing but his black eyes and looking absolutely non-human. This image and my fear entered into a species of combination with each other. *That shape am I*, I felt, potentially. Nothing that I possess can defend me against that fate, if the hour for it should strike for me as it struck for him. There was such a horror of him, and such a perception of my own merely momentary discrepancy from him, that it was as if something hitherto solid within my breast gave way entirely, and I became a mass of quivering fear. After this the universe was changed for me altogether. I awoke morning after morning with a horrible dread at the pit of my stomach, and with a sense of the insecurity of life that I never knew before, and that I have never felt since. It was like a revelation; and although the immediate feelings passed away, the experience has made me sympathetic with the morbid feelings of others ever since. It gradually faded, but for months I was unable to go out into the dark alone.
>
> In general I dreaded to be left alone. I remember wondering how other people could live, how I myself had ever lived, so unconscious of the pit of insecurity beneath the surface of life.[9]

Ralph B. Perry, the biographer of James, relates this panic to the "ebbing of the will to live." James' materialism could not save him

[8] Ralph Barton Perry, *The Thought and Character of William James* (Boston: Little Brown, 1935) 1:286-287.

[9] The experience is described in *The Varieties of Religious Experience*, 157-158, where it is attributed to "an anonymous French correspondent." James' son identified the experience as that of William James and dated it in the spring of 1870; Gay W. Allen, *William James, a Biography* (New York: Viking Press, 1967), 165.

from the feeling of pointlessness in life because it lacked a vision of human purposes as participating in a cosmic purpose.[10] Of course there were no doubt deeper roots to his experience, but his philosophical outlook was of no assistance in counteracting the tendencies of his temperament. James' later writings do show he felt this to be an inadequacy in materialism. In addition I suggest this crisis shows a second inadequacy in materialism as perceived by James, and that is its view that the will is determined and the mind is epiphenomenal. For if we are unfree, then we are mere spectators at the growth of our own neurotic symptoms and our final suicide or insanity; but if we are free, we can counteract these tendencies. It is as if James' question were, "Can I choose to live, or is my despair the first sign of a determined psychological process which will end in self-death?" A typically Jamesian view of the situation would say, if we assume the epiphenomenal view of mind, then we are more likely to give in to our despair and the obsessive thought of suicide, than if we assume we are free.

This interpretation of James' crisis is born out in his own diary entries for the period. His recovery is related to the reading of Charles Renouvier's *Essais*. Here James discovers the defense of free will as "the sustaining of a thought because I choose to when I might have other thoughts."[11] James perceived the issue in his crisis as the choice between giving in to despair or affirming a life of moral effort.

> Today I about touched bottom, and perceive plainly that I must face the choice with open eyes: shall I *frankly* throw the moral business overboard, as one unsuited to my innate aptitudes, or shall I follow it, and it alone, making everything else merely stuff for it.[12]

This last phrase can be taken as a statement of James' philosophical aim: a world view is to be developed that provides a sustaining and encouraging basis for the life of moral effort.

So James constructed a philosophy of free will, and he affirmed belief in an evolving, struggling God who requires our strenuous efforts in the perfecting of a growing, unfinished world. Belief in the finite, evolving God overcame the first felt inadequacy of materialism mentioned above; for if such a God exists, our striving may be part of a cosmic struggle, thus gaining meaning and a chance of success. Belief in free will counteracted for James the second inadequacy in materialism, its deterministic view of the self. Both beliefs are affirmed through "the will to believe" because they are necessary to encourage

[10] Perry, *Thought and Character of James*, 322-323.

[11] *Ibid.*, 323.

[12] *Ibid.*

life-affirmation and to energize effort after personal growth and social progress.

The point in mentioning James' crisis and his resolution of it is not to condemn materialism or to recommend James' alternative. It is merely to show how his own approach to moral and religious life is a typical example of the Victorian, will-centered attitude. In James' opinion, there is no decisive evidence for either free will or a God, finite or otherwise; both are affirmed because they are required by "the strenuous mood" of nineteenth century moralism and progressivism. This shows the poignant irony of James' interest in the idea of fulfillment through letting go of effort.

The free exercise of the will in energetic moral effort is James' way of affirming life and of counteracting recurrent moods of despair. It is understandable that such a disciple of the strenuous mood would be fascinated by and drawn to the idea which he encountered in his studies of the psychology of religion, that one may come to "accept the universe" with serenity through the very different way of surrender. For the same reason, James was intrigued by the new "mind-cure" movement manifest in Christian Science and a variety of related late nineteenth century tendencies. Being himself what he called a "sick soul" who must be "twice born" to come to affirm life, he was puzzled by the "healthy minded" who seemingly denied the reality of evil and darkness. He concluded that such a view of life is fine as long as it works, but it may easily break down in the face of tragedy and melancholy. To him the most complete religions would be those that admit the truth about the world as it is revealed in experiences of anxiety and despair, teaching us to overcome this rather than deny it. For James, Christianity and Buddhism, "the religions of deliverance," are truest and deepest because they center on despair and rebirth.

Nevertheless, James concluded that the healthy mindedness of the mind-cure movement and the crisis of rebirth cultivated in Protestant conversion were both predicated on the same paradox of surrender.

> On the whole, one is struck by a psychological similarity between the mind-cure movement and the Lutheran and Wesleyan movements. To the believer in moralism and works, with his anxious query, "What shall I do to be saved?" Luther and Wesley replied: "You are saved now, if you would but believe it." And the mind-curers come with precisely similar words of emancipation. They speak, it is true, to persons for whom the conception of salvation has lost its ancient theological meaning, but who labor nevertheless with the same eternal human difficulty. *Things are wrong with them*; and "What shall I do to be clear, right, sound, whole, well?" is the form of their question. And the answer is: "You *are* well,

sound, and clear already, if you did but know it."[13]

Both mind-cure and Christian conversion are based on the assurance that effort is unnecessary because the solution to our life problem is already at hand, either in the form of God's offer of forgiveness for sin or in the fact that the real self is perfect and only suffers due to its ignorance of this.

> Now the history of Lutheran salvation by faith, of Methodistic conversions, and of what I call the mind-cure movement seems to prove the existence of numerous persons in whom — at any rate at a certain stage in their development — a change of character for the better, so far from being facilitated by the rules laid down by official moralists, will take place all the more successfully if those rules be exactly reversed. Official moralists advise us never to relax our strenuousness. "Be vigilant, day and night," they adjure us; "hold your passive tendencies in check; shrink from no effort; keep your will like a bow always bent." But the persons I speak of find that all this conscious effort leads to nothing but failure and vexation in their hands, and only makes them twofold more the children of hell they were before. The tense and voluntary attitude becomes in them an impossible fever and torment. Their machinery refuses to run at all when the bearings are made so hot and the belts so tight.
>
> Under these circumstances the way to success, as vouched for by innumerable authentic personal narrations, is by an anti-moralistic method, by surrender. . . . Passivity, not activity; relaxation, not intentness, should be now the rule. Give up the feeling of responsibility, let go your hold, resign the care of your destiny to higher powers, be genuinely indifferent as to what becomes of it all, and you will find not only that you gain a perfect inward relief, but often also, in addition, the particular goods you sincerely thought you were renouncing. This is salvation through self-despair, the dying to be truly born, of Lutheran theology, the passage into *nothing* of which Jacob [Boehme] writes. To get it, a critical point must usually be passed, a corner turned within one. Something must give way, a native hardness must break down and liquefy; and this event . . . is frequently sudden and automatic, and leaves on the subject an impression that he has been wrought on by an external power.
>
> The mind-curers have given the widest scope to this sort of experience. They have demonstrated that a form of regeneration by relaxing, by letting go, psychologically indistinguishable from the Lutheran justification by faith and the Wesleyan acceptance of free grace, is within the reach of persons who have no conviction of sin and care nothing for the Lutheran theology. It is but giving your little private convulsive self a rest, and finding that a greater Self is there. [14]

What interests James is that what he calls "salvation by relaxation" or

[13] James, *Varieties*, 106.
[14] *Ibid.*, 107-108.

"regeneration by letting go" does not require as its premise the pessimistic view of the self as helpless sinner, *unable* to achieve through effort; for in mind-cure optimism as opposed to evangelical conversion, the point is merely that you *need not* seek to achieve through effort because you are already perfect. This recurrence of the paradox of intention in belief-systems which are very different will be a concern at many points in our study.

Reflections of this sort led James to the conclusion that reaching peace and affirmation through letting go was compatible with a variety of different beliefs and could be explained in a number of ways. In a footnote, he suggested three types of explanation.

> The theistic explanation is by divine grace, which creates a new nature within one the moment the old nature is sincerely given up. The pantheistic explanation (which is that of most mind-curers) is by the merging of the narrower private self into the wider or greater self, the spirit of the universe (which is your own 'subconscious' self), the moment the isolating barriers of mistrust and anxiety are removed. The medico-materialistic explanation is that simpler cerebral processes act more freely where they are left to act automatically by the shunting-out of physiologically . . . 'higher' ones which, seeking to regulate, only succeed in inhibiting results.[15]

The theistic and the pantheistic explanations posit different views of God as either transcendent of the world or as wholly immanent within it, and they are thus mutually exclusive in James' view; but either might be compatible with the naturalistic view.

James was sympathetic to Starbuck's explanation, feeling that it was compatible with his own belief in God. This explanation was based largely on reports from revival meetings and rescue missions, and therefore it centers on moral change and the emergence of a "better self." In this view, the troubled self is the so-far-developed and consciously known aspect of the person. Therefore, conscious, willful efforts on the part of the present self cannot give rise to a new consciousness free of the troubles and problems of the sick soul. Unconsciously a new, more constructive, responsible, and mature set of attitudes are forming through a variety of influences, including the learning involved in observing that one's present life doesn't work. When in despair the mastery of the present organization of the personality is finally relaxed, that which was forming subliminally may emerge. In this way one is reborn not through moral effort, but through the relaxation of effort.

> "Man's extremity is God's opportunity" is the theological way of putting

[15] *Ibid.*, 109-110, footnote.

> this fact of the need of self-surrender; whilst the physiological way of stating it would be, "let one do all in one's power, and one's nervous system will do the rest." Both statements acknowledge the same fact.[16]

We may well find that the problem to which letting go is the solution is not always, or even usually, "moral reform," but what is of interest here is the attempt of Starbuck and James to see the process as universally human and understandable.

Even if "salvation by relaxation" is open to naturalistic explanation, James believed that this explanation is compatible with belief in real divine influence in the unconscious birth of the new self. The mere fact that the reversal of effort appears as a universal human experience led the early psychologists of religion to conclude that the process is not dependent on a single, privileged set of religious beliefs. This is implied within James' claim of the similarity of Christian Science and evangelistic conversion. James quotes Coe, with approval, to the effect that what is important in the process of conversion is "what is attained" in the way of affirmation of life and personal growth. James therefore goes on to accept Leuba's conclusion that the power of reversed effort does not depend on Christian beliefs, but rather the subjective certainty of belief was due to the association of these beliefs with the sense of liberation and transformation which accompany letting go. One was formerly fearful and defensive, but now opens outward in trust, and this is understandably expressed in beliefs about the experience of God or oneness with the soul of the universe.

> The transition from tenseness, self-responsibility, and worry, to equanimity, receptivity, and peace, is the most wonderful of all those shiftings of inner equilibrium, those changes of the personal center of energy, which I have analyzed so often; and the chief wonder of it is that it so often comes about, not by doing but by simply relaxing and throwing the burden down. This abandonment of self-responsibility seems to be the fundamental act in specifically religious, as distinguished from moral practice. It antedates theologies and is independent of philosophies. Mind-cure, theosophy, stoicism, ordinary neurological hygiene, insist on it as emphatically as Christianity does, and it is capable of entering into closest marriage with every speculative creed.[17]

Note the contrast between moralistic change through will power, and rebirth through letting go.

James' acceptance of the independence of the paradox of intention from any particular belief-system is seen further in his use of the following two cases as examples of conversions. He regards the conver-

[16] *Ibid.*, 208.
[17] *Ibid.*, 284.

sion of the Russian novelist Leo Tolstoi from a condition of despondency to a new life as being based on ethical insight rather than religious belief. Tolstoi had been preoccupied with the meaninglessness of his life as an aristocrat and a successful writer. After returning to the Russian Orthodox faith of his childhood, Tolstoi moved on to a religious position that involved the rejection of belief in the divinity of Jesus and the personal, supernatural God. He found release from his sense of the emptiness of his personal life in the discovery of the ethical teaching of Jesus, "Resist not evil" (Matt. 5.39). As Tolstoi understood this, if we offer no opposition to that which opposes and threatens our aims, we are actually renouncing concern for self and commencing to live a life of service to others and to the life-force. In this letting go of self-concern, including the concern for the meaning of one's personal life, Tolstoi found a sense of fulfillment that he could not grasp through seeking it.

Secondly, James mentions elsewhere the case of the French philosopher Jouffroy who was released from torturing doubt about religious beliefs when he simply let go and admitted that he was no longer a believer. That sense of settlement and resolution, which could not be achieved through the effort to prop up traditional beliefs and crank up an affirmative attitude toward them, arose on its own when he let go. Jouffroy found freedom from doubt in skepticism, as did the ancient philosophers who first recommended this path and gave it its name. Here, peace arises through the reversal of effort in the case of a conversion from religion.

The point here is not that it doesn't matter what you believe, for James' personal attitude was precisely the opposite. For James, the active, creative, affirmative style of life was possible only if we believe it is part of a cosmic process of growth in which God participates and we are co-workers with the divine. His agreement with Coe and Leuba is merely that what is important in various instances of what he called "salvation by relaxation" is the outcome. This is precisely the point of his idea of the will to believe, that we are justified in our belief because of its result in affirmation and action.

This sketch of James as a man and as a representative of early psychological efforts to grasp the elusive paradox of intention and its role in the fulfillment of life will serve as an introduction to the terrain over which the following study will attempt to pass. For in his story we have seen that the paradox of intention, in at least some instances, is related to the experience of despair; that it leads to the end of defensive insularity and to an affirmation of and opening outward toward life; that it results in a new vigor, freedom, and carelessness in action; that it is compatible with a variety of different beliefs; and that it involves a total reorientation of the self.

* * * * *

A word should be said about the arrangement of this study as a whole. In the first part, five examples of ancient and modern embodiments of the paradox of intention are encountered. These are four ancient, classical religious or philosophical texts, *The Manual* of the Stoic philosopher Epictetus, the letters of Paul the Apostle, the *Tao Teh Ching* of Lao Tzu, and the *Dohakosha* of the Buddhist sage Saraha; the modern representative is the existentialist psychotherapist Viktor Frankl. (The thought of the philosopher Martin Heidegger provides a second modern example of the paradox, but discussion of this is postponed until the second part of the study for a reason which will become apparent later.)

The second part of the study seeks to "unscrew the inscrutable," to understand the law of the reversal of effort, by raising a series of questions about it and following these wherever they may lead. The questions dealt with are: (1) What experiences lead to the recurrent discovery of the paradox of intention? (2) To what problem is it supposed to be the solution? (3) Does letting go of self-effort mean passivity? Is it the life-style called "dropping-out?" (4) Isn't the reversal of effort a sign of weakness, incapacity, or even self-destructiveness? (5) Since it is found in connection with many belief-systems and even apart from religious or philosophical doctrines altogether, what is its relation to the beliefs that are used to express and undergird it? (6) How should we understand the process of letting go itself? Is it an act of will, something you do?

Each of the four classical expressions of the ethic of consolation to be taken up in the next four chapters will be found to include three things. Firstly, each includes an attack on some form of the ethic of attainment current in its world as necessarily futile and, in fact, leading away from the goal of life's fulfillment. Secondly, each substitutes for this some form of the paradox of intention, the claim that the goal is reached by giving up the attempt to reach it. And thirdly, each undergirds the paradox of intention with a particular belief-system; claims about the nature of reality are offered that show just why effort fails and which assure us that letting go of effort must succeed. Because of the presence of these three themes within each text, each chapter will begin with an overview of the doctrine of the text, will continue with an examination of the attack made on the ethic of attainment, and will conclude with a statement of the particular way in which the law of reversed effort is presented.

Emphasis in dealing with the four ancient texts is placed on frequent quotation so that the reader may end with some feeling of familiarity with the sources themselves. No assumption is made that the reader has prior historical or philosophical knowledge, and so the exposition may repeat what is well known to some. In these four chapters, comments, comparisons, and criticisms are minimized so that the texts can speak for themselves. Yet, the study of these texts is not comprehensive, but is only sufficient to show the particular way in which they bear within them the paradox of intention; each text contains much else besides this, and one cannot assume an understanding of, say, Stoicism or Paul, merely from a reading of these chapters. Lastly, all of the sources are polemical and argumentative, intending in one way or another to attack a form of the ethic of attainment; the views opposed are not presented by our texts with either completeness or fairness, and it is not wise to try to learn about an opinion mainly from its critics. Thus, for example, one cannot assume to have understood Judaism or Confucianism from the criticisms made of them by Paul or the *Tao Teh Ching* respectively.

Throughout, an attempt has been made to be clear and explicit. But clarity is deceptive, for nothing worthwhile in this area of inquiry can be as clear as a sentence about it. Perhaps the reason really profound writers write so obscurely is both to not falsify the unyielding mysteriousness that surrounds the most important questions and to not sound merely inspirational. For this reason this introduction must end with the Japanese proverb, "If you believe everything you read, better not read."

Part One:
The Law of the Reversal of Effort in Ancient and Modern Thought

Chapter 2

THE MANUAL OF EPICTETUS: IF YOU WANT WHAT YOU GET, YOU WILL GET WHAT YOU WANT

> We must abstain from the will to get, and not attempt any of those things which are not in our power.
>
> —attributed to Epictetus
> *Marcus Aurelius* 11.37

The Manual of Epictetus represents a concise summary of ancient Stoic ethics and was probably compiled by Arrius, a student of Epictetus, as a means of popularizing the Stoic message. Epictetus had been a slave, but we are assured that he came to be regarded as a philosopher by no less an authority than the Emperor Domitian who banished all philosophers in the year A.D. 89, thus forcing Epictetus to leave the city of Rome where he had taught. He is usually said to have lived from about A.D. 55 to 135.

Every great traditional expression of the law of the reversal of effort is developed in opposition to some form of the ethic of attainment. Behind the Stoicism of Epictetus lies the ethic of the aristocracy of the Greek city-states as formulated by Aristotle (384-322 B.C.) in the *Nichomachaean Ethics*. Expressing the vigorous and self-confident mentality of the Greek aristocracy, Aristotle maintained that the good of human life is the perfected functioning of the unique human potential of reason through its full application in the guidance of all of the activities of life. The good life was seen as a work of conscious art, perfected by reason; in every situation, reason was to choose the most rational alternative, the median between extremes. The good is thus an attainment of effort directed by thought and eventually fixed in character or habit. It is present in that life in which passions, vital energies, and powers are constructively channeled and reach their appropriate goal guided by reason. The context in which life reaches this fulfillment is the social and political life of the Greek city-state, in the activities of deliberating and governing. Aristotle knew well that this life required certain conditions of material and social well-being; the prerequisites of the fulfilled life are material comfort, leisure, education, justice, and social stability.

However, the social conditions upon which this particular form of the ethic of attainment depended underwent rapid change in the Hellenistic period, preparing the way for both the late phase of Stoicism represented by Epictetus and the spread of Pauline Christianity. The unrest characteristic of the Hellenistic period commences with the Peloponnesian War in which the Greek city-states lost their independence through conquest by Sparta. Shortly all of Greece was subdued by Philip II of Macedon (382-336 B.C.), and the great Persian Empire was conquered by his son Alexander (356-323 B.C.), called on this account "the Great." After his death, this immense Macedonian Empire, which included all of the Near East was divided among his generals, and within a century much of it had fallen to Rome. This history, the context in which Stoicism developed, brings us down to the time of Epictetus and Paul.

In this period, the integrity of the Greek aristocratic tradition, which Aristotle's ethic assumed, was eroded by contact with alternative traditions in the form of the seemingly exotic cultures of the Near East; this is simply because contact with other ways of being human tends to erode people's confidence and trust in the superiority and validity of their own ways. The political stability on which this ethic was based was threatened by revolution and warfare; life as a work of rational art assumes a stable context in which we can trust that predicted outcomes of our actions will indeed come to pass. Thus there was a widespread "failure of nerve," a loss of confidence in the ability of persons to secure the good of life by their own effort.

To understand this crisis, it is necessary to see certain political events as also spiritual events. Conquest by another people is not merely an external and military event, but a disaster for a people's self-understanding. It seems to show that one's gods are weak and one's values and institutions unable to produce a nation which can withstand assault and survive. The sense of military defeat as a religious crisis is hard for secular persons to recapture, but we can attempt to empathize with the Japanese who saw the divine emperor, descendent of the sun goddess Ameterasu, publicly admit to defeat by the occidental barbarians. The fall of ancient political orders is also the erosion of traditional religious belief.

A second way in which Hellenistic political events are also spiritual events is through acculturation caused by contact with diverse peoples. The natural assumption of every culture developing in isolation is that there is really only one way to be human. Forced and sustained contact with different ways thus has the effect of discrediting this traditional confidence. Alexander's project of a cosmopolitan world empire in which traders and the military moved about freely and at least the local aristocracies benefited from an infusion of Greek civilization had the effect of leading to acculturation. This pattern can be seen among some Native American people who at first came to distrust their inherited traditions due to contact with the technologically more dazzling European culture. That this loss of confidence in one's ancestral ways is painful and disorienting and, in some cases, worse than death is seen in the high statistics for suicide, alcoholism, disruption of families, and what the larger culture calls emotional illness among acculturated, conquered peoples. The technical term acculturation masks thousands of individual experiences of hurt and humiliation, moments of dread at not knowing who one is, what one can expect, or what one should do, and of sorrow and emptiness at the loss of the cherished and familiar.

The crisis of old patterns led to a widespread feeling of estrangement and impotence; familiar patterns and symbols were disappearing, and people felt powerless to bring order into their lives.

> Any one who turns from the great writers of classical Athens, say Sophocles or Aristotle, to those of the Christian era must be conscious of a great difference in tone. There is a change in the whole relation of the writer to the world about him. It is hard to describe. It is a rise of ascetism, of mysticism, in a sense of pessimism; a loss of self-confidence, of hope in this life and of faith in normal human effort; a despair of patient inquiry, a cry for infallible revelation; an indifference to the welfare of the state, a conversion of the soul to God. It is an atmosphere in which the aim of the good man is not so much to live justly, to help the society to which he belongs and enjoy the esteem of his fellow creatures; but rather, by means of a burning faith, by contempt for the world and its standards, by ecstasy, suffering, martyrdom, to be granted pardon for his unspeakable unworthiness, his immeasurable sins. There is an intensifying of certain spiritual emotions; an increase of sensitiveness, a failure of nerve.[1]

It is this mood which is expressed in Epictetus' sense of our helplessness before the impersonal laws and forces that govern our external lives, and of Paul's sense of our sinful alienation from God and of our inability to find a remedy in our own efforts. It is this which separates the ethic of Epictetus from that of Aristotle, and Paul's from that of Judaism.

Conquest and acculturation through cross-cultural contact generated an experience of the impossibility of fulfillment through effort. A similar experience arises in late medieval Europe and ancient China, and in our own time and place. It is safe to say certain historical periods are rich in the experience of impossibility through the interposing

[1] Gilbert Murray, *Five Stages of Greek Religion* (New York: Doubleday, n.d. [1951]), 119.

of historical crisis in countless individual lives, and they will therefore generate forms of the ethic of consolation. It may be that the term failure of nerve seems judgmental and disapproving; whether you feel that this is so ultimately depends on how you view yourself and the world. We may just as well say more approvingly that the Hellenistic crisis is "the birth of humility."[2] After all, the early church understood this crisis as *praeparatio evangelica*, the providential "preparation for the Gospel."

Stoicism arose as one of the responses to the felt need for stability in the midst of this chaos. It offered a thorough-going criticism of the ethic of attainment no longer found functional, and it offered consolation in the face of cultural crisis. Its rooting in a time of bewildering change and disorder is seen in its conviction that that which befalls us in the world of events is the working out of impersonal forces and laws, and simply must be accepted. Events are ruled by destiny and can be little affected by our action.

According to the popular Stoic market place teachers, both the quest for wealth and security as the prerequisite of the good life, and the attempt to rationally order our actions and affairs, are bound to lead to frustration. For the course of history and our individual fates are completely determined, and destiny will realize itself whether we struggle against it or not. All of the goods promised by the ethic of attainment are illusory, simply because they all lie beyond our grasp in the realm of that which we cannot control. Whether one achieves that thorough education and material well-being, which are necessary to the good life, and whether the results of one's actions will follow as planned from one's rational intentions, are both beyond our power and are subject to destiny. What happens to us in external affairs is not a result of our rational intention, but of powers beyond our control.

But we would be without hope if the good of our life lies in that realm which is not subject to our own power, the realm of external events. Rather, it must lie in that area which is within our power, the realm of our personal desires and responses. While we are powerless to affect the course of events and thereby rationally build the good life of Aristotle, we do have power over our desires and over the emotional response we make to that which befalls us. We cannot order the working of history, but we can control the way we respond to it, and what we hope for within it. Here popular Stoicism has retreated from the goal of perfecting social life and is content to achieve the inner freedom of the individual; this too is typical of the Hellenistic crisis.

This reordering of our feelings and desires must be based on a new perception of the way the world works. The world of events is gov-

[2] *Ibid.*, 120.

erned by its natural law structure, which is in a sense an indwelling divinity. Thus, we must come to see that nature is a rational and law-abiding process in which everything occurs for the rational good of the whole. If we see the reasonableness of destiny, we will be led to accept it. Stoic liberation is based on a certain claim about the nature of the world. To desire what destiny does not decree and to attempt to attain what destiny does not intend to bestow is futile and irrational. Rather, we ought to align our desires and feelings with the divine course of nature, accepting whatever occurs as necessary, reasonable, and right. For when we desire only that which actually comes to pass, then nothing ever comes to pass but that we desire it; if you want what you get, you will get what you want. Our apprehensions and frustrations will disappear when we cease attempting to establish the good of our lives by our own efforts in a realm where our efforts are powerless. We achieve peace and serenity only when we resign ourselves to accept whatever occurs as ordained by a higher divine rationality, and therefore both inevitable and right. In short, we must abandon our personal point of view, with its private desires and feelings, and adopt the point of view of the rational order of the universe.

In later Stoicism the ethic of attainment is criticized for urging persons to act on the basis of their own limited and partial knowledge of the good, that is, on the basis of that which seems good to them. For this limited knowledge of the good is based on ignorance of the higher good, the good of the whole. The ethic of attainment is further criticized for urging us to expend our efforts in an attempt to contrive the fulfillment of our lives in an area where all is determined and exertion is futile. To *know* the good is to know that all events obey a rational destiny, and to *do* the good is to accept this and thus be in harmony with nature. One achieves the good of life by renouncing the attempt to achieve it.

This expression of the law of the reversal of effort was offered as consolation in the midst of the Hellenistic crisis. Here fulfillment has ceased to mean the full realization of human powers and potentialities through rational action and has come to mean *ataraxia*, "the experience of inner calm and freedom" through the renunciation of personal desire and emotion. The goal of the ethic of attainment cannot be achieved in unsettled Hellenistic times, and Stoicism offers an ethic of consolation.

* * * * *

Turning now to the text of *The Manual* itself, we notice it includes a vigorous attack upon the ethic of attainment. *The Manual* repeatedly contrasts the futility of the attempt to attain the good of human life by one's own efforts with the wisdom of accepting that which occurs inevitably. The illusory good life offered by the ethic of attainment lies in the realm of things beyond our power, while the inner peace offered by the Stoic teacher is entirely within our grasp.

> Of all existing things some are in our power, and others are not in our power. In our power are thought, impulse, will to get and will to avoid, and, in a word, everything which is our own doing. Things not in our power include the body, property, reputation, office, and in a word, everything which is not our own doing. Things in our power are by nature free, unhindered, untrammeled; things not in our power are weak, servile, subject to hindrance, dependent on others. (1)[3]

This distinction is basic to all that follows; the good life must be sought where it can be found, in the realm within our control, and not in the realm which is beyond our power.

The conventional orientation embodied in the ethic of attainment is vulnerable to frustration in that it places its emotional investment in the region beyond our power to control. It desires that which it lacks power to secure.

> Remember that the will to get promises attainment of what you will, and the will to avoid promises escape from what you avoid; and he who fails to get what he wills is unfortunate, and he who does not escape what he wills to avoid is miserable. (2)

Especially dangerous is the tendency to have unrealistic desires regarding possessions and persons to which we have strong attachments.

> It is silly to want your children and your wife and your friends to live forever, for that means that you want what is not in your control to be in your control, and what is not your own to be your own. (14)

Attachments make one vulnerable to suffering when the object is lost. Only the one who seeks to attain or possess beyond his or her power can ever suffer loss. Therefore,

> Never say of anything, "I lost it," but say, "I gave it back." (11)

The opposition between the attempt to attain and the real good of human life is seen in section 24 of *The Manual*. Here it is pointed out that to seek the conventional good life of honor, wealth, and knowledge necessarily involves the loss of the true goods of inner peace and security. The law of the reversal of effort is clearly seen in this. Refer-

[3] All subsequent quotations from Epictetus are from "The Manual of Epictetus," trans. P. E. Matheson, in *The Stoic and Epicurean Philosophers*, ed. W. J. Oates (New York: Random House, 1940), 468-484.

ring to the so-called goods of the ethic of attainment, a friend or family member may say to us:

> "Get them . . . that we may have them." If I can get them and keep my self-respect, honour, magnanimity, show the way and I will get them. But if you call on me to lose the good things that are mine, in order that you may win things that are not good, look how unfair and thoughtless you are. (24)

The good is not achieved by the attempt to achieve it, but is rather destroyed by this attempt.

The ethic of attainment is oriented outward toward the world and seeks its fulfillment in the active attempt to master the world by knowing it and possessing its goods. But this is a false hope, based on ignorance of where the true good lies.

> The ignorant man's position and character is this: he never looks to himself for benefit or harm, but to the world outside him. The philosopher's position and character is that he always looks to himself for benefit and harm. (48)

For the good of human life is in the right adjustment of the desires and feelings to that which *is*, based on a recognition of its necessity and rightness, and it does not lie in the attempt to compel events to fit one's desires.

In short, the ethic of attainment is doomed to failure and frustration because it seeks fulfillment in an area beyond human control. In seeking the good in action in the world, it loses all hope of finding the real good of human life.

> If you try to act a part beyond your powers, you not only disgrace yourself in it, but you neglect the part you could have fulfilled with success. (37)

* * * * *

To this criticism of the ethic of attainment *The Manual* adds its positive teaching about the truly fruitful approach to the good of human life. As will become apparent, this positive teaching is an instance of the law of the reversal of effort.

The fulfillment of human life lies not in the attempt to achieve it, for this attempt has been shown to lead us into the region where the outcome is beyond our control. Rather, it lies in the renunciation of the attempt to achieve it. Thus we are to count what lies beyond our power as nothing and seek the good only in what we can control ourselves.

> And if it is concerned with what is not in our power, be ready with the answer that it is nothing to you. (1)

We cannot succeed in the attempt to attain the good by controlling events, but only by abandoning this effort and aligning our feelings and desires with destiny.

> What disturbs men's minds is not events but their judgements on events. For instance, death is nothing dreadful, or else Socrates would have thought it so. No, the only dreadful thing about it is men's judgement that it is dreadful. (5)

> What distresses him is not the event, for that does not distress another, but his judgement on the event. (16)

> But for me, all omens are favorable if I will, for, whatever the issue may be, it is in my power to get benefit therefrom. (18)

> For no one shall harm you without your consent; you will only be harmed when you think you are harmed. (30)

Far from achieving the good life, the ethic of attainment, with its aggressive desire and futile activity, causes increased frustration and suffering by seeking that which cannot be attained. Therefore, we are to renounce this attempt to attain the good of life, and in this very act we discover that we have it. The key to this reversal is to seek control only over what is within one's power, that is, one's feelings about that which occurs inevitably.

> Ask not that events should happen as you will, but let your will be that events should happen as they do, and you shall have peace. (8)

> Sickness is a hindrance to the body, but not to the will, unless the will consent. Lameness is a hindrance to the leg, but not to the will. Say this to yourself at each event that happens, for you shall find that though it hinders something else it will not hinder you. (9)

One is not to allow one's peace of mind to depend on what cannot be controlled, and thus one must abandon the concern and ambition at the root of the attempt to attain.

> If you wish to make progress, abandon reasoning of this sort: "If I neglect my affairs I shall have nothing to live on." . . . For it is better to die of hunger, so that you may be free from pain and free from fear, than to live in plenty and be troubled in mind. . . . Wherefore, begin with little things. Is your drop of oil spilt? Is your cup of wine stolen? Say to yourself, "This is the price paid for freedom from passion, this is the price of a quiet mind." (12)

> Let him who wishes to be free not wish for anything or avoid anything that depends on others; or else he is bound to be a slave. (14)

> There is but one way to freedom — to despise what is not in your power. (19)

That is to say, the only way to achieve the good is to cease attempting to achieve it by desire and action in the world. For the very cessation of this effort is itself the attainment of the only true good, which is acceptance and inner calm. Yet paradoxically, this cannot be regarded as my attainment, for it arises of itself on the condition that I give up all efforts to attain. Thus the normal order of cause and effect, intention and outcome, is reversed.

The key to this renunciation of the attempt to attain fulfillment through effort is the realization that events are inevitable, and they occur according to a divine rational order. This is the teaching about the nature of reality which is the basis of Stoic ethics. An image conveying this meaning is that of life as the enactment of a play written by another.

> Remember that you are an actor in a play, and the Playwright chooses the manner of it; if he wants it short, it is short; if long, it is long. If he wants you to act a poor man you must act the part with all your powers; and so if your part be a cripple or a magistrate or a plain man. For your business is to act the character that is given you and act it well; the choice of the cast is another's. (17)

In this understanding of the way the world works, it is clear that the ethic of attainment cannot succeed and, indeed, that it must lead only to suffering and frustration. For it asserts its own wishes and desires against destiny. The fulfillment of human life is found only in renouncing the attempt to run counter to nature's course and in accepting in trust that which occurs as being inevitable and right. The good is not attained by the attempt to achieve it, but by the abandonment of that attempt. The price of the genuine goods of freedom, peace, and inner strength is giving up the quest for attainment of what conventional thought calls good.

> You must be one man, good or bad; you must develop either your Governing Principle, or outward things — in a word, you must choose between the position of a philosopher and that of a mere outsider. (29)

To seek the good of harmony with the natural course of events absolutely excludes the seeking of those goods promised by the ethic of attainment.

> Remember that if you want to get what is not in your power, you cannot

> earn the same reward as others unless you act as they do. . . . What is the price of a lettuce? An obol perhaps. If then a man pays his obol and gets his lettuce, and you do not pay and do not get it, do not think you are defrauded. (25)

The true good of human life is secured only by the cessation of the attempt to achieve it. When the effort to attain what everyday thought calls good is abandoned, the resulting freedom, peace, and inner strength are found to be the only good worth possessing. In the very act of ceasing to assert and strive, the good is discovered.

Thus the teaching of Epictetus, a man who in his own eyes was twice set free from slavery, can be summarized in this statement: the good of human life is not achieved by attempting to achieve it, but by the paradoxically indirect method of not attempting to achieve it, for on this condition it is discovered to be already in one's possession.

Chapter 3

THE LETTERS OF PAUL: SALVATION IS NOT AN ACCOMPLISHMENT BUT A GIFT

For our argument is that man is justified by faith quite apart from success in keeping the law.

—Rom. 3.28

The letters of Paul the Apostle were written between A.D. 50 and 58 while he was in the midst of his mission to the gentiles or from prison when his activities offended local officials. All are genuine "occasional letters" written to specific churches founded by Paul in Asia Minor, Macedonia, and Greece to deal with specific problems. The exceptions are Philemon, which is written to an individual, and the *Letter to the Romans*, which is addressed in its present form to a church not founded by Paul. Romans is therefore a general introduction to the teaching of Paul addressed to Christians not familiar with his thought; and it may have served also as a "circular epistle" passed about among a number of Paul's churches afterwards, due to its character as a summary of his message. For this reason a sketch of Paul's thought may well focus on Romans.[1]

Born with the Jewish name of Saul in Tarsus, a city in southeastern Asia Minor, Paul was a Hellenistic Jew in touch with both Jewish tradition and the cosmopolitan Greek language culture of the Roman Empire. In a sense, Paul represents an alternative response to that same "failure of nerve" which drew forth the message of late Stoic ethics. His sense of our utter powerlessness in the awful state of alienation from God is typically Hellenistic and parallels the Stoic's sense of our impotence before destiny. On the other hand, it stands in contrast to both the classical Greek view of human nature in Plato and Aristotle, and Judaism, neither of which saw the human situation as one of total helplessness.

For Paul, the problem of human life is the justification of sinful humanity before a righteous God who has fully stated his requirement of

[1] This observation and the general approach taken in summarizing Paul's thought are from Rudolf Bultmann, *Theology of the New Testament*, vol. 1 (New York: Charles Scribner's Sons, 1951).

obedience in the *Torah*, the Law of Moses. Like others whose thought embodies the law of the reversal of effort, his reaction is against a form of the ethic of attainment, and he criticizes it as a false and futile approach to the problem of righteousness. Paul rejects what he perceived as legalism in certain sectors of Judaism. As he understood it, Judaism maintained that the good of human life lies in the scrupulous fulfillment of every ritual and ethical requirement of the *Torah*, and this seemed to mean that we become righteous and acceptable to God through our own efforts. In his polemic against this form of the ethic of attainment, Paul asserted that absolute righteousness is not a possible human attainment, and that even by the most thorough and energetic attempt to fulfill the *Torah*, persons cannot justify themselves before God. Indeed, the very attempt to attain righteousness and to justify oneself by one's own endeavor is itself an expression of sinful pride. Note that the point is not merely that it is impossibly difficult to fulfill the *Torah*, but rather that we must fall into sin if we try through our own powers, precisely because reliance on our own power is the essence of sin.

For Paul, as for Judaism generally, sin is a willful rebellion of the creature against the Creator; it is the attempt to live from oneself rather than from God. In sin we attempt to secure the good of our lives by our own efforts, rather than to receive fulfillment as a gift of God. Paul here depicts sin as a state of character, a total attitude to life, and not merely as individual disobedient deeds; sins follow from the state of sin, and it is this state which is our problem. This view of sin as a willful and disobedient turning away from God and seeking to live by one's own power and knowledge is typically Hebraic. The intense awareness of our inability to overcome this is more characteristic of the Hellenistic religious crisis.

As a Jew, Paul regards the flesh, that is, the body and the world as its sphere of action, as created by God and therefore good. But the flesh may become the occasion for sin, for through it we may be tempted to turn away from the Creator and seek to live wholly within our own power and action. Thus in Paul, "life according to the flesh" can be a term for the state of sin. It is not that the flesh itself is evil, but that it may become sinful if by choice we put the sphere of the flesh in the place of God. It seems that by life according to the flesh Paul does not mean merely the lust and immorality of the pagan world; he also includes in this the Greek philosophic quest for wisdom and goodness and the zealous pursuit of righteousness in Judaism. All of these represent the human attempt to live from ourselves rather than from God. Paul thus condemns all forms of the ethic of attainment as prideful self-reliance, or sin. Life according to the flesh is opposed to "life according to the spirit" in which the creature recognizes and turns toward the Creator as the sole source and ground of life.

In short, sin is self-reliance, the attempt to fulfill life by one's own effort; as such it leads to anxiety. For one comes to worry about one's ability to make life truly secure and complete through one's own efforts. The life of sinful self-reliance leads to pride, boasting of one's own accomplishments in wisdom or righteousness or happiness, as if all of the goods of human life were not really gifts of God. True life, life lived as a gift of God, would be free from both anxiety and pride, for one would be living by God's power and not one's own efforts.

This distinction between true life as dependence on the Creator and false life as the rebellious independence of the creature is revealed, according to Paul, in the *Torah*. The Law of Moses in his view is a genuine and eternal revelation of God's will for humanity. It reveals that true life would be a life of obedience to the Creator as the source of life. The danger of the *Torah* is not that it is an inferior revelation, but that it tempts us to justify ourselves before God by our own strenuous efforts to fulfill it. But the *Torah* cannot be fully obeyed by unaided human effort, and the attempt to do so is just another form of rebellion against God. Thus the *Torah* reveals what is required of humanity, righteousness and obedience to God; and it shows that we cannot attain to this by our own self-reliant efforts.

In this dual way the Law prepares persons for the Christian Gospel, which is the gracious offer of the right relation with God as a gift. Divine grace is the free and unmerited offer of God of both forgiveness and a new divine-human relationship. God offers to do for humanity what it cannot do for itself. God will accept persons as if they were righteous and make them righteous. The specific and visible sign that God is offering his grace to us is the death and resurrection of Jesus Christ. Paul has very little interest in the life and teachings of Jesus apart from this single episode and its meaning as the historical manifestation of divine grace. The notion of a dying and rising savior is similar to ideas in the pagan mystery religions, which like late Stoicism had arisen in response to the Hellenistic crisis, but in the Gospel the savior is a recent historical individual rather than a figure in "mythic time." Paul speaks of the way in which Christ accomplishes our salvation through a variety of different metaphors, one of which is taken from Jewish temple ritual: Jesus is a propitiatory sacrifice, a sin offering to God.

Through the Christ-event, God offers a choice between two forms of life. We can accept the gift of forgiveness and give up the attempt to live by our own efforts, or we can reject the offer and continue to live as if by our own power. To decide for God's offer of true life is faith, *pistis* in Paul's Greek. Faith is the opposite of sin, for sin is self-reliance, and faith is reliance on divine grace. It is the attitude of trust and belief in which God's gift of salvation is accepted. It is an act of obedience and submission, and as such it is a total rejection of the attempt to save oneself, to live by one's own attainments. Faith is not itself an act of human will that earns salvation, but a moment of surrender in which self-reliance is renounced and one comes to rely totally on God's grace. God accepts faith, the giving up of the attempt to save oneself, in lieu of righteousness, and justifies the sinner.

This is clearly an instance of the law of the reversal of effort. The right relation of creature to Creator cannot be a human achievement, but arises only when we set aside the attempt to achieve it by our own efforts and receive it as a gift. Faith as trust in divine grace is the cessation of the effort of self-salvation, and through this very cessation of effort, that which was sought is received.

Since faith is reliance on God's grace, it is free of both anxiety and pride. Now one relies only on grace and not on one's own efforts, and anxiety about how things will turn out is lifted; letting go of self-reliance brings anxious care to an end because that care was rooted in the notion that life depends solely on our own efforts. Of course since we owe our new right relation to God to grace and not to our own accomplishments, there is nothing which we may boast or feel proud about. The gifts of the spirit follow faith, including a new life of love and righteousness, but since these are gifts, there is no basis for our taking pride in them. Paul calls on his new converts to exert themselves in the moral life, but now righteousness is no longer accompanied with self-congratulation; nor is it burdened with the weight of having to prove one's acceptability to God. The effort to do good is thus liberated from self-interest, and one is free simply to do good in thankfulness to God, with nothing to prove and no reason for self-righteous superiority.

This sketch is sufficient to show that Paul opposes the ethic of attainment as a means of restoring the right relation to God and that his positive message is an instance of the law of the reversal of effort. That righteousness, which is not possible to attain by human effort, is to be received as a free gift of God. The only condition of the receipt of this gift is that one renounce the prideful attempt to justify oneself by moral and religious effort. Thus one is made righteous by abandoning the effort to attain righteousness. One is justified before God not by the effort to attain justification, but paradoxically, by the renunciation of this effort, by the trusting receptiveness to God's gift of salvation. This reversal of the normal relation of intention and outcome is based in Paul's thought on the belief-system which centers on the revelation of God's will in the Law of Moses and the embodiment of grace in Jesus Christ.

* * * * *

These themes are emphasized again and again in the letters. It is impossible for a person to wholly fulfill the *Torah*, for even knowing the righteousness required by God, one is not able to perform it.

> We know that the law is spiritual; but I am not: I am unspiritual, the purchased slave of sin. I do not even acknowledge my own actions as mine, for what I do is not what I want to do, but what I detest. But if what I do is against my will, it means that I agree with the law and hold it to be admirable. But as things are, it is no longer I who perform the action, but sin that lodges in me. For I know that nothing good lodges in me — in my unspiritual nature I mean — for though the will to do good is there, the deed is not. The good which I want to do, I fail to do; but what I do is the wrong which is against my will, clearly it is no longer I who am the agent, but sin that has its lodging in me. (Rom. 7.14-20; cf. Gal. 5.17)[2]

This sense of powerlessness in the state of sin is of course the basis for discovering that only God's grace can deliver us. It seems typical of the Hellenistic loss of confidence, reminding us of Epictetus' helplessness before destiny. So deeply involved are we in rebellion that we are powerless to do what we know would be good.

The purpose of the *Torah* then seems to be to announce the righteousness required by God as something so complete as to be unattainable to sinful, self-reliant humans.

> Now all the words of the law are addressed, as we know, to those who are within the pale of the law, so that no one may have anything to say in self-defense, but the whole world may be exposed to the judgement of God. For (again from Scripture) "no human being can be justified in the sight of God" for having kept the law: law brings only the consciousness of sin. (Rom. 3.19-20; cf. Gal. 3.10-12)

Indeed, the attempt to justify oneself by scrupulous adherence to the demands of the Law is an instance of sinful self-reliance and rebellion against God, and leads to trust in one's own strength and boasting of one's own righteousness. In this sense, the *Torah* is a temptation to sin.

> Israel made great efforts after a law of righteousness, but never attained to it. Why was this? Because their efforts were not based on faith, but (as they supposed) on deeds. . . . They ignore God's way of righteousness and try to set up their own. (Rom. 9.31-32, 10.3)

[2] *New English Bible* (Oxford: Oxford University Press; Cambridge: Cambridge University Press, 1961).

> The keeping of the law would not exclude [pride], but faith does. (Rom. 3.27)

To seek to justify oneself through one's own righteous deeds is the essence of sin, and this leads away from that spirit in which we can receive justification as the gift of God. The effort of self-justification through deeds is in fact a rejection of God's grace.

> When you seek to be justified by way of law, your relation with Christ is completely severed: you have fallen out of the domain of God's grace. For to us, our hope of attaining that righteousness which we eagerly await is the work of the Spirit through faith. (Gal. 5.4-5)

Thus the ethic of attainment leads away from the goal.

* * * * *

To this criticism of the ethic of attainment, Paul adds the message of a different approach embodying the reversal of effort theme. Righteousness is not attained through self-effort, but is received as a free gift of God by means of our faith in Christ. There is no basis for pride, for our righteousness is not our own.

> I count [my own attainment] so much dung, for the sake of gaining Christ, and in him finding that, though I have no righteousness of my own, no legal rectitude, I have the righteousness which comes from faith in Christ, given by God in response to faith. (Phil. 3.8-9, alternate reading; cf. I Cor. 1.29)

The goal that cannot be attained through effort can be received as a gift.

> Thus it [righteousness] does not depend on man's will or effort, but on God's mercy. (Rom. 9.16)

This gift is given in response to faith, which is precisely the cessation of the effort to attain.

> For Christ ends the law and brings righteousness for everyone who has faith. (Rom. 10.4)

The contrast between the ethic of attainment and the Pauline ethic of consolation is clearly seen in the relation of the following two passages.

> I will not nullify the grace of God; if righteousness comes by law, then Christ died for nothing (Gal. 2.21; cf. 3.21)

> But if it is by grace, then it does not rest on deeds done, or grace would cease to be grace. (Rom. 11.6)

Justification, the restoration of the right relation of the creature to the Creator, does not come about through human action, but by faith, which is the abandonment of the effort of self-justification and the trusting reception of the gift of forgiveness. The movement is from activity to receptivity. The possibility of this reversal rests upon specific beliefs about the nature of reality. Specifically, faith involves the belief that the obedience of Jesus in his crucifixion is a sacrifice which satisfies the divine justice and restores the right relation between God and humanity in principle. All that is required is that each individual accept the gift of justification personally through faith.

> For God designed him to be the means of expiating sin by his sacrificial death, effective through faith. (Rom. 3.25)

Faith, which is the renunciation of the effort of self-salvation and the trust that God's grace is sufficient to do for us what we cannot do for ourselves, is accepted instead of the attainment of righteousness. This reversal of the usual relation between effort and result is identical in its inner logic with that found in Stoicism, although of course the belief-systems differ. For Paul, the attempt to make oneself righteous is counted as sin, but the renunciation of this effort is counted as righteousness. This is the meaning of the reference to the faith of Abraham who trusted God's promise that a great people would spring from his descendants and left his home in Mesopotamia to wander across the desert to Palestine, and who was ready to sacrifice his son Isaac at God's command.

> If Abraham was justified by anything he had done, then he has a ground for pride. But he has no such ground before God; for what does Scripture say? "Abraham put his faith in God, and that faith was counted to him as righteousness." Now if a man does a piece of work, his wages are not "counted" as a favor; they are paid as a debt. But if without any work to his credit he simply puts his faith in him who acquits the guilty, then his faith is indeed "counted as righteousness!" (Rom. 4.1-5)

It is not that we first make ourselves acceptable to God through our own deeds and then God must accept us, but merely that we trust that God has already accepted us as sinners. As with Abraham's faith, so it is with the Christian's faith in Christ.

> It is to be "counted" in the same way to us who have faith in the God who raised Jesus our Lord from the dead; for he was delivered to death for our misdeeds, and raised to life to justify us. (Rom. 4.23-25; cf. 5.18-19; 10.5-10)

Numerous passages repeat this paradox that the justification of sinners before God comes about not through the effort to overcome sin and achieve righteousness, but by the abandonment of this effort and the trusting acceptance of justification as a gift. What the ethic of attainment cannot do, the ethic of consolation can, through the reversal of effort.

> But we know that no man is ever justified by doing what the law demands, but only through faith in Christ Jesus; so we too have put our faith in Jesus Christ, in order that we might be justified through this faith, and not through deeds dictated by law; for by such deeds, Scripture says, no mortal man shall be justified. (Gal. 2.15-16; cf. 3.1-6, Rom. 1.16-17, 3.22-24, 3.30, 8.3-4)

A great sense of unburdening and relief follows the realization of the power of the reversal of effort. For Paul, life under the ethic of attainment would involve constant anxiety about avoiding evil and doing good, and about the sufficiency of one's will to the task. One had sought peace through this effort at righteousness, but there is no peace this way. Peace is not discovered through the effort to attain it, but in the quiet resulting from the cessation of that effort. Thus Paul found the goal is received through the renunciation of the attempt to grasp it.

> Therefore, now that we have been justified through faith, we are at peace with God through our Lord Jesus Christ, through whom we have been allowed to enter the sphere of God's grace, where we now stand. We exult in the hope of the divine splendour that is to be ours. (Rom. 5.1-2, alternate reading)

There is a certain carelessness in this state of justification which allows Paul to say:

> For no one of us lives, and equally no one of us dies, for himself alone. If we live, we live for the Lord; and if we die, we die for the Lord. Whether, therefore we live or die, we belong to the Lord. (Rom. 14.7-8)

In terms of the law of the reversal of effort, the self whose security does not lie in its attainment, but in its renunciation of attainment, is invulnerable to historical events. This same invulnerability was observed in Stoicism in which all possible turns of events are accepted in advance as inevitable, so that one remains above the threatening eventfulness of history. It is as if in times of disorder it becomes obvious that the life built on the ethic of attainment is terribly vulnerable to unforeseen adversity, and so forms of the ethic of consolation arise to transcend the risk and threat of living in an eventful world.

An interesting corollary of this application of the paradox of intention to the problem of moral righteousness is the reversal of the order of wisdom and ignorance. Human wisdom, which the eighteenth century Enlightenment might call "autonomous reason," is seen as an aspect of the ethic of attainment, and as such it cannot achieve what it seeks. It therefore amounts to foolishness. On the other hand, what seems ignorant and paradoxical to self-reliant human reason constitutes the true wisdom. Therefore, if you think yourself wise, you are foolish; and if you content yourself to be foolish in the world's terms, you are wise.

> God has made the wisdom of this world look foolish. As God in his wisdom ordained, the world failed to find him by its wisdom, and he chose to save those who have faith by the folly of the Gospel. . . . Divine folly is wiser than the wisdom of man, and divine weakness stronger than man's strength. (I Cor. 1.20-21, 25)

Worldly wisdom would expect that all goals, including the right relation to God, are the outcome of effort, and thus it never could have predicted what God has revealed, that salvation is a gift and the condition of the receipt of this gift is that we abandon the effort to achieve.

Like Epictetus, Paul sees himself as a liberated slave. His message to his gentile hearers was simple: the right relation to God is not achieved by attempting to achieve it, but by the paradoxically indirect method of not attempting to achieve it, for on this condition, called faith, it is received as a gift of God's grace.

Chapter 4

THE TAO TEH CHING OF LAO TZU: YIELDING IS STRONGEST

For sometimes things are benefited by being taken away from, and suffer by being added to.

—*Tao Teh Ching*, 42

The *Tao Teh Ching*, or "Book of the Way and Its Power," constitutes the written basis of philosophical Taoism. It was traditionally attributed to Lao Tzu (Old Master or Sage), an imperial archivist and older contemporary of Confucius living in the late sixth century B.C. While the tendency of the text and even several passages may trace back to this semi-legendary figure, the book itself is a composite work that took its final form in the third century B.C.

The elaborations of the legends of Lao Tzu and the attribution of the book to him may be an attempt to establish the priority of Taoism over Confucianism, since the two represent opposing and competing philosophies. In the legends, Lao Tzu tries gently to set the meddlesome Confucius on the right path, but his dark aphorisms have no effect. Confucianism then represents a form of the ethic of attainment which *Tao Teh Ching* rejects.

Taoism and Confucianism pose opposite solutions to the problem of social disruption of the Warring States Period (403-221 B.C.). The period began with the Tartar invasions and continued in a time of civil war, which fractured the Chinese Empire into competing, predatory duchies. Clearly, this was a time like the Hellenistic period in the Mediterranean and the Near East, in which ancient feudal order was in decay and tradition and authority had lost their unifying power. The social ways of the ancients and the political power of the Chou emperors were discredited, and traditional distinctions of class and rank were blurred, posing the question of how society could be saved and order restored. The Taoist answer is, like late Stoicism and Pauline Christianity, a form of the ethic of consolation. And like them, it involves a criticism of a form of the ethic of attainment, in this case Confucianism.

For Confucianism, the disorder of the Warring States Period can be overcome by the intelligent and active attempt to understand and propagate the values embodied in classical Chinese feudal society. First, these ancient values were to be rediscovered through the collection and study of the ancient classics. Then these values are to be taught to the young, written into law, and lived out as an example by rulers and teachers. The basic value of the ancient order was said to be *li*, "propriety or decorum;" it is this which defines the correct form of every relationship in a feudal order. The specific meaning of *li* was worked out for all of the five basic relationships (ruler-subject, father-son, husband-wife, older brother-younger brother, older friend-younger friend), and this was to be the basis of social education. The whole project involves the "rectification of names," the active restoration of the traditional feudal meaning of the basic roles played by each member of society; rulers, fathers, subjects, and sons must be educated to embody the true meaning of these terms as defined by the golden age of feudal order. The teaching of *li* was an activist movement aiming at restoration. Confucianism was a complete outline of the rationally ordered hierarchical society and an educational program to establish it, with minute prescriptions for the proper conduct of life based on obligations of ritual propriety and social courtesy.

The *Tao Teh Ching* reacts against the doctrine which says the good of human life can be achieved through the establishment and maintenance of rational order by human action. It criticizes this form of the ethic of attainment as meddling interference that upsets the natural balance of life and obstructs the natural flow of things, the *Tao* or "way." The doctrine of *li* confuses people with a host of prohibitions and admonitions and distracts them from the natural course of life they would follow if left alone. As soon as we begin to worry about contriving the best possible society, the number of details calling for conscious rational determination and regulation becomes overwhelming. Therefore, all attempts to contrive the good life must fail, for no human knowledge however complete and no human effort however constant can contrive a harmony so inclusive and self-sustaining as that already present in nature. In fact, all of our attempts to impose our own order on life actually obstruct the natural flow and harmony of nature. At best, Confucianism is foolish tinkering, an attempt to improve what cannot be improved; at worst, it is disastrous obstruction of the natural order, which can only lead to disorder. As interference with natural harmony, the ethic of attainment is counter-productive.

As an alternative to the Confucian ethic of attainment, the *Tao Teh Ching* offers *wu-wei*, "non-interference." When we renounce the effort to contrive the good of human life by our knowledge and effort and seek only to act in harmony with the course of nature, we find that nature bestows the good we sought. True virtue is therefore not the attempt to act according to some conception of order. Rather, it is the abandonment of the attempt to achieve the good by knowledge and effort, and the adoption of the way of non-interference. One is simply to let things be as they are and let processes tend toward the goals they naturally seek. When one no longer interferes with the natural course of things, one finds that the good of human life is bestowed by the *Tao*.

This attitude of non-interference is made possible by the recognition of the fact that in nature there is a natural flow or harmony, the *Tao*, which overcomes all discord and bestows fulfillment upon all things, on the condition of non-interference. The *Tao* is not a force external to humanity and natural objects, which orders them like a divine monarch; rather, it seems to be the very internal characteristic that all things exhibit if left alone, of being themselves all by themselves. It is the way the universe operates, the path taken by natural events, which through effortless action reach their goals. This is the teaching about the nature of reality on which Taoist ethics rests.

The Taoist claims, in effect, that the disorder of the Warring States Period comes from the violent assertiveness of ambitious rulers, and that the solution of the Confucians is the genteel assertiveness of meddlesome scholars. Both groups alike are assertive; if they would simply let the world be, then whatever order there is supposed to be in society would return without anyone planning or contriving it. When one no longer attempts to manipulate nature and contrive the good life, one is at harmony with nature and experiences peace, strength, and freedom in the manner appropriate to one's being. In short, the good of human life is found in the cessation of the attempt to attain it.

* * * * *

The contrast between the true virtue of non-interference and the Confucian ethic of attainment is stated in this way.

> The man of superior virtue is not conscious of his virtue, hence he is virtuous. The man of inferior virtue is intent on not losing virtue, hence he is devoid of virtue. (38)[1]

The *Tao Teh Ching* continues with the accusation that Confucians force their conception of the good on nature, even though it does not give a supportive response to this effort.

[1] All subsequent quotations from *Tao Teh Ching* are from "Laotse: the Book of Tao," trans. Lin Yu-tang, in *The Wisdom of China and India*, ed. Lin Yu-tang (New York: Random House, 1942), 583-624. Parentheses ( ) are from the translator, but square brackets [ ] indicate the substitution of words by the author. Occasionally, the translator's capitalization has been removed.

> But when the man of superior *li* acts and finds no response, he rolls up his sleeves to force it on others. (38)

Confucian rationalism and activism are thus rejected as running counter to the natural flow.

> There are those who will conquer the world and make of it what they conceive or desire. I see that they will not succeed, for the world is [a sacred] vessel. It cannot be made by human interference. He who makes it spoils it. He who holds it loses it. (29)

For

> . . . to improve upon life is called an ill omen; . . . [assertiveness] would be against the *Tao*. (55)

Conscious knowledge and efforts at morality are artificial and only were thought to be necessary in the first place because people lost touch with the natural way.

> On the decline of the great *Tao*, the doctrines of "love" and "justice" arose. When knowledge and cleverness appeared, great hypocrisy followed in its wake. When the six relationships no longer lived at peace, there was praise of "kind parents" and "filial sons." When a country fell into chaos and misrule, there was praise of "loyal ministers." (18)

Here, specific Confucian doctrines are mentioned by name. The point is that the very existence of the concern for right action is evidence that people have wandered from the natural way. Indeed, the concern with right action, being unnatural, leads not to success but to failure.

> He who stands on tip-toe does not stand firm; he who strains his strides does not walk well; . . . he who boasts of himself is not given credit; he who prides himself is not chief among men. (24)

This paradox that effort and action necessarily fail to reach their goal is given repeated expression. The effort to achieve the good through activism is self-defeating and is the source of evil.

> He who acts, spoils, he who grasps, lets slip. Because the Sage does not act, he does not spoil, because he does not grasp, he does not let slip. (64) The reason it is difficult for the people to live in peace is because of too much knowledge. Those who seek to rule a country by knowledge are the nation's curse. Those who seek not to rule a country by knowledge, are the nation's blessing. (65)

> The more prohibitions there are, the poorer the people become. The

> more sharp weapons there are, the more prevailing chaos there is in the state. . . . The greater the number of statutes, the greater the number of thieves and brigands. (57; cf. 75)

> Be busy about its affairs, and one's whole life is beyond redemption. (52)

Consistent with this is a strong disapproval of violence and militarism in chapters 30 and 31. The principle at work in all of this is that the meddlesome attempt to improve on nature always goes too far and does too much.

> Stretch a bow to the very full, and you will wish you had stopped in time. Temper a sword edge to its very sharpest, and the edge will not last long. (9)

Further, all those things sought as goods by the activist are illusory, hollow, and ultimately unsatisfying. The attainment of success, power, wealth, or fame is a worrisome exertion and makes one vulnerable to loss. And since these goods are unnatural, they do not truly satisfy.

> When gold and jade fill your hall, you will not be able to keep them safe. To be proud with wealth and honor is to sow the seeds of your own downfall. (9)

> The five colors blind the eyes of man; the five musical notes deafen the ears of man; the five flavors dull the taste of man; horse-racing, hunting and chasing madden the minds of man; rare valuable goods keep their owners awake at night. (12)

Attainment of what the world considers good makes one vulnerable and leaves one unsatisfied. More important, the very effort of attainment leads us away from true fulfillment that only harmony with the *Tao* can bestow.

> Fame, or one's own self, which does one love more? One's own self or material goods, which has more worth? Loss (of self) or possession (of goods), which is the greater evil? Therefore, he who loves most, spends most, he who hoards much, loses much. The contented man meets no disgrace; who knows when to stop runs into no danger. (44)

In the very effort to attain the good of human life, one loses all hope of finding it.

Even the attempt to know is futile. For all knowledge is based on rational discrimination of the objects of the universe. But the path that all things follow in effortlessly becoming what they are is hidden. Within all things is the unknowable mystery of *Tao*, which is their source. *Tao* as the way things naturally become is logically, though not necessarily chronologically, prior to knowable things. Thus,

> Out of *Tao*, one is born; out of one, two; out of two, three; out of three, the created universe. (42)

Because of this priority there can be no conscious knowledge of the natural way of all things, for processes follow this path automatically and unconsciously.

> The *Tao* that can be told of is not the absolute *Tao*; the names that can be given are not absolute names. (1)

This is expressed paradoxically in a way reminiscent of Paul.

> Who knows that he does not know is the highest; who (pretends to) know what he does not know is sick-minded. (71)

What the world considers as knowledge cannot be knowledge of the hidden *Tao* and thus is foolishness; therefore, to truly know is to know that one does not know.

* * * * *

In addition to this rejection of what is perceived as the meddling of the Confucian ethic of attainment, the *Tao Teh Ching* presents a constructive teaching in the form of non-interference, or life in harmony with *Tao*. This will be seen to be an instance of the reversal of effort theme, that the good is achieved on the condition we cease the effort to achieve it.

The posture of non-interference is variously described as being soft, yielding, pliable, passive, receptive, and empty; and as being like a reed, a vessel, a valley, water, or the female. It is described as "holding to the core" (5) and as "action without deeds" (3) and as inaction.

> The best of men is like water; water benefits all things and does not compete with them. It dwells in (the lowly) places that all disdain — wherein it comes near to the *Tao*. (8)

> The softest substance of the world goes through the hardest. That-which-is-without-form penetrates that-which-has-no-crevice; through this I know the benefit of taking no action. (43)

> The Female overcomes the Male by quietude. (61)

The central paradox presented in these images is that yielding is strongest.

> To yield is to be preserved whole. To be bent is to become straight. To be hollow is to be filled. To be tattered is to be renewed. To be in want is to possess. (22)

> The student of knowledge (aims at) learning day by day; the student of

> *Tao* (aims at) losing day by day. By continual losing one reaches doing nothing. By doing nothing everything is done. He who conquers the world often does so by doing nothing. (48; cf. 57)

> When the things and plants are alive, they are soft and supple; when they are dead, they are brittle and dry. Therefore hardness and stiffness are the companions of death, and softness and gentleness are the companions of life. (76)

That is, assertive action runs counter to the *Tao*, and being brittle and rigid it will ultimately be broken while natural, effortless action is in harmony with the *Tao* and will flourish.

> There is nothing weaker than water, but none is superior to it in overcoming the hard . . . . weakness overcomes strength and gentleness overcomes rigidity. (78)

Again, the central image of water appears; meditation on its ways reveals the power that non-interference and letting be can bestow.

Throughout these various attempts to depict the attitude of non-interference runs a sense of the power (*teh*), which is appropriated by receptivity.

> He who is aware of the Male, but keeps to the Female becomes the ravine of the world. . . . He has eternal power that never fails. (28)

While the mountain loses the water that falls upon it and is worn down in the process, the ravine, being empty is filled. The passive, receptive attitude makes one a channel of the power of the *Tao* quietly active in all things.

> If kings and barons can keep (this unspoiled nature) the whole world shall yield them lordship of (its) own accord. (32)

Power is not the result of our own knowledge and effort, but comes to us spontaneously when we are unobstructed channels of the power of nature. The way to become a fulfilled person with all the appropriate powers is not through contrivance and exertion, but in the effortless way in which natural things come to possess their powers. On this account the Taoist Sage lays no claim to whatever good comes and takes no pride in so-called accomplishments.

> Therefore the Sage acts, but does not possess, accomplishes, but lays claim to no credit. (77)

As in the letters of Paul, if you accomplish without trying, there is no basis for pride.

Since so much of the Confucian teaching of *li* was concerned with the rational ordering of social and political affairs, the *Tao Teh Ching* repeatedly shows how the best order of society comes from "rule without interference" (10). The more regulation there is, the more disturbed is the natural harmony, and disorder grows (56). The proper method of rule by non-interference is shown in the aphorism:

> Rule a big country as you would fry small fish. (60)

For if tested and turned too much, the small fish crumbles in the pan. A peaceful and prosperous land results from the non-interference of its rulers (75).

> Therefore the Sage says: I do nothing and the people are reformed of themselves. I love quietude and the people are righteous of themselves. I deal in no business and the people grow rich by themselves. I have no desires and the people are simple and honest by themselves. (57)

That order, which Confucian ministers cannot contrive, comes of itself if people are let be.

As pointed out above, what common sense considers knowledge is in the final analysis foolishness. The corollary to this is that to common sense, the teaching of the *Tao* seems foolish. To seek the good through not attempting to know or work for it seems foolish to common sense.

> When the lowest type (of men) hear the *Tao*, they break into loud laughter, — if it were not laughed at it would not be *Tao*. Therefore there is the established saying: "Who understands *Tao* seems dull of comprehension; who is advanced in *Tao* seems to slip backwards." (41)

> The highest perfection is like imperfection, . . . the greatest abundance seems meager. . . . What is most straight appears devious; the greatest cleverness appears like stupidity; the greatest eloquence seems like stuttering. (45)

> All the world says: my teaching greatly resembles folly. Because it is great, therefore it resembles folly. If it did not resemble folly, it would have long ago become petty indeed! (67)

The pursuit of what the world terms wisdom is fruitless and self-defeating, for what can be known cannot be the hidden working of *Tao*; the true wisdom of *Tao* comes by not seeking to know or understand.

> The farther one pursues knowledge, the less one knows. Therefore the Sage knows without running about, understands without seeing, accomplishes without doing. (47)

The contrast of what is usually called knowledge and Taoist wisdom is succinctly stated in this aphorism.

> He who knows does not speak; he who speaks does not know. (56)

To "know" the *Tao* is simply to live in harmony with it by non-interference and letting be, without conscious knowledge of its nature or course.

As with Stoicism and Pauline Christianity, the reversal of effort depends in Taoism on a specific teaching about the nature of reality. That is, non-interference is based upon a particular description of the world and the way it works, which involves the notion that within and beneath the many things of this world there is at work a process which seeks to balance all opposition, harmonize all dissonance, and bring all incompleteness to fulfillment. All things have within them the ability to follow this way if no one interferes; everything in nature including men and women, "knows" how to be itself, how to grow, how to heal, how to prosper, how to wain, and how to fade away and die. In fact, non-interference is precisely the way the *Tao* itself acts.

> The *Tao* never does, yet through it everything is done. (37)

> *Tao* is good at conquest without strife, . . . achieving results without obvious design. (73)

The pervasive tendency toward fulfillment active throughout nature is the Great *Tao*, the source of all.

> The Great *Tao* flows everywhere, like a flood it may go left or right. The myriad things derive their life from it, and it does not deny them. When its work is accomplished, it does not take possession. It clothes and feeds the myriad things, yet does not claim them as its own. Often (regarded) without mind or passion, it may be considered small. Being the home of all things, yet claiming not, it may be considered great. Because to the end it does not claim greatness, its greatness is achieved. (34)

Yet the all-pervading activity of *Tao* is itself nameless and cannot be known except through its "named" manifestations.

> The thing that is called *Tao* is elusive, evasive. Evasive, elusive, yet latent in it are forms. Elusive, evasive, yet latent in it are objects. Dark and dim, yet latent in it is the life force. From the days of old till now its named (manifested) forms have never ceased, by which we may view the father of all things. How do I know the shape of the father of all things? Through these! (21; cf. 1)

Since the *Tao* is the path things naturally follow in effortlessly reaching their proper state, all things come from the *Tao* and derive their life and strength from it. Therefore, to cut ourselves off from this way of being through self-assertiveness leads to disaster. The good of human life consists in returning to the root of life through non-interference and effortless action.

> The myriad things take shape and rise to activity, but I watch them fall back to their repose. Like vegetation that luxuriantly grows, but returns to the root from which it springs. To return to the root is repose. It is called going back to one's destiny. Going back to one's destiny is to find the eternal law. To know the eternal law is enlightenment. (16)

In living naturally, we do not assert our partial knowledge and our limited conception of the good against the larger natural good that the *Tao* is working out in the whole of the universe. In not insisting on our consciously chosen desires and plans, and in giving ourselves away in non-assertive being, we follow nature, which is ever abundant and ever-living because it constantly bestows itself.

> The universe is everlasting. The reason the universe is everlasting is that it does not live for self. Therefore it can long endure. (7)

Non-interference as an attitude to living is thus possible because one has come to see fulfillment as bestowed by the *Tao* and not contrived by self-effort; now one does not exert oneself to secure the good of one's own personal life apart from the total system of nature. The attitude of non-interference and natural action then puts one in harmony with the flow of nature, which fulfills the being of everything in nature in a way appropriate to each thing, and creates a harmony of all things in the whole. The power and life and wisdom of *Tao* are appropriated through letting be; it fosters our greatest good when we are open to it, giving ourselves over to natural, effortless action, and not obstructing its natural flow with attempts to know, plan, and manage.

> *Tao* is hidden, without a name. It is this *Tao* that is adept at lending (its power) and bringing fulfillment. (41)

> Looked at, it cannot be seen; listened to, it cannot be heard; applied, its supply never fails. (35)

> Therefore *Tao* gives them birth, . . . fosters them, makes them grow, develops them, gives them a harbor, a place to dwell in peace, feeds them and shelters them. It gives them birth and does not own them, is superior and does not control them. This is the mystic virtue. (51)

It seems in this concept, we have neither the transcendent, personal monarchial God of Paul, nor the Absolute Reality of some Hindu and Buddhist thought, the supreme unity in which particular things lose their separate identities. The concept of *Tao* represents the naturalism and common sense of China. It does not obliterate the separate reality of the many particular objects of the world. It is not transcendent of nature, but immanent within it. It is not mere stillness, but the way of pervasive activity and process, the pattern of all change and the impetus to completion. And it is not *a* being, some person or thing that acts on other things from outside them, but the mysterious way through which all being comes to be. For ancient China, every seemingly stable object is a process of interaction, and *Tao* is the natural way every process, the self, the universe and everything in it, reaches completion.

The criticism of the ethic of attainment and the assertion of a form of the law of the reversal of effort can be summarized through these lines, which incidentally cite specific Confucian doctrines.

> Banish wisdom, discard knowledge, and the people shall profit a hundredfold; banish "love," discard "justice," and the people shall recover love of their kin; banish cunning, discard [wealth] and thieves and brigands shall disappear. (19)

The proper order of personal and societal life, and the proper harmony with nature, are not achieved by attempting to achieve them but by the paradoxically indirect method of not attempting to achieve them, for on this condition these goods are discovered to be already in our possession, bestowed by the *Tao*.

Chapter 5

SARAHA'S TREASURY OF SONGS: FIND TRUTH BY LETTING GO OF ILLUSION

The nature of the sky is originally clear, but by gazing and gazing the sight becomes obscured; then when the sky appears deformed in this way, the fool does not know that the fault's in his own mind.

—*Dohakosha*, 188.34

The *Treasury of Songs*, or *Dohakosha*, represents Tantric Buddhism, the last phase in the development of Buddhism in India before its virtual extinction in the land of its origin. It is attributed to Saraha, one of the "eighty-four perfect ones" who are the founders of Tantrism, and was written in the Apabhramsha, or Old Bengali language, a dialect of eastern India, in the eleventh and twelfth centuries A.D. As Tantric Buddhism survived largely in and across the Himalayas, Tibetan versions also exist and are useful in translation and interpretation.

Saraha belonged to the Sahajayana or "Vehicle of the Innate" school of Tantrism and believed the ultimate reality is present in all things. What follows from this belief is, firstly, there is in one sense only one single identity in the universe, and thus it is not strictly true there are distinct objects; on the other hand, within the frame of mind which recognizes separate objects, you can now see them as really being manifestations of the ultimate reality. Thus there is good news, the ultimate is close at hand, nearer than hands and feet, and any person not just monastics, saints, and philosophers, can readily come to see this.

Indeed, according to Saraha, the energetic and learned pursuers of enlightenment are for a very subtle reason not as likely to see the ultimate in everyday reality as the common person. The *Treasury of Songs* specifically and directly attacks various forms of the ethic of attainment, which were being set forth at the time of its composition. The Brahmin or priestly caste of Hindu society, sought the good of human life in the full and scrupulous observance of the ritual obligations of the sacred *Veda* texts. Purity and the favor of the gods are to be attained, and thus life is fulfilled. The monks of the Jain sect sought the good in a strenuous and intense effort to subdue and thus find release from the material body and its world, which enslave the spirit. Their dualistic view of reality taught them to see themselves as discrete, upward-striving spirits, each trapped in an evil, burdensome physical body. Scholars of the Hinayana, or Old School sects of Buddhism, sought the good in the elaboration of a systematic understanding of Buddhist metaphysics. Each embodies a form of striving and aims at attaining the good as a direct outcome of action. The Brahmin sees the good as the direct result of prayer-words and acts of worship, the Jain sees it as the direct result of the effort to attain release from the encumbrance of matter through ascetic discipline, and the scholastic Buddhist sees it as the direct result of a proper and thorough intellectual understanding of the nature of the self and the world. But the author of the *Treasury* insists that each of these efforts is doomed to failure by the fact that it misunderstands the nature of the good and therefore leads us away from the good by its very attempt to achieve it.

The good of human life is by nature a state that cannot be attained by effort, since it requires the cessation of all effort. The good is immediate recognition of the ultimate unity of all seemingly distinct subjects and objects in the supreme reality, the Innate Buddha. This recognition is experienced as release and freedom from all of the worries and struggles that one experiences when taking the illusory world of discrete persons and objects as if it were ultimately real. One then sees that the discrete self, struggling for its own good and ultimately threatened by death, is an illusion, and one's anxiety and concern melt away. There is no little self to be protected and fulfilled. Now one is free to act naturally and engage in everyday activities, knowing that one's good is not won through effort in a precarious existence, but that it lies in one's own present identity with the still, eternal Innate. This is the condition called nirvana. Note, as in the case of the other classical expressions of the law of the reversal of effort, letting go of self-effort is based on a certain perception of the nature of reality, in this case, the belief in the unity of all things.

In the light of this understanding of the good of human life, all attempts to attain the good, whether through ritualism, ascetism, or intellectualism, lead directly away from it. One can never recognize the illusory nature of the idea of the discrete self while one is busily engaged in attempting to enhance it. All attempts to attain the good fail because they are based on the idea of the distinct self acting to maintain and fulfill itself. The ethic of attainment seeks to maintain the self and secure it against all threats. This, of course, is based on illusion and cannot succeed; meanwhile it leads away from the recognition of the provisional nature of the world of subject and object. Therefore, the good lies precisely in abandoning all attempts to achieve it, since these attempts presuppose and help to sustain a misleading view of the self. When we cease seeking to fulfill the little self, we may then perceive its lack of ultimacy and our true identity with the Innate Buddha. The true nature of the self is known, and the resulting bliss experienced, only when all striving for the good ceases.

* * * * *

In the *Treasury of Songs* considerable attention is given to the direct and explicit criticism of the attempt to attain or contrive the good. All such attempts are based on the illusion of a discrete self acting to secure its own permanence and security, and its effect is simply to reinforce such illusions. But in fact, the good of life is already in our possession because each self is actually identical with the supreme reality; all that is necessary is that one come to recognize this. This involves abandoning the illusion of the distinct self and those activities that seek the good in the enhancement of this illusion.

> *Mantras* and *tantras*, meditation and concentration, they are all a cause of self-deception. Do not defile in contemplation thought that is pure in its own nature, but abide in the bliss of yourself and cease those torments. (23)[1]

This is the basic form of the attack on the ethic of attainment.

Specifically, an attack is made upon Brahmin ritualism in terms of the strongest ridicule and caricature.

> The Brahmin who do not know the truth, vainly recite the *Vedas* four. With earth and water and *kusha*-grass they make preparations, and seated at home they kindle fire, and from the senseless offerings that they make, they burn their eyes with the pungent smoke. . . . With ashes these masters smear their bodies, and on their heads they wear matted hair. Seated within the house they kindle lamps. Seated in a corner they tinkle bells. They adopt a posture and fix their eyes, whispering in ears and deceiving folk, teaching widows and bald-headed nuns and such like, initiating them as they take their fee. (1, 2, 3, 5)

The dualistic Jain ascetics are handled with the same kind of mockery and humor.

> The *Jain* monks mock the Way with their appearance, with their long nails and their filthy clothes, or else naked and with disheveled hair, en-

[1] All subsequent quotations from Saraha are from "Saraha's Treasury of Songs, chap. 188," trans. David S. Snellgrove, in *Buddhist Texts through the Ages*, ed. Edward Conze (Oxford: Bruno Cassirer, 1954), 224-239. The numbers in parenthesis after quotations refer to sections within chap. 188.

> slaving themselves with their doctrine of release. If by nakedness one is released, then dogs and jackals must be so. If from absence of hair there comes perfection, then the hips of maidens must be so. . . . For these *Jain* monks there is no release, Saraha says. Deprived of the truth of happiness, they do but afflict their own bodies. (6, 7, 9)

(The "Way" mentioned in the first line of this quotation refers to the *dharma*, the "path or teaching" of the historical Buddha, the enlightened one.) Neither the scrupulous attention to Vedic ritual, nor the world-fleeing ascetic discipline of the Jains leads to release from the illusion of the ultimacy of the self or to the discovery of one's true identity with the Innate. Rather, ritualism and ascetism are mere foolishness, which with their striving only further enslave us to our illusions.

Even within Buddhism, Saraha finds those who have begun to fall into the error of seeking enlightenment through the action of the self.

> Then there are the novices and *bhikshus* with the teaching of the Old School, who renounce the world to be monks. Some are seen sitting and reading the scriptures. Some wither away in their concentration on thought. . . . Others just meditate on *mandala*-circles. Others strive to define the fourth stage of bliss. With such investigation they fall from the Way. Some would envisage it as space, others endow it with the nature of voidness, and thus they are generally in disagreement. (10, 11, 12)

The criticism here is two-fold. First, there are those who seek to reduce the attainment of enlightenment to a method of monastic discipline and meditation. This must fail as it is based on the illusion of the self striving through this method to secure its own good, and it cannot therefore lead to freedom from the illusion of the separate self. Further, there is special condemnation for those who develop a particular method, the method of the intellect. The attempt to know the nature of enlightenment cannot succeed because the awareness of the ultimate unity takes one beyond all distinction of knowing subject and object known; the ultimate unity includes both subject and object and thus cannot itself become an object of knowledge. The nature of enlightenment awareness cannot be a subject of knowledge, which proceeds by making distinctions, for there are no distinctions within the supreme reality. And of course, the intellectual approach assumes and maintains the illusion of the knowing, inquiring self, and thus only enmeshes us more deeply in error.

This criticism of worship, ascetic discipline, meditation, and intellectual inquiry as all leading away from the true good of human life is repeated throughout the *Treasury*. Worship may be valid, but according to Saraha it leaves unsettled the question of the nature of the self; faithfulness in ritual will not lead to the realization of the provisional nature of the self and the unity of all things in the Innate. Indeed, ritual moves in the world in which subject (the worshiper) and object (the deity) are separate, thus maintaining this fictitious distinction. It therefore cannot answer our deepest problem or lead to a genuine solution.

> One may worship a divinity, and (in trance) even his form may be seen. But one is still oneself subject to death, for what can he do? (65)

The same point is made with respect to the physical discipline of yoga. The practice of yoga cannot lead to enlightenment since it presumes the illusion of the self acting to attain the good, and it cannot therefore lead to the realization that the self is illusory as a discrete entity.

> "One fixes the eyes, obstructs the thought, restrains the breath. This is the teaching of our lord and master." But when the flow of his breath is quite motionless, and the *yogin* is dead, what then? (66)

The mention of death in these last two quotations is important. Saraha is saying if we identify ourselves with that which perishes, and seek to build up and secure the self, we will be lost; we must learn our real identity is that which is eternal. As long as release is sought in the context of the fictitious self, one retains all of the problems of the self. Neither can meditation lead to enlightenment, for its practice keeps alive the idea of a self who meditates and seeks release.

> How by meditation should one . . . gain release? And why accept such falsehood? (33)

Finally, release from the illusion of the self cannot lie in the self's acquisition of knowledge. If one seeks the good through knowledge, one is committed to actively maintaining the idea of the self as knower, therefore experiencing all of the suffering to which the self is vulnerable.

> One thing is so, another is not so. . . . Strange how these *pandits* go to grief through their own errors. . . . In this house and that the matter is discussed, but the basis of the great bliss is unknown. The world is enslaved by thought, Saraha says, and no one has known this non-thought. (76, 78)

Thought lives on distinctions and therefore cannot know the basic unity beneath distinctions; thus enlightenment could only come by a process of unknowing.

> It is devoid of names and other qualities; I have said it cannot be known by

> discussion. So how may the Supreme Lord be described? It is like a maiden's experiencing bliss. (58)

What is needed is not discursive knowledge of this view of reality, but our immediate and ecstatic awareness of reality itself.

> All these pundits expound the treatises, but the Buddha who resides within the body is not known. (68)

> The whole world is confused by schools of thought, and no one perceives his true nature. (35)

This last criticism of intellectualization as leading to confusion and obscuring what would otherwise be apparent summarizes the logic of the criticism of all efforts to attain the good. All effort, whether in ritual, meditation, ascetism, or knowing, obscures the simple and obvious truth and leads to confusion and frustration.

> The nature of the sky is originally clear, but by gazing and gazing the sight becomes obscured; then when the sky becomes deformed in this way, the fool does not know that the fault's in his own mind. (34)

Thus efforts to attain the good lead away from it, foolishly ignoring what would otherwise be obvious and near at hand. In seeking the good in the action of the self, one is further implicated in the fictitious world of subject and object, and one seeks the good where it cannot be found.

> He is at home, but she goes outside and looks. She sees her husband, but still asks the neighbors. (62)

The effort to attain the good maintains the illusion of the discrete self, and it leads away from the realization of one's inner unity with the Innate. This in turn implies that if the effort to save the self were relaxed, the illusions would dissolve and one's true nature would become apparent.

> Whoever deprived of the Innate, seeks nirvana, can in no wise acquire the absolute truth. (13)

The important word here is "seeks." Nirvana is enlightenment conceived as the "snuffing-out" of our selfish clinging to the idea of the little self; to strive for nirvana as an object of selfish desire cannot lead to enlightenment. All forms of the ethic of attainment manifest this selfish clinging, which prevents us from discovering our real identity. This criticism of the ethic of attainment implies the form of the ethic of consolation, which the *Treasury* will offer: the good of life lies in the abandonment of the attempt to secure it.

* * * * *

Subsequent to this criticism of the ethic of attainment, and implied within it, is the positive teaching of the *Treasury*, which is a form of the law of the reversal of effort. Since it is the misdirected attempt to contrive the good as the outcome of the self's effort that keeps us from realizing the good, the cessation of this effort must be the condition on which the good is based.

> Thought bound brings bondage, and released brings release. . . . When so bound it dashes in all directions, but released, it stays still. Just consider the camel, my friend. I see there a similar paradox. (42, 43)

The active attempt to attain the good of the separate self binds one more firmly to this fictitious understanding and involves one in the futile and frustrating struggle to preserve and sustain something that is not abidingly real. Release from this bondage to an illusion through the cessation of effort brings peace, just as the camel struggles against a tether, but remains at peace in one place when untied.

When the misdirected striving to make the illusory self secure ceases, the true self becomes apparent.

> When the mind ceases thus to be mind, the true nature of the Innate shines forth. (77)

When the mind ceases to see itself as its own end and gives up the struggle to save itself through knowing and acting, its true identity with the whole becomes apparent.

This letting go of effort is made possible by the specific doctrine of the *Treasury* concerning the nature of reality. This teaching provides the rationale for the abandonment of striving. The doctrine is simply this: ultimately, that which is alone real is the Innate Buddha. Of course, separate objects, including the self, have a provisional kind of reality in that they at least appear real to us and we must live among them and take account of them. Their reality is not ultimate for they do not abide, and we cling to the illusion of the substantial and permanent being of the self and its world only out of selfishness and the fear of letting go. When we come to see things as they are and know the Innate Buddha as the true identity and essence of all things, then we can see the world of separate objects in a new way, as bearers of the ultimate reality. But what we see is the Innate in things and not things as ends in themselves.

Thus the self is not a permanent and discrete entity, and so the good cannot consist in the effort to save or fulfill the self. Rather, the self is a manifestation of the ultimate essence or mind of all things. The good therefore consists in ceasing to identify ourselves with this little self and in coming to identify with the whole. The result is freedom from anxiety and struggle. We are freed from the illusion of the separate self by realizing that it is even now identical with the ultimate, that it has innate within it the essence of the whole of reality. On this basis, we can let go of the self without fear of loss. We already possess all there is in our identity with the Innate Buddha, and so we need seek no further gain nor fear any loss.

The identity of self and whole is obscured by the structure of conventional thought, which hypostasizes parts of the whole (the individual mind, separate objects, etc.) and treats them as ends in themselves.

> They do not perceive the true basis of mind, for upon the Innate they impose a three-fold falsification. (36)

In this case the falsification is the fictitious separation of perceiver, object and perception, and the Innate is the identity that is thereby obscured.

The realization of the ultimate unity as the basis of the true good of human life is well summarized in the sixtieth stanza.

> So long as you do not recognize the Supreme One in yourself, how should you gain this incomparable form? I have taught that when error ceases, you know yourself for what you are. (60)

The good consists in the realization of one's identity with the ultimate reality and therefore requires the abandonment of all thought and action that obscures or denies this identity. Fictitious distinctions, and the actions which follow from them and help maintain them, must be overcome so that one's true nature will become apparent.

> Do not conceive differences in yourself. When there is no distinction between Body, Speech and Mind, then the true nature of the Innate shines forth. (83)

> The bodiless form is concealed in the body. He who knows this is therein released. (89)

> Who does not comprehend that everything is of his own nature? He is like a thirsty deer that runs for water which is but a mirage. (91)

In short, the doctrinal basis of the *Treasury* is the contrast between the fictitious and provisional distinctions imposed upon reality by erroneous thought (88), and the ultimate unity of all in the Innate Buddha.

> "This is myself and this is another." Be free of this bond which encompasses you about, and your own self is thereby released. (105)
>
> Do not err in this matter of self and other. Everything is Buddha without exception. (106)
>
> It is profound, it is vast. It is neither self nor other. (96)
>
> Mind is the universal seed. (41)

Realization of this is the basis of freedom and peace. This realization does not occur unless we ". . . renounce the idea of a self" (112). This implies the paradox of intention, for the good is achieved only by renouncing the attempt to achieve it as the goal of a striving self.

It seems that enlightenment involves not an ecstatic vision of hidden realms, but a new way of perceiving everyday reality. This is expressed in the doctrine that "*Samsara* is *Nirvana*," or that common experience, when viewed correctly becomes transparent and reveals the ultimate (102, 103, 110). This obviates reliance upon occult and ascetic practices that promise visions and transports (19). The *Treasury* even recommends full involvement in common physical experience for the enlightened, not in the way of the unenlightened who are driven by cravings and become addicted to the senses, but in a way that celebrates each physical object and person as a disclosure of the Innate Buddha. This is a middle way between worldliness and ascetism. The common person sees the world as full of separate objects to be consumed and enjoyed for themselves and becomes enmeshed in the pursuit of sensation, not seeing the ultimate in each object of desire. On the other hand, the ascetic fails to see the ultimate near at hand in every object and turns away from everyday physical experience. In keeping with Tantric Buddhism, Saraha advises that the enlightened engage in physical action and enjoyment, particularly sexual intercourse, in order to deepen one's experience of the hidden presence of the Innate.

> Enjoying the world of sense, one is undefiled by the world of sense. One plucks the lotus without touching the water. So the *yogin* who has gone to the root of things is not enslaved by the senses, although he enjoys them. (64)
>
> He who does not enjoy the senses purified, and practices only the void, is like a bird that flies up from a ship and then wheels round and lands back there again. But do not be caught by attachment to the senses, Saraha says. (70, 71)

The released enjoy the delights of everyday experience, including the sharing of sexual pleasure, without compulsion or anxiety, knowing that their final good does not depend upon their attainment of pleasure and their avoidance of pain. Physical enjoyment is freed from the negative evaluation often placed on it in systems of spiritual growth. And it is released from the burden of having to fulfill life as a whole and give it meaning; it is allowed to be simply what it is. (While the comparison may seem strange at first, this is not unlike the way in which Paul's idea of salvation by grace through faith allows moral action to be just what it is, freeing it from the burden of having to prove one's acceptability; of course Paul's views on sexuality are not the same as Saraha's.) The point is simply that in the end, all experience tastes of the supreme reality.

> When the mind goes to rest, and bonds of the body are destroyed, then the one flavour of the Innate pours forth and there is neither outcaste nor Brahmin. (46)

At this point it is clear that the *Treasury of Songs* exemplifies an ethic of consolation, the inner logic of which is the law of the reversal of effort. The good of human life is not achieved by the attempt to achieve it, but by the paradoxically indirect method of giving up the attempt to achieve it, for on that condition one finds it is already in one's possession in the form of our identity with the Innate Buddha.

Chapter 6

VICTOR FRANKL'S LOGOTHERAPY: HEALING THROUGH PARADOXICAL INTENTION

> If we succeed in bringing the patient to the point where he ceases to flee from or to fight his symptoms, . . . then we may observe that the symptoms diminish and that the patient is no longer haunted by them.
>
> —Viktor Frankl
> *The Doctor and the Soul*

The writings of Viktor Frankl, founder of the school of depth psychology called logotherapy, contain the most explicit expression and self-conscious use of the reversal of effort theme in recent literature. The term "logotherapy" is derived from the Greek word *logos*, "word or meaning," and therefore signifies "healing through meaning."[1] As a school of psychotherapy it treats the usual physically and emotionally caused psychic problems, but it also identifies certain other neuroses as of spiritual or philosophical origin. According to Frankl, psychic distress may arise from physical dysfunction, emotional trauma or conflict, as well as from problems in the realm of meaning; we have a need for a sense of meaning, and the lack of meaningfulness or a conflict between this need and received beliefs may lead to symptoms like depression and even to suicide.

In the treatment of both problems of meaning and problems of physical and emotional origin, logotherapy employs concepts embodying the reversal of effort theme. Firstly, in connection with the neuroses of meaning, logotherapy maintains that the fulfillment of the self cannot arise as the outcome of direct action, which treats this as a goal; rather, it comes about as a a by-product of our commitment to a meaning or value outside the self, such as a task or a loved person. Secondly, in the treatment of strictly emotional conflicts, two methods called "paradoxical intention" and "dereflection" are used which clearly involve reversal of effort; in paradoxical intention, for example, a stutterer may be instructed to stutter intentionally, with the frequent result that stuttering becomes impossible.

[1] Viktor E. Frankl, *The Will to Meaning, Foundations and Applications of Logotherapy* (New York: World Publishing, 1969), 9.

Viktor Frankl, born in 1905, received Doctor of Medicine and Doctor of Philosophy degrees from the University of Vienna, and was professor of neurology and psychiatry at the Medical School of that university and head of the neurological department of the Poliklinik Hospital in Vienna. As a Jew, Professor Frankl was subject to persecution by the German occupation, and after declining an opportunity to flee to the United States in order to remain with his aged parents, he was imprisoned for three years and was at both Auschwitz and Dachau. It is especially significant and poignant that Professor Frankl experienced the Nazi death camps, for in three earlier chapters it was suggested that letting go of self-effort may be a response to extremity and disaster, and to the collapse of our control over events.

* * * * *

Frankl proposes a view of human nature which is holistic and counteracts the tendency of our analytic time to reduce the person to something less than what we really know ourselves to be. To Frankl, Freud's concept of the human as dominated by the will to pleasure and Adler's idea of the will to power both reduce the whole person to that which is but a part, but for Frankl the will to meaning includes and supersedes these parts, and it is this which shapes human character. Of course we are bodies with physical needs, and we are likewise psychological beings with social needs, and thus pleasure and self-esteem are important motives of human action, as Freud and Adler saw. But what is unique about the human is that we can take a stand toward the physical and psychological aspects of our selves; the person is shaped not merely by what is given in biology and by what occurs in social experience, but by the attitude taken toward them. This insight reveals the "noetic sphere" beyond the biological and psychological; this is the realm of the meanings or values we find in experience and is called "noetic" from *nous*, the Greek word for reason or mind. Persons characteristically ask what a situation means, and their fulfillment requires they find and fulfill meaning and purpose in what they experience and do. This is our "intentionality," the demand that what we do and undergo must bear meaning or embody purpose or have value. "What I call the will to meaning could be defined as the basic striving of man to find and fulfill meaning and purpose."[2] If this will to meaning is unfulfilled, life itself is blunted.

Our intentionality, our seeking and finding meanings in experience, is the way we transcend ourselves. Through self-detachment we can step outside of our situation and assess it, and through self-transcendence we ask about its meaning. The human is unique in needing

[2] *Ibid.*, 35.

to find his or her situation meaningful; we do not simply act and experience, but transcend experience and look back at it, requiring that it contribute to a purpose and have a value. The sense of humor and heroism in the face of hopeless defeat are examples respectively of self-detachment and self-transcendence; in these examples we look at our lives as if from outside, and we find a meaning which transcends the given. That this dimension of the person transcends the sphere of pleasure and power on which Freud and Adler focused is seen in the dual fact that one may be unfulfilled and in despair even if pleasure and social adjustment are possessed, and one may find meaning and fulfillment even if they are absent. Only to the extent that we commit ourselves to the fulfillment of a meaning in life are we whole. Frankl insists that a truly human life is not found within the self as if it were a closed system, but only in commitment to something which transcends the self and the moment. This is clearly a criticism of the widespread popular movement in which self-realization is made a goal.

If the uniquely human need is for a sense of meaning or purpose, then there is danger in acting primarily to achieve satisfaction of our physical and emotional needs; the common phenomenon of "success with despair" shows that our drives may be satisfied and our lives still unfulfilled. Indeed, we cannot aim at pleasure or happiness with any hope of success, for they cannot be attained if they are made ends in themselves; they are only possible as by-products of self-transcendence through the discovery of meaning or commitment to a value. Pleasure, happiness, or fulfillment must be side effects and not goals.

> If there is a reason for happiness, *happiness ensues*, automatically and spontaneously, as it were. And that is why one *need not pursue happiness.* One need not care for it once there is a reason for it.[3]

According to Frankl, we cannot pursue happiness, for if it is our objective, we lose sight of the reason for happiness and happiness itself fades away. Concentration on pleasure and happiness and neglect of the dimension of meaning is counter-productive. Fulfillment thus cannot be a goal; it must be the effect of our finding a purpose, value or meaning. It is an "unintentional effect of life's intentionality."[4]

Clearly in Frankl we find a theme of the classical texts examined above, the goal cannot be reached by attempting to reach it.

> Pleasure establishes itself automatically as soon as one has fulfilled a meaning or realized a value. Moreover, if a man really attempted to gain pleasure by making it his target, he would necessarily fail, for he would miss

[3] *Ibid.*, 34.
[4] *Ibid.*, 38.

> what he aimed at.[5]

Fulfillment for humans accompanies a sense of meaningfulness; to turn away from this toward pleasure for its own sake cannot lead to fulfillment. This is true also of the preoccupation with peace of mind or the pursuit of happiness. "The pursuit of happiness amounts to a self-contradiction: the more we strive for happiness, the less we attain it."[6] It is a side-effect which is destroyed if made an intention. Frankl often uses the case of striving for a good conscience as an example of the counterproductive character of effort.

> A man who is striving for a condition in which he can rightly say, "I possess a good conscience" would already represent a case of Pharisaism. A really good conscience can never be reached by grasping for it, but solely by doing a deed for the sake of a cause, or for the sake of the person involved, or for God's sake. A good conscience is one of those things which can be brought about only as an unintended side effect and is destroyed at the moment that it is sought after directly.[7]

True goodness would not be action to earn reputation or a good feeling about oneself, or to avoid the pain of guilt and rejection; it would be to act for the sake of a person or a meaning, someone or something beyond the self. Since the basic fact of human nature is self-transcendence, the fulfillment of human life cannot be found through making it the object of intention. Here Frankl repeats that critique of the ethic of attainment which characterized the great traditional expressions of the law of the reversal of effort. He has shown why there cannot be a self-help book on how to achieve happiness and peace of mind.

Even if all of our physical and emotional needs be met, the will to meaning may be unsatisfied. This can lead to neurotic illness manifest as boredom, apathy, despair, and suicide. But this neurosis is *noogenic*, "rooted in the noetic sphere," as opposed to those *somatogenic* and *psychogenic* neuroses rooted in physical dysfunction or emotional conflict. To Frankl, this is the characteristic neurosis of our time, precisely because we concentrate so completely in our psychology, religion, and life styles on achieving satisfaction within ourselves. Meaning is found in relation and commitment to something outside the self, and self-preoccupation therefore must frustrate the will to meaning. In Frankl's view, the collective neurosis of our time is this "existential vacuum," or emptiness of meaning, that frustrated longing for a mean-

[5] Viktor E. Frankl, *Psychotherapy and Existentialism, Selected Papers on Logotherapy* (New York: Washington Square Press, 1967), 40.

[6] *Ibid.*, 41.

[7] *Ibid.*

ing to life which could only come from commitment to a value outside oneself. It is manifest in the panicked quest for self-actualization and self-expression, in the lurking despair that comes about in the "Sunday neurosis" or "vacation malaise" when the compulsively busy are faced with unstructured time, in compulsive conformity which looks alike and talks alike and fears deviation, and we might add to Frankl's list, in the rush to unload our responsibility to find meaning in our own lives through the joining of authoritarian churches and cults with ready-made answers.

Specifically, noogenic neuroses arise from frustration of the will to meaning, either in the form of failure to find meaning, or in the form of conflict between imposed, ready-made and often inherited meaning-patterns and our own need. Our time is peculiar in that for an increasing number of people, traditional universal meanings do not satisfy, and their decline as cultural forces throws us into a noetic vacuum. Thus meaning becomes very much an individual task and responsibility, and this is both burdensome and liberating. Meaning must be found individually and contextually, by each person and for each situation. Frankl feels meaning is found by the intuitive faculty he calls "conscience." Logotherapy as a therapy for noogenic neurosis is a process in which the therapist does not impose his or her own meaning, but encourages the conscience of the patient to perceive purposes and meanings within the life situation; for "meaning must be found, it cannot be given."[8]

Meaning is found in three ways: (1) by doing a deed, which is the way of achievement or accomplishment; (2) by experiencing a value, as in love, through which we become aware of the inner core of the being of another person or an object; and (3) by suffering in a situation which is inescapable, and yet being able to suffer well and give it meaning. In short, meaning is found in what we give, in what we take, and in the stand we take toward a fate that cannot be changed. The values for life that arise in each of these contexts Frankl refers to as the creative, the experiential and the attitudinal.

Creative values are the meanings that arise by the goals we seek and the tasks we complete. This is the realm in which the ethic of attainment seeks the whole of life's fulfillment, as seen in earlier chapters. Frankl has provided in this concept a way of understanding the validity in the ethic of attainment; for when effort is not self-defeating, it can give genuine meaning to life. But as noted in the earlier chapters, personal and historical circumstances may make attainment impossible, and, in addition, may deprive us of those objects of love that are the source of experiential values. It was, in fact, in just such crises

[8] *Will to Meaning*, 67.

that the ethic of consolation developed. Therefore, we will be especially interested in Frankl's understanding of the third way of finding meaning. For what he calls attitudinal values arise in just those situations in which the ethic of attainment cannot operate, and in which the ethic of consolation arises again and again in history.

Meaning is found in deeds, in love, and in suffering. Even if we are deprived of the ability to act and denied that which we love, meaning can be found in the attitude we take to our suffering; even if we lose the creative and experiential values of life, the attitudinal remains possible, and thus a meaning can always be found in life.

> This is why life never ceases to hold a meaning, for even a person who is deprived of both creative and experiential values is still challenged by a meaning to fulfill, that is, by the meaning inherent in the right, in an upright way of suffering.[9]

That this affirmation is not cheap and untried appears when we recall that it grows out of Frankl's survival of the holocaust.

> Whenever one is confronted with an inescapable, unavoidable situation, whenever one has to face a fate that cannot be changed, e.g., an incurable disease, such as an inoperable cancer, just then is one given a last chance to actualize the highest value, to fulfill the deepest meaning, the meaning of suffering. For what matters above all is the attitude we take toward suffering, the attitude in which we take our suffering upon ourselves.[10]

When suffering finds a meaning, as in the meaning of sacrifice or courage, then it ceases to be merely suffering.

> As soon as a painful fate cannot be changed, it not only must be accepted, but may be transmuted into something meaningful, into an achievement.[11]

In this thought, that whatever comes, we are always free in the attitude we take, we find repeated the message of Epictetus and the Stoics.

Frankl had said our most fundamental need as humans is not to achieve pleasure and avoid pain, but to find meaning; it follows that we can be willing to suffer on the condition that it have meaning. That this is possible even in hopeless situations shows that attitudinal values are higher and more perdurable than the creative or the experiential. Just as attention to physical and emotional satisfactions alone was said

[9] *Ibid.*, 70.

[10] Viktor E. Frankl, *Man's Search for Meaning, an Introduction to Logotherapy*, rev. ed. (New York: Washington Square Press, 1963), 178.

[11] *Will to Meaning*, 72.

above to lead to the phenomenon of "despair despite success," so through attitudinal values we may find "fulfillment despite failure."[12] This phrase of Frankl's can be taken as a precise statement of the core of the ethic of consolation.

Frankl complains that at present, psychology is dominated by a view which centers on physical and emotional satisfaction and ignores the noetic dimension, and that therefore takes all unhappiness as a sign of maladjustment. This simply adds a second burden, "unhappiness about being unhappy," to those whose suffering is inescapable.[13] Here the incurable sufferer is deprived of the possibility of seeing suffering as ennobling. The simple fact is, in some situations one cannot do one's work and enjoy one's life, but one can still suffer well.

It shouldn't be necessary to add that Frankl is not advising that suffering be sought, for he recognizes this as an illness. He is only discussing a possible response to the inescapable. Nevertheless, his concept of attitudinal values as the finding of meaning in suffering has been criticized as showing a "regressive tendency to self-destructive submissiveness."[14] Perhaps this is understandable coming from a traditional Freudian psychologist. Freud had said life is fulfilled in love and work, in Frankl's terms, the experiential and the creative values. Freud provides little theoretical basis for understanding the attitude that accepts unavoidable suffering, for his image of the person centers on the struggle to achieve pleasure, acted out against one's own regressive tendencies toward passivity and a restrictive, punishing conscience within a hostile and grudging environment. (In spite of this, as a person, Freud knew quite well how to live with a prolonged and finally fatal cancer of the jaw.) Thus the Freudian critic of Frankl can only find his notion masochistic. Whether the ethic of consolation is such will be discussed in a later chapter. For now it is sufficient to point out that Frankl's view is indeed a form of the ethic of consolation and the reversal of effort theme is clearly present. To attempt to fulfill life by seeking pleasure, happiness, serenity, or self-actualization as immediate objectives is always a failure, for human life can only be fulfilled when you spend it, give it away, in commitment to a meaning beyond the immediate satisfaction of the self. But when meaning is fulfilled in commitment to something beyond the self, then pleasure, happiness, or serenity may well follow as side-effects, if and to the degree appropriate. You cannot get the goal by attempting to get it, but only by giving up direct concern for it, and on that condition, you receive it.

[12] *Ibid.*, 76.

[13] *Search for Meaning*, 180.

[14] Richard Trautman, Review of Frankl's *Homo Patiens* in *American Journal of Psychotherapy*, (1952), 5.821, quoted in *Will to Meaning*, 72.

* * * * *

Frankl insists that it is an error of traditional psychotherapy to treat the above problems of meaning as if they were manifestations of emotional disturbance; we have a need for meaning, which if frustrated manifests itself in psychic distress. Similarly, it would be an error to treat emotionally or physically based problems through philosophical understanding, and so logotherapy has developed techniques for dealing with these. As will be seen, these also manifest the reversal of effort motif.

Frankl is an existentialist and, as such, is concerned with the way in which the influence of science, technology, and the competitive industrial economic order influence our thought patterns so that we tend to lose sight of the uniqueness of the human; we fall into the habit of "reification," treating persons as things by applying to them patterns of analysis and manipulation so dominant in the rest of our lives. Logotherapy has been complemented as being the only existentialist school of psychotherapy that has developed definite techniques, but Frankl is quick to warn that therapy is based on encounter; that which heals is the patient-therapist relationship, and thus technique must not be understood mechanistically.

> Reification has become the original sin of psychotherapy. But a human being is no thing. This no-thingness rather than nothingness, is the lesson to learn from existentialism.[15]

The ego can only become an ego through a You, and thus a purely technological and manipulative approach to psychotherapy would block its therapeutic effect, in Frankl's view. Nevertheless, logotherapy has techniques; when these are shown below to embody the reversal of effort, the question will have arisen for the first time as to whether one can intend to suspend intention, and whether giving up the ethic of attainment is itself a kind of "doing."

In his approach to emotional illness, Frankl recognizes two pathogenic patterns, two modes of thought and feeling that give rise to distress. These are anticipatory anxiety and the compulsion to self-observation. Anticipatory anxiety produces that which is feared. A person tends to blush and fears that he or she will blush on an important social occasion; but this very fear of blushing causes it to happen. Thus one is involved in a vicious circle: the symptom evokes a fear and the fear provokes the symptom; then the occurrence of the symptom reinforces the fear, and so on. A feedback mechanism is at work. The

[15] *Will to Meaning*, 6.

patient suffers from "fear of fear,"[16] and the flight from those situations provoking the fear itself provokes fear. Frankl calls the pattern following from anticipatory anxiety "hyperintention," an excess of intention which leads to precisely what is feared.

The above example dealt with a phobia, the fear of blushing, and showed how the "flight from fear" provoked the fear. But anticipatory anxiety and hyperintention are also operative in the "fight against obsessions and compulsions." A person may be obsessed with the thought of suicide, or the fear that one will do an act of violence or murder or blurt out an obscenity; thoughts one judges to be bizarre may force themselves forward and are feared as signs of abnormality and a coming breakdown. Here the problem is not fear of fear provoked by something external, but fear of oneself. The more one fights the symptoms the stronger they become. Pressure of the compulsion or obsession elicits a counterpressure, and the counterpressure increases the pressure. Thus in the obsessive-compulsive neurosis, the same feedback mechanism seen in the phobias is at work. The problem is one of excessive intention; willing to avoid the fear or control the compulsion is counterproductive, simply intensifying the problem.

Along with flight from fear and the fight against obsessions and compulsions, a third pattern expressing anticipatory anxiety is the "fight for pleasure," which is one factor in most sexual neuroses. This is simply the hyperintention of pleasure, derived from the underlying anxiety that one will not "perform well" or attain or give an orgasm. But hyperintention is always counterproductive.

> The more a man tries to demonstrate his sexual potency or a woman her ability to experience orgasm, the less they are able to succeed. Pleasure is, and must remain, a side-effect or by-product, and is destroyed and spoiled to the degree to which it is made a goal in itself.[17]

"The more one strives for pleasure, the less one is able to attain it."[18]

In addition to anticipatory anxiety and its three expressions, a second pathogenic pattern is the compulsion to self-observation. Thus parallel with hyperintention, there is hyperreflection; as suffering may be caused by excessive *in*tention, it may also be caused by excessive *at*tention. Hyperreflection is implicated in most sexual neuroses along with the fight for pleasure, for sexual spontaneity and enjoyment can be blocked if made either the object of attention or the object of intention. Hyperreflection impedes any activity by the constantly inter-

[16] Viktor E. Frankl, *The Doctor and the Soul, from Psychotherapy to Logotherapy*, 2nd ed. (New York: Alfred A. Knopf, 1966), 221.
[17] *Search for Meaning*, 194.
[18] *Doctor and the Soul*, 223.

rupting question, "How am I doing?" Precisely because you ask, you cannot do well. Frankl illustrates the way in which hyperreflection impedes action and blocks spontaneity with the story of the centipede,

> who was asked by his enemy in what sequence he moved his legs. When the centipede paid attention to the problem, he was unable to move his legs at all. He is said to have died from starvation. Should we say that he died from fatal hyperreflection?[19]

Here in the case of psychogenic neuroses as in the case of the noogenic, Frankl has shown that effort fails to achieve its goal.

> Anticipatory anxiety brings about precisely what the patient fears, while excessive intention, as well as excessive self-observation with regard to one's own functioning, makes this functioning impossible.[20]

This insight of the psychotherapist is simply the repeated criticism directed against the ethic of attainment by the ethic of consolation. Paradoxically, efforts to escape fear, efforts to overcome obsessions and compulsions, and efforts to achieve pleasure and performance necessarily fail; since hyperintention is the cause, we may assume that some kind of "deintention" must be the cure. Further, efforts to become aware of our action in order to improve it end in blocking and distorting it; since hyperreflection is the cause, the solution must be "dereflection."

Notice that in identifying these two pathogenic patterns, Frankl does not seek underlying causes in the patient's past; such causes certainly exist, but knowledge of them is not necessary to the solution of the patient's problem. In fact, Frankl claims that often insight into the cause of a problem left the patient unrelieved of the symptoms, while his own methods brought relief, whether accompanied by insight into causes and origins or not. Having identified the two pathogenic patterns, Frankl offers a method for dealing with each. Hyperintention is to be treated with the method of paradoxical intention, and hyperreflection is to be treated with the method of dereflection. Each of these methods is made possible by an underlying capability of the human being. We are capable of paradoxical intention because of our capacity for self-detachment: we are able to stand aside from our situation and see ourselves as if from outside, as when we see the humor in our plight and take a playful attitude toward it. We are capable of dereflection due to our capacity of self-transcendence; we can direct our attention away from an immediate involvement by grasping the vision of a larger meaning or purpose of which it is a part.

[19] *Will to Meaning*, 100.
[20] *Psychotherapy and Existentialism*, 146.

Paradoxical intention is based on "the two-fold fact that fear makes come true that which one is afraid of, and that hyperintention makes impossible what one wishes."[21] This paradox that intention cannot accomplish what it seeks calls for a paradoxical solution, the reversal of one's intention. "Paradoxical intention means that the patient is encouraged to do, or to wish to happen, the very thing he fears."[22] The inversion of intention in the case of a phobia removes the fear of fear, for one is to replace the fear of, say, sweating in public with the wish to do so. The vicious circle is broken, the feedback mechanism removed.

> Encouraging the patient to do, or wish to happen the very thing he fears engenders an inversion of intention. The pathogenic fear is replaced by a paradoxical wish. By the same token, however, the wind is taken out of the sails of anticipatory anxiety.[23]

So the patient is encouraged to say, "I sweated out a quart before, but now I'm going to pour out at least ten quarts!" In this way, an embarrassing problem of four years standing was removed in one week, and after only one consultation. Here the phobia is replaced with a wish, and the feared symptom disappears. Similarly, the obsessive-compulsive is invited to wish for the acting-out of the feared compulsion. A man who feared that he would smash any large window he saw was instructed to "Go right up to the window with the intention of smashing it!" His compulsion had been absent for twenty years at the time Frankl wrote of this. The energy directed to controlling the compulsion kept it active, and when withdrawn through paradoxical intention the compulsion disappeared. For twenty years a woman had been seriously hampered by the necessity to check and double-check drawers, windows, and doors to see if they were locked. She was invited to think to herself, "What if the door *is* open! Let them steal everything in the whole apartment!" When what was feared was willed, the obsession disappeared.[24]

Frankl insists this approach is appropriately logotherapy, healing through meaning, because paradoxical intention works without reference to the underlying causes; it is precisely the adopting of a new attitude toward or interpretation of the neurosis. This change is possible due to the specifically human capacity for self-detachment in humor. Frankl points out that the paradoxical intention should be formulated in a humorous way; a playful attitude toward oneself is invited. Humor creates perspective, a distance between yourself and

[21] *Search for Meaning*, 195-196.
[22] *Will to Meaning*, 102.
[23] *Ibid.*, 103.
[24] *Doctor and the Soul*, 223-224; *Psychotherapy and Existentialism*, 155-156; the essay containing this example was written in 1960.

that which confronts you; in allowing us to detach ourselves from ourselves and to let go of our efforts at self-management, paradoxically it enables us to gain control over ourselves.

A person was anxious and upset about a coming trip to distant and unfamiliar places, fearing that he would be rendered helpless far from home and friends by an anxiety attack. These attacks had occurred before in response to provocation, but now the fear of an attack was a cause in its own right. He was obsessed with the image of a foreign student who had committed suicide after a welcoming party at her new university, apparently depressed and disoriented by her isolation in strange surroundings. The therapist simply shrugged and said, "Right, you may sit and shiver for the whole month. So what?" Subtly, this amounted to the method of paradoxical intention, and it had the effect of breaking the hold of anticipatory anxiety and the hyperintention to fight against and flee from anxiety, thus removing its major cause. In the future, if signs of an attack arose, a quickened pulse, shallow breathing, etc., instead of increasing the anxiety by hyperreflection ("Here it comes!") and hyperintention ("Run!"), the patient would relax, accept the anxiety and will the experience of it, which had the effect of ending the episode. In this way fear of attacks as a cause of the attacks was permanently removed.

The paradox that increased self-awareness and self-analysis distort the very action being observed is handled by Frankl in the paradoxical way of dereflection. Attention is directed from the immediate situation to a more inclusive concept or meaning. For example, a patient's eating was disturbed by an acute consciousness of the mechanism of swallowing and the fear of choking by swallowing the wrong way. The patient was told to think "I don't need to watch my swallowing, because I don't really need to swallow, for actually *I* don't swallow, but rather *it* does." The "it," of course, refers to the unconscious and unintentional act of swallowing.[25]

Dereflection is helpful in removing secondary emotional symptoms caused by an awareness of one's neurosis or psychosis. In these cases, not only does the patient suffer from the disability itself, but from anxiety and self-contempt derived from the awareness of being ill. Dereflection helps the patient stop fighting the illness and spares the patient the secondary suffering.

Frankl describes the treatment of a psychotic whose problem was complicated by hyperreflection; being aware of her bizarre behavior and thoughts caused secondary anxiety. In asking, "How am I doing?" she became increasingly aware of her illness, which in turn made her worse; again we see the feedback mechanism. Part of her treatment

[25] *Doctor and the Soul*, 256.

involved dereflection, directing her attention toward her career and what she hoped to accomplish; in this way, concern for a larger purpose directs attention away from the immediate situation. Dereflection is possible only by reorientation toward a vocation or mission and is thus appropriately logotherapy, healing through meaning. "The cure is self-commitment."[26]

A person may be "depressed about being depressed;"[27] or a depression of surprising depth may provoke an attack of anxiety as in the "suicide fright." In both cases, hyperreflection is operative. In such a situation, a patient found that diverting his attention to a larger meaning latent within the situation of depression lessened the problem; he thought of himself not as ill and debilitated, but as one who courageously and self-responsibly lives with depression, and is made more insightful and sensitive by it. The secondary symptom of anxiety and depression about depression was removed. Incidentally, paradoxical intention also played a role; fighting depression worsened it, but willingly accepting it lessened it and made possible the integration of it within a concept of himself which he could value.

The treatment of insomnia is an interesting example of the combination of the two techniques because it often is the result of both excessive intention and attention. Since sleep presupposes relaxation, the hyperintention of sleep prevents sleep; one cannot relax by trying, in the usual sense of the word. Of course, one can learn to relax, but this is not effort in the usual meaning of effort, but an end of effort.

> Dubois, the famous French psychiatrist, once compared sleep to a dove which has landed near one's hand and stays there as long as one does not pay any attention to it; if one attempts to grab it, it quietly flies away.[28]

The basis of this hyperintention which prevents sleep is the anticipatory anxiety that one will say awake. Frankl deflates this fear by the paradoxical intention to stay awake. Sleep is further complicated by hyperreflection, for the insomniac is constantly aware of being sleepless and of the inability to relax. Thus dereflection is used; one must not think of sleep or sleeplessness. But this instruction cannot be given in negative form. If I am instructed not to think of a chameleon, though I never have in the past, now I will. Therefore, the instruction is put in positive form, "Think of something else." In dereflection, one's symptom is ignored, and in paradoxical intention it is ridiculed.

Frankl quotes one interpreter as explaining the mechanism operat-

[26] *Search for Meaning*, 201.
[27] *Will to Meaning*, 132.
[28] *Doctor and the Soul*, 253; cf. *Will to Meaning*, 158. For other examples of treatment, see *The Doctor and the Soul*, 241-251.

ing in these two techniques as "super-ego modification" in which the therapist gives the patient a more permissive conscience. Elsewhere, he refers to another interpreter as claiming that paradoxical intention cheats the punitive super-ego which uses the symptom as a punishment by having the patient affirm the symptom; if it is chosen, it isn't punishment.[29] I would expand on these essentially identical suggestions in this way. In paradoxical intention, the symptom of anxiety is accepted as part of oneself, and the fear of fear no longer operates; to intend what is feared is to accept it. Or, if a forbidden impulse is willed to appear, then it too has been accepted, and the energizing fear and resistance are gone. In both of these instances, the end of the fear of and resistance to the symptom through accepting it removes the feedback mechanism that energizes it. Also, in dereflection, one's primary symptom is accepted as part of one's larger life, and the secondary symptom of fear and self-rejection due to the primary symptom is gone. And in each case, it would seem to me, acceptance of oneself is a reflex of being accepted by another, in agreement with Frankl's belief that the I becomes an I only through a You.

The conflict of the ethic of attainment and the ethic of consolation is over activity and passivity; but obviously both are appropriate in different contexts and life could not be based on a choice of one over the other. This is made clear in Frankl's concept of right activity and passivity, and wrong activity and passivity.[30] Wrong passivity is seen in the withdrawal from situations that provoke anxiety, as in the phobias. Wrong activity occurs in the obsessive-compulsive neuroses in which one fights against compulsion and obsessions and thus reinforces them; and it occurs in the sexual neuroses in which one struggles for pleasure or performance and thus blocks them. Right passivity is exemplified by paradoxical intention in which we ridicule or play with symptoms, rather than flee from them or fight them. Right activity is found in dereflection in which we ignore our symptoms and focus attention away from the self or at least away from the immediate situation through reorientation of one's meaning in life.

Thus in Frankl's logotherapy we see a modern rediscovery of the law of the reversal of effort. The concepts of hyperintention and hyperreflection refer to ways in which the active attempt to fulfill life is counterproductive and must necessarily fail. The success of the techniques of paradoxical intention and dereflection show that a goal may be reached by giving up the attempt to reach it.

29 *Will to Meaning*, 112-113; *Doctor and the Soul*, 236-237.
30 *Doctor and the Soul*, 258-259; *Psychotherapy and Existentialism*, 161-162.

Part Two:
Questions About the Reversal of Intention

Chapter 7

HOW DOES INSIGHT INTO THE REVERSAL OF INTENTION ARISE? WHEN THERE IS NOTHING YOU CAN DO, THERE IS NOTHING YOU NEED DO

> To ultimate situations we react either by obfuscation or, if we really apprehend them, by despair and rebirth.
>
> —Karl Jaspers
> *The Way to Wisdom*

> To give up pretensions is as blessed a relief as to get them gratified; and where disappointment is incessant and the struggle unending, this is what we will always do. . . . There is the strangest lightness about the heart when one's nothingness in a particular line is once accepted in good faith.
>
> —William James
> *Psychology*

According to the four ancient religious and philosophical texts we have examined, some great good can come about in our lives through the reversal of intention. Each agreed that unhappiness and spiritual discontent are inevitable when we try to achieve fulfillment, precisely because we are trying. Each promised that the greatest good which humans can experience follows from letting go of our exertions to attain the good. Of course, the traditional expressions of this theme disagree profoundly on just what a fulfilled life is and just why letting go of self-effort leads to it. "Absence of painful emotion due to the acceptance of whatever comes" is a very different description of fulfillment from "the right relation to the personal, transcendent God," and this in turn differs from "awareness of our identity with the Innate Buddha." But each classical text agreed at least in this single fact, they advocate the psychological maneuver we have been calling the reversal of effort.

We found a modern psychologist who was very self-conscious about the reversal theme. This reinforces the intuition that this insight is universal and recurs again and again in different times and places. Frankl locates the source of both noogenic and psychogenic problems in the excessive intention of some desired goal, and he suggests the reversal of intention as a solution. Your problem comes from trying too hard; let go of that intense striving for the goal, even go so far as to will the opposite, and you arrive at the point you couldn't reach through concentration and striving.

If this insight is indeed universal and constantly rediscovered when needed, then the first step in understanding it may be the question, "How does insight into the reversal of effort arise? That is, what kinds of experiences and conditions have led to the discovery of the paradox of intention?"

* * * * *

As exotic and distant from common sense as the reversal of effort may seem as an idea, it is not uncommon as an experience. In every life, there are spontaneous occurrences of the reversal of intention, unnoticed uses of the principle that yielding is strongest. Frankl mentions several instances in which paradoxical intention was demonstrated outside of clinical practice.

> Unwillingly and unwittingly, paradoxical intention has always existed. An example of unwilling use was reported to me by the head of the Department of Psychiatry at the University of Mainz in West Germany. When he was in junior high school his class was to present a play. One of the characters was a stutterer, so they gave this role to a student who actually stuttered. Soon, however, he had to give up the role because it turned out that when standing on the stage he was completely unable to stutter. He had to be replaced by another boy.[1]

Every time he spoke, the stutterer was trying not to stutter and failed; when once he relaxed this effort, accepted that he was a stutterer and tried to stutter, he no longer could.

Not only was the usefulness of paradoxical intention stumbled upon, but it was raised to the level of self-conscious technique prior to modern empirical psychology. William James reports this use of the technique.

> It is the very badness of the act that gives it then its vertiginous fascination. Remove the prohibition, and the attraction stops. In my university days a student threw himself from an upper entry window of one of the college buildings and was nearly killed. Another student, a friend of my own, had to pass the window daily in coming and going from his room, and experienced a dreadful temptation to imitate the deed. Being a Catholic, he told his director, who said, "All right! if you must, you must," and added, "Go ahead and do it," thereby instantly quenching his desire. This

[1] Viktor Frankl, *Will to Meaning*, 107.

director knew how to minister to a mind diseased.[2]

This shows that in the 1880s James was aware of the nature of compulsions and recognized the power of paradoxical intention: "remove the prohibition, and the attraction stops." It demonstrates the paradox was part of the lore of a much more ancient tradition of psychological insight, the Roman Catholic confessional.

I can mention two instances of the spontaneous occurrence of the reversal of intention from personal experience. When I was thirteen, I went with a friend who was a year younger to an amusement park. We had ridden on streetcars for nearly two hours to travel the thirty miles from downtown Los Angeles to Long Beach. The first ride we saw on entering the amusement zone was a new attraction imported from Germany, and in our eagerness to get right into the adventure, we paid fifty cents and entered. We were led up an incline to a circular gallery looking down into a drum about twenty feet in diameter with its axis perpendicular to the ground. As we looked down on the people in the drum it began to turn faster and faster, and when they were pinned against the sides of the drum by centrifugal force, the floor dropped out. Through loudspeakers, an accented voice told us we could stay and watch, leave, or enter the drum for a ride when it stopped. My fear diminished as I decided that I would watch for a while and then leave, but when I looked at my friend we shrugged and went down from the gallery to enter the drum. Inside, I knew I had made a mistake, but the door closed and I was trapped. As we began to move my terror increased, and the screams of others multiplied it. As we reached what seemed an incredible speed, the floor dropped away without a sound and I was suspended against the wall. I had never felt such intense panic and helplessness. But then it occurred to me that regardless of what I did, everything would be the same. There was nothing to do but relax and trust to the spinning centrifuge. This was not a process of reasoning, but an event in which I suddenly became calm. Then I found delight in the feeling of motion and of being pinned to the wall. I laughed, rolled over, and drew up my knees while I pushed away from the wall with my arms, and found I could crawl up and down the wall. I was the only one doing this and wondered why no one else was playing with their plight. The drum slowed, and as the centrifugal force diminished, I jumped to the floor. I rode again and even attempted for the first time a rollercoaster ride which had always terrified me.

At first, this example seems different from that of the stutterer who couldn't intentionally stutter. It is easy to show that written texts

[2] William James, *Psychology* (New York: Henry Holt, 1893), 447.

agree, but harder to see that experiences are similar. The operations are the same in both examples. Each involved letting go of some kind of counterproductive effort and finding a value that couldn't be reached by trying. In the centrifuge, the goal of feeling safe and at ease and being able to function and play, which could not be secured by effort, was received by letting go of effort. I had been trapped and helpless and fought this situation with intensity, becoming increasingly anxious; but unable to do anything to change my situation anyway, I relaxed and accepted it, and the feelings of panic and helplessness disappeared. In fact, energy was released, which made the playful and active use of my situation possible; this shows that letting go is not despair and inaction, but a means to more appropriate and effective action.

As a graduate student at Columbia University, I was surprised to be selected to teach something called "Religion V3202y, Section 2," which was merely an introduction to the modern, critical study of the New Testament. The regular instructor had been assigned other duties, and even though I was not a specialist in biblical studies, I was selected to teach the course. I was both excited to have a chance to try out my ideas on introducing undergraduates to a fascinating subject and afraid that while I had ideas to communicate, I might lack that grasp of detail which the specialist has. And there was the undercurrent of student discontent, which I had shared at other times, with being taught by a graduate student at a university with some of the finest scholars in the world. So on the day of each class meeting, I prepared a lecture and discussion outline with great care, usually finishing about five o'clock in the evening; then in order to fill the void of the next two hours before class and to deal with my apprehension about details, I would range through the library looking up miscellaneous bits of useless and irrelevant information so as to be able to handle questions from my exceedingly bright students. The information was unrelated to the large and impressive ideas I thought I wanted to communicate, but what if some one asked? Of course, I had set a trap for myself. The classes went well, and I discovered the exhilaration of thinking on my feet, finding new ways to explain and vivify ideas, and responding to the insights of really superb students. But then one night one of my favorite students asked a perfectly marvelous question, relevant, insightful, well expressed, based on a genuine understanding of the problems and methods of the subject, and entirely beyond my preparation and competence. As I hesitated, panic arose; I simply didn't have a good, helpful answer, and my ability to improvise or direct the student to other sources for an answer was blocked by my apprehension. I not only didn't have an answer, I was no help at all. But then it occurred to me that I simply had nothing to say, and, in fact, I could not have hoped to have all the answers. When I admitted I did not know, calmness and composure came to me, and the classroom became a different kind of place.

Clearly, I attempted to be or appear omniscient as a way of feeling capable and at ease in the classroom, but this cannot work. When effort at this impossible task was abandoned, a feeling of ease followed, and also greater capability. For once I accepted that I do not and cannot have all the answers, I was sufficiently at ease to better perform my real function in the classroom. So letting go of counter-productive effort is not quitting, and it does not lead to failure to reach the goal.

In these examples, a barrier is encountered that frustrates a certain intention and shows efforts toward its fulfillment to be impossible; then when one lets go of this intention, a state is reached which was impossible through effort. This new state is not passive and despairing, but is one which is capable of accomplishing something, if that is appropriate; for after all, the stutterer talked, the boy enjoyed and exploited the spinning drum, and the teacher was more open and effective. There are spontaneous discoveries of the value of the reversal of intention, and thus it is not an esoteric idea but a common experience. These discoveries seem to arise when we encounter an impossibility.

As so often turns out to be the case, William James already knew all of this. Of special relevance to the example of the "all-knowing teacher" above is James' formula:

$$\text{Self-esteem} = \frac{\text{Success}}{\text{Pretensions}}$$

> Such a fraction may be increased as well by diminishing the denominator as by increasing the numerator. To give up pretensions is as blessed a relief as to get them gratified; and where disappointment is incessant and the struggle unending, this is what we will always do. The history of evangelical theology, with its conviction of sin, its self-despair, and its abandonment of salvation by works, is the deepest of possible examples, but we meet others in every walk of life. There is the strangest lightness about the heart when one's nothingness in a particular line is once accepted in good faith. *All* is not bitterness in the lot of the lover sent away by the final inexorable "No." Many Bostonians . . . would be happier women and men today, if they could once for all abandon the notion of keeping up a Musical Self, and without shame let people hear them call a symphony a nuisance. How pleasant is the day when we give up striving to be young, or slender! Thank God! we say, *those* illusions are gone. Everything added to the Self is a burden as well as a pride. A certain man who lost every penny during our civil war went and actually rolled in the dust, saying he

had not felt so free and happy since he was born.[3]

"Decreasing the denominator" is acceptance of yourself as you are; this makes clear a claim of the preceding chapter that reversal of effort often involves self-acceptance. Maintenance of some pretension or desire, in the above examples, to be fluent in speech, to be safe from harm and anxiety, and to be effective in the classroom by being all-knowing, is burdensome and counterproductive, and the impossibility of reaching the goal and continuing to live in this way provokes the discovery of the paradox of intention.

* * * * *

In the cases of three of the ancient texts embodying the notion of the reversal of intention, it was noted that historical crises of social disorder may be related to the rise of this idea. If encounter with impossibility is the context in which the idea is discovered, then historical calamities like the disorder of the Warring States Period in China or the Hellenistic religious crisis might be examined. Of course Confucianism as well as Taoism arose in the Warring States Period. Conversely, it is likely that the idea may arise in orderly times and supportive societies in some individuals. In any case, some individual must feel addressed by impossibility for the notion to be discovered.

The enlightenment experience of Siddhartha Gautama (563-483 B.C.), through which he became the Buddha, "the enlightened one," may be taken as an example of a personal crisis in which impossibility was encountered and insight into the reversal of intention arose. Gautama was born in northern India near Benares to a chieftain of the Shakya clan of the *kshatriya*, or "warrior caste." According to the *Jataka* tales, his father was a king with ambitions for his son, and he was dismayed at the birth-prophecy that the boy would either be a great ruler or a monk and a great liberator; so he deliberately isolated the boy from those experiences of impossibility, of limits, that lead to introspection and spiritual unrest. The child was to be preserved from knowledge of old age, disease, and death. Gautama was raised in great luxury, attended only by the young, living in three palaces as the seasons changed, and having the road cleared before him as he rode through the countryside. But the legend tells of the Four Passing Sights that broke Gautama's isolation from life. As the future Buddha rode in a chariot, a god appeared by the roadside, first as an aged man, then as a diseased man, next as a corpse, and finally as a monk. Troubled by the first three sights and knowing himself to be subject to old age, disease, and death for the first time, he found the idea of retire-

[3] *Ibid.*, 187.

ment from the world attractive, for perhaps in the meditation of the monastic life he would find peace. He could not be consoled with feasts, music, and dancing. At the birth of his son he felt his duty to his clan was fulfilled, and leaving his sleeping wife and child, he rode away from the palace. This turning aside from wealth, pleasure, and rule is called the Great Retirement; it has great didactic value for Buddhists, for the Buddha shows that what can be attained in the world, he has tried, and it fails to console and give peace.

Next in the traditional story there follows the Great Struggle of six arduous years, living as a wandering beggar. Gautama studied with Alara Kalama and Uddaka, the disciple of Rama, learning the eight stages of meditation accepted in brahmanistic Hinduism. Just as he had tried worldly delight, now he tried brahmin meditation and learning, and this too was of no value. Next he tried the extreme austerities of Jain-style ascetism in which the monk seeks to liberate the soul from the contamination and limitation of the body by vigorously denying the body. From the Buddhist point of view, the self-defeating aim of this life is peace through striving. Gautama took up residence in a grove near a city, near water and a source of alms, and began his task, saying:

> This surely is a fit place for the striving of a high-born one intent on striving. Then I sat down there; a fit place is this for striving.[4]

The *Mahasaccaka-sutta* vividly describes Gautama's ascetic discipline.

> Then I thought, what if I now set my teeth, press my tongue to my palate, and restrain, crush, and burn out my mind with my mind. (I did so) and sweat flowed from my armpits. Just as if a strong man were to seize a weaker man by the head or shoulder . . . so did I set my teeth . . . and sweat flowed from my armpits. I undertook resolute effort, unconfused mindfulness was set up but my body was unquiet and uncalmed, even through the painful striving that overwhelmed me. Nevertheless such painful feeling as arose did not overpower my mind.[5]

He practiced restraint of breath until he heard of violent roaring in his ears, he felt as if a strap were being tightened around his head, as if a butcher were carving up his body, as if he were being suspended over burning coals. He fell into unconsciousness and was thought dead.

Gautama is said to have lived on but one sesame seed or one grain of rice a day, according to the *Jataka*, and in the *Mahasaccaka-sutta* his emaciation is described.

[4] *Mahasaccaka-sutta, Majjhima*, 1.240, quoted in Edward J. Thomas, *The Life of the Buddha as Legend and History* (New York: Barnes and Noble, 1952), 64.
[5] *Ibid.*

> My body became extremely lean. . . . The mark of my seat was like a camel's footprint through the little food. The bones of my spine when bent and straightened were like a row of spindles through the little food. As the beams of an old shed stick out, so did my ribs stick out through the little food. And as in a deep well the deep low-lying sparkling of the waters is seen, so in my eye-sockets was seen the deep low-lying sparkling of my eyes through the little food. And as a bitter gourd cut off raw is cracked and withered through wind and sun, so was the skin on my head withered through the little food. When I thought I would touch the skin of my stomach, I actually took hold of my spine, and when I thought I would touch my spine, I took hold of the skin of my stomach, so much did the skin of my stomach cling to my spine through the little food.[6]

But the future Buddha concluded that all of this exertion in seeking self-mastery and release from distress was "like time spent in endeavoring to tie the air into knots."[7]

> By this severe mortification I do not attain superhuman noble knowledge and insight. Perhaps there is another way to enlightenment.[8]

He resolved to abandon ascetic discipline, and taking up his begging bowl, he returned to the life of a mendicant. Since the legend of the enlightenment of the Buddha is itself a means of conveying the Buddhist message, it is intended that the hearer draw the lesson that Gautama tried ascetic exertion and found that it too does not bring peace.

The climax of Gautama's striving for peace came on the day when, according to the tradition, he seated himself beneath a bo-tree facing east and vowed to achieve enlightenment or die.

> Let my skin, and sinews, and bones become dry and let all the flesh and blood in my body dry up! but never from this seat will I stir, until I have attained the supreme and absolute wisdom![9]

At this point the *Jataka* introduces a severe temptation by the evil god Mara, who attempts to arouse desire and to distract Gautama, and finally to destroy him. But Gautama perseveres in his grim resolve to fight for serenity. Suddenly enlightenment comes to him in the form of a cessation of desire, together with the realization that all his suffering has come from wrong desire.

It seems the tradition understands that Gautama's liberating insight arose from the frustration of all of his efforts to achieve release; in de-

[6] *Ibid.*, 65.
[7] *Jataka*, 1.65.29, in Henry Clarke Warren, *Buddhism in Translation* (Cambridge: Harvard University Press, 1922), 70-71.
[8] Thomas, *Life of the Buddha*, 66.
[9] Warren, *Buddhism in Translation*, 76.

spair, he abandoned the effort to attain peace, and in this very act he discovered it. Thus there arose awareness that the search for enlightenment had failed up to this point simply because it was based on desire for enlightenment.

> He had tried too hard altogether, so that his very determination stood between him and the state of consciousness he desired, but now, in the face of self-defeat, his will relaxed. . . . And suddenly, the answer came. His inability to experience release from his suffering was due to desire.[10]

Discovery of the impossibility of achieving peace through striving provoked the further discovery that peace comes by relaxation, giving up of the urgent pursuit of it. The experience of impossibility is the source of the reversal of intention theme in the teaching of the Buddha.

The rejection of striving and the idea of salvation by relaxation of the effort to attain it are contained in what was traditionally taken to be the earliest address of the newly enlightened Gautama, the Sermon in the Deer Park at Benares.

> There are two ends not to be served by a wanderer. What are these two? The pursuit of desires and of pleasure which springs from desire, which is base, common, leading to rebirth, ignoble and unprofitable. And the pursuit of pain and hardship, which is grievous, ignoble, and unprofitable. The Middle Way of [the Buddha] avoids both these ends. It is enlightened, it brings clear vision, it makes for wisdom, and leads to peace, insight, enlightenment and nirvana.[11]

The middle way is thus one of letting be, between the extremes of striving for pleasure and striving for enlightenment. For all striving is based on *tanha*, "selfish desire or craving," and it destroys peace, while enlightenment is precisely the abandonment of this desire. Selfish desire is shown to be the root of all suffering in the Four Noble Truths in the Deer Park Sermon.

> And this is the Noble Truth of Sorrow. Birth is sorrow, age is sorrow, disease is sorrow, death is sorrow, contact with the unpleasant is sorrow, separation from the pleasant is sorrow, every wish unfulfilled is sorrow. . . .
>
> And this is the Noble Truth of the Arising of Sorrow. It arises from craving, which leads to rebirth, which brings delight and passion, and seeks pleasure now here, now there, the craving for sensual pleasure, the craving for continued life, the craving for power.

[10] John Noss, *Man's Religions*, 7th ed. (New York: Macmillan, 1984), 110.

[11] *Samyatta Nikaya*, 5.421 ff., in ed. Theodore de Bary, *The Buddhist Tradition in India, China and Japan* (New York: Random House, 1969), 16.

> And this is the Noble Truth of the Stopping of Sorrow. It is the complete stopping of that craving, so that no passion remains, leaving it, being emancipated from it, being released from it, giving no place to it.
>
> And this is the Noble Truth of the Way which Leads to the Stopping of Sorrow. It is the Noble Eightfold Path: Right Views, Right Resolve, Right Speech, Right Conduct, Right Livelihood, Right Effort, Right Mindfulness, and Right Concentration.[12]

All life is vulnerable to suffering, all suffering comes from selfish desire and ceases when it ceases, and selfish desire can be removed when right desire and action replace it. Just because craving is the root of our problem, craving for enlightenment and peace must be self-defeating. Enlightenment, or nirvana, is blocked by the desire for it because it is a state in which selfish desire is blown out like a candle. The Eightfold Path makes clear that what is extinguished is not all desire, but wrong desire.

The extinction of wrong desire is the solution to Gautama's problem of anguish over the facts of suffering and death; all suffering is from selfish craving, and if this is extinguished, suffering ceases.

* * * * *

A similar sketch can be drawn of a personal crisis in which impossibility is encountered and salvation by relaxation of the effort to achieve it is discovered, if we look at the experience of Martin Luther (1483-1546). Luther's experience in the Augustinian monastery parallels the Buddha's practice of ascetism, and his Tower Experience parallels the Buddha's experience under the bo-tree. The tendency to legendary exaggeration is present in both stories, though in Luther's to a much smaller degree, but both can surely be trusted to the extent that the pattern of despair over effort can be seen.

Luther was born in Eisleben in central Germany. His father Hans had been a miner in the new copper mines; eventually, he became a shareholder and a foreman in the mine. He came to own property and was a member of the town council; he was thus a part of a newly emerging class that lived by trade and manufacturing and centered in the cities. Hans was ambitious for his son Martin; since there were many opportunities in the expanding field of commerce, and in the newly developed local governments, he decided Martin should become a lawyer. Martin attended Latin school and went on to the University of Erfurt, where he completed the Master of Arts degree in 1505. His father's joy was destroyed, however, when Martin announced he would join the Augustinian hermits, an unusually strict

[12] *Ibid.*, 16-17.

monastic community, following a vow made during a frightening thunderstorm. This sudden decision reveals an underlying religious discontent more compelling than any storm; Luther later said he hoped he could win God's mercy in the monastic life.

This problem is seen again when after a year's training he celebrated his first mass. In the introduction to the mass, the bread and wine are offered to God through the Prayer of Consecration: "Receive, O sacred Father, omnipotent and eternal, this Sacred Host which I Thine unworthy servant offer to Thee, my living and true God. . . ." Luther later wrote:

> At these words I was utterly stupefied and terror-stricken. I thought to myself, "With what tongue shall I address such Majesty, seeing that all men ought to tremble in the presence of even an earthly prince? Who am I, that I should lift up mine eyes or raise my hands to the divine Majesty? The angels surround him. At his nod the earth trembles. And shall I, a miserable little pygmy, say "I want this, I ask for that"? For I am dust and ashes and full of sin and I am speaking to the living, eternal and the true God.[13]

The problem then is the feeling of unworthiness before the righteous God; this parallels the anguish of Gautama over the Four Passing Sights.

Brother Martin experienced a continuing spiritual discontent in the monastery, and he attempted to win divine favor and attain contentment through the energetic use of discipline and confession. Luther used the monastic rule, mistakenly some of his superiors held, as a means of coping with inner turmoil; he went beyond the requirements of the rule in extra vigils and prayers. He fasted for as long as three days, slept without blankets in cold weather, wore disciplinary clothing.

> I was a good monk, and I kept the rule of my order so strictly that I may say that if ever a monk got to heaven by his monkery it was I. All of my brothers in the monastery who knew me will bear me out. If I had kept on any longer, I should have killed myself with vigils, prayers, reading, and other work.[14]

Brother Martin extended confessions into reviews of his whole life; it was said that once after confessing for six hours, he returned because he had forgotten something. In his later years, Luther used the story

[13] Otto Scheel, ed. *Dokumente zu Luthers Entwicklung*, quoted in Roland Bainton, *Here I Stand, a Life of Martin Luther* (New York: Abingdon Press, 1950), 41.

[14] J. K. F. Knaake, et al., *Martin Luthers Werke*, 38:143, quoted in Bainton, *Here I Stand*, 45; cf. Robert H. Fife, *The Revolt of Martin Luther* (New York: Columbia University Press, 1957), 94.

of his life in the monastery and his Tower Experience as a way of communicating the message of divine grace, just as the story of the Buddha's enlightenment is a teaching device; and so we may allow for an element of stylizing and even exaggeration. But the pattern is clear; Luther sought peace through effort.

After being transferred to Wittenberg, Brother Martin was informed by John of Staupitz, the head of the Augustinian Order in Germany, that he had been chosen to study for the Doctor of Theology degree and would become professor of biblical theology at the university. In 1512 he received the degree, and in 1516 was selected as supervisor of training over a dozen Augustinian monasteries. But with every increase in outward success, his inner discontent grew. This is the phenomenon Frankl called "success with despair." The more Luther strove to overcome the feeling of unworthiness through accomplishments, the more the feeling grew; each success that should have proven his worth was instead a source of mounting despair, precisely because it failed to bring peace.

As Luther experienced the failure of efforts to bring him peace, he came to feel God was his enemy. If effort in the religious life is self-defeating, then God demands the impossible. We should love God, but the divine demands are oppressive and cannot be fulfilled; such a God is a tyrant and cannot be the object of our love.

> I was myself more than once driven to the very abyss of despair so that I wished I had never been created. Love God? I hated him![15]

But one cannot hate God, for we are all dependent on God and receive our lives through divine power. Brother Martin was caught within a dilemma; characteristically, he devoted himself to discipline and study with greater energy.

This experience in the monastery, which parallels Gautama's fruitless attempt to fight through to peace, is the source of Luther's later conception of "works righteousness." Effort in the religious life is self-defeating because it is self-seeking; every seeming achievement of effort leads to pride, which is sin! Works righteousness is thus the sinful attempt to prove our acceptability to God by our own efforts; far from leading to holiness, it is the essence of sin. For sin is the self-reliant refusal of the creature to live in dependence on the creator, the rebellious self-assertion of the creature.

In 1513, in the midst of studies in a tower in the monastery, Luther underwent an experience in which he received the resolution to his problem

[15] *Ibid.*, 18:719, in Bainton, *Here I Stand*, 59.

> In this tower in the Black Monastery at Wittenberg the Holy Ghost imparted to me his understanding.[16]

Luther came to see that it is impossible to earn God's love; rather, it is to be received as a free gift. While we cannot make ourselves righteous and worthy of God's love through self-reliance, God is willing to accept us *as if* we were righteous because of the divine mercy. We need not first become worthy of divine love in order to be in relation to God, for God already accepts us as we are, as sinners. God has revealed this in the death and resurrection of Jesus Christ. We are accepted, not because of our own merits, but through God's grace; all that is necessary is that we accept this acceptance. In such a faith, Luther's problem was resolved.

The attitude in which we accept God's free offer of forgiveness is faith, which is the abandoning of the effort of self-salvation and trust in God's forgiveness. Salvation that cannot be achieved through effort is received as a gift, on the condition that we give up our self-reliant rebellion. This conception of "salvation by faith alone" came to Luther through his study of the Psalms and the letters of Paul, but we can also assume that this discovery of the reversal of effort theme is a direct outcome of Luther's experience of the futility of striving toward salvation. As in the case of the experience of the Buddha, attempts to grasp peace through effort were frustrated, and in despair these efforts were abandoned; in this very experience of letting go, what was sought was found.

* * * * *

There is at least one instance in the history of the spiritual life in which despair of self-effort is deliberately provoked through contrived experiences of frustration. The Japanese Buddhist sect called Zen, especially in its Rinzai form, uses methods which seem well suited to lead the student to recapitulate the Buddha's experience of energetic striving for peace, in order that they find for themselves his experience of frustration and letting go.

Zen developed in China, where it was known as Chan, and was influenced by both the Tibetan Tantric Buddhist idea of the Innate Buddha and the Chinese Taoist concept of *wu-wei*, or "noninterference." Zen is an approach to enlightenment through meditation, and its goal is *satori*, an experience of "the direct seeing of reality." The paradox that effort spoils while relaxation of effort fulfills is well understood in Zen. Our problem is that by striving we keep alive our primary identification with the separate self; therefore, striving to escape

[16] Quoted in Heinrich Boehmer, *Luther and the Reformation in the Light of Modern Research*, trans. E. S. G. Potter (London: G. Bell and Sons, 1930), 46.

this illusion cannot help. We live in and through thought, which operates by making distinctions, and thus thought cannot lead us to see the Buddha Essence as the one reality. Even a sound grasp of Buddhist doctrine is of no avail, because what is called for is an experience of seeing the Buddha Essence, which takes us beyond thought and action.

Zen has several unique ways of non-intellectual pointing to the Innate Buddha already present in everyday experience, such as calligraphy, tea-ceremony and flower arranging. These all aim not at imparting knowledge, but at a new orientation of the self to reality, so that what was always present, but unknown due to our assertive thought and action, can now be seen. Of special relevance to our question about how the reversal of intention arises is the use of the *koan* in the interview between the monk and master. The master knows that nothing needs to be added to the student; the monk already is one with the Innate, embedded within it at every moment. Rather, what is required is the cessation of that reliance on thought and action which keeps the monk from seeing this. Therefore, the monk is given experiences which show the painful futility of reliance on effort, so that through frustration the monk gives up. At that point, with the self no longer being maintained through assertion, *satori* may arise.[17] As in Saraha, to find truth, merely let go of illusion.

When the master gives a student a *koan* on which to meditate, it may seem like a problem inviting reflection and resolution. The problems that seem to be contained in the *koan* reflect the very intellectual questions the student brings to the master. Here are three such *koans*.

> A monk asked Kassan Osho, "What is the Dharmakaya?" "The Dharmakaya is without form," Kassan replied.
>
> The Sixth Patriarch asked the head monk Myo, "Thinking neither of good nor of evil, at this very moment what was your original aspect before your father and mother were born?"
>
> Tosotsu Etsu Osho gave this test to his students: "One who has realized his own original nature escapes from birth-and-death. When the light of your eyes falls to the ground, how will you escape?"[18]

Questions about the Innate Buddha (the Dharmakaya), our eternal nature, and the problem of death appear to be worthy of thought. But "thoughtful" explanations are rejected because they reflect a view of

[17] Daisetz Teitaro Suzuki, *An Introduction to Zen Buddhism* (London: Rider, 1949), chap. 8.

[18] Isshu Miura and Ruth Fuller Sasaki, *The Zen Koan, Its History and Use in Rinzai Zen* (New York: Harcourt, Brace and World, 1965), 44, 48, 50.

the self as a discrete entity seeking to understand the world. Thus in responding to them, the master may speak and act in paradoxical, nonsensical, or contradictory ways, even replying with an insult or a blow. This rejection, week after week, recapitulates the Buddha's frustration in working at enlightenment, and for that matter, Luther's experience in the monastery.

To demonstrate that intellection leads away from a clear and immediate vision of reality into complexity and confusion, the master confounds the students intellect. In the above examples, frustration of effort was supplied by the master's response to the student's explanation; but some *koans* are frustrating in themselves. The master may reply to the student's questions about the teaching of Buddhism with *koans* giving examples of the handling of similar questions in the past.

> When Ummon was asked, "What is the pure Dharmakaya?" he replied, "The flowering hedge surrounding the privy."
>
> A monk asked Master Joshu, "What is the meaning of Bodhidharma's coming from the West?" "The cypress tree in the garden," Joshu replied.
>
> A monk once said to Fuketsu Osho, "Speech and silence tend toward separation from It or concealment of It. How shall we proceed so as not to violate It?" Fuketsu replied with the following verse:
> I always remember Konan in the spring,
> The partridges crying and flowers spilling
> their fragrance.
>
> A monk once said to Dairyo Osho, "The physical body decomposes. What is the indestructible Dharmakaya?" Dairyo answered with this verse.
> Blooming mountain flowers
> Are like golden brocade;
> Brimming mountain waters
> Are blue as indigo.
>
> A monk asked Master Joshu, "What is Joshu?" "East gate, west gate, south gate, north gate," Joshu replied.
>
> To Jun Osho's verse on the Dharmakaya was this:
> When the cows of Eshu are well fed with grain
> The horses of Ekishu have full stomachs.
>
> Hakuin Zenji used to say to his disciples, "Listen for the sound of one hand clapping."[19]

The student is asked to meditate on *koans* containing replies to questions much like his own, and he finds these replies are not responsive

[19] *Ibid.*, 44, 48, 50, 54, 55.

and contain nonsense, humor, and irreverence. *Koans* may even confound Buddhist doctrine.

> A monk asked Master Joshu, "Has the dog Buddha Nature or not?" Joshu answered, "Mu!"[20]

The answer means "no" or "none," and it is surely not what we have learned about the Innate Buddha.

But the clever student will not relinquish effort so easily and will likely treat the *koan* as a problem to be solved. After all, great Zen masters gave these responses, and so they must contain some hidden meaning. But even a "correct" explanation of the seeming nonsense will be rejected by the master. "The Innate Buddha is all things, and so is clearly the privy hedge, the cypress tree, Konan in the spring, blooming mountain flowers, etc. Since each is one with all reality, the master is not distinct from the four gates, and the four directions make a fitting symbol for the all-inclusive. All things are one, and one might express this as cows eating and horses becoming full. One hand clapping is a sign of non-duality; all is one and there is no opposition. As to the dog's Buddha Nature, everyone knows he has it, so Master Joshu must have meant he doesn't have it in a way excluding others from having it, or maybe that he doesn't have it but *is* it." Each of these answers seeks to remove the offense to reason, seeking to keep active the illusion of the rational and competent self mastering its situation. Finding clever resolutions to the *koan* builds up the illusion of the little self solving problems and securing its existence by its own efforts. So "answers" are rejected, and effort is found again and again to be counter-productive.

Frankl would understand the use of humor, both in the *koans* and in the masters' outrageous responses to them. Humor enables us to distance ourselves from our situation and to see ourselves; the hyperintensive student is made to see the comic aspect of taking play seriously and fighting toward serenity.

Then what would be an acceptable response to a *koan*? Any answer based on the logical analysis of the *koan* as a problem, so as to demonstrate a doctrine, clearly shows non-enlightenment, even if the doctrine is "true." The correct reply would be enlightenment itself, and this might be expressed in a spontaneous, uncontrived response in which the little self is no longer in control and the Buddha Nature itself answers. The last eight *koans* are examples of just this kind of response. What is the message of Bodhidharma, the first Buddhist teacher to come from India to China with the saving message? Cypress tree. (The danger in knowing this is that now we can fake it;

[20] *Ibid.*, 44.

thus the clever student may adopt the rule for responding to koans: "Be spontaneous!")

Thus in the use of the *koan*, frustration and the despair of effort are induced, and the discovery of the merit of the reversal of intention is intentionally provoked. (Apparently, we can intend to provoke letting go in others, but not to achieve it ourselves.) This is the second time we have encountered technique in examining the thought of those who say our problem is an excess of contrivance in our lives. Here the Zen master says, break down hyperintention by placing before it impossible tasks.

Life places before each of us at least one impossible task: to avoid death. This brings us to a last approach to the question of how the idea of reversal arises.

* * * * *

An answer to our question about how the idea of the reversal of intention arises is thus emerging: the discovery flows from an experience of impossibility in which efforts to achieve a goal are found to be useless; in frustration these efforts are abandoned, and this very letting go is found to yield the sought for result. Not everyone is beset by Luther's sense of sinful alienation from a personal God, and not everyone is as sensitive as Gautama to the vulnerability of life to suffering and death prior to an actual experience of it. But there is a near universal crisis in which almost everyone encounters impossibility, and thus may learn to let go of self-effort, and that is the crisis created by knowledge of our own imminent death; only those dying suddenly and unexpectedly are exempt. Elizabeth Kubler-Ross has described five stages through which the dying often proceed, and the last stage, "acceptance," appears very much like a spontaneous, personal discovery of the value of the paradox of intention.

Dr. Kubler-Ross came to understand these stages through her experience as a psychiatrist counseling hundreds of terminally ill patients. The almost universal first response to the knowledge that one is going to die is *denial*. One says, "No, not me, it cannot be true." This is a useful buffer against the ultimate shock to the self and simply the continuation of a lifelong pattern of fear and denial of death. Since Dr. Kubler-Ross recognizes the necessity of denial, she does not oppose it; the notion of stages does not imply that the patient is to be rushed along. With understanding and conversation, almost all patients move beyond this first stage.

The second state involves *anger* and rage at one's situation, and envy and resentment at those who do not have to face imminent death. One says, "Why me? Why not someone else? It's not fair!" If the patient's needs and importance are respected, and if the naturalness and predictability of his or her anger are recognized, this will pass, although like all of the stages, it may recur intermittently.

A third stage often encountered is that of *bargaining*, the attempt to postpone death by promising something in return. One patient said she would be wholly cooperative if the staff could only help her survive long enough and regain her strength sufficiently to attend her son's wedding. Postponement is seen as a prize for good behavior, and a self-imposed deadline is often involved. Usually the bargaining is done with God rather than the medical staff, and one promises "a life dedicated to God or to the service of the church" in exchange for time.

The fourth stage is *depression*, which is related to the loss of strength and the advance of the signs of the illness. First, there is reactive depression, depression in response to actual losses; the dying lose their appearance, their freedom of action, their sense of manhood or womanhood, their usefulness, and they are separated from home and family. But there is secondly what Kubler-Ross calls "preparatory depression," which is much like the grief felt after the patient's death by the survivors. This is a letting go of life, a turning away from the past toward the future, which is to say, toward death. While reactive depression can be dealt with through encouragement, temporarily restorative treatment, involvement in tasks, visits of friends and family, etc., these methods are not very helpful in dealing with preparatory depression. Indeed, they are not even desirable in the case of preparatory depression because they distract the patient from a necessary task. To accomplish its function, this sorrow must be expressed and experienced.

> This type of depression is necessary and beneficial if the patient is to die in a stage of acceptance and peace. Only patients who have been able to work through their anguish and anxieties are able to achieve this stage.[21]

This stage assumes the overcoming of denial and anger and prepares for the fifth stage, *acceptance*.

Kubler-Ross describes acceptance of one's death as something different from mere resignation and hopelessness, though these attitudes may be expressed too.

> If a patient has had enough time (i.e., not a sudden, unexpected death) and has been given some help in working through the previously described stages, he will reach a stage during which he is neither depressed nor angry about his "fate." He will have been able to express his previous feelings, and his envy for the living and the healthy, his anger at those who do not have to face their end so soon. He will have mourned the impending loss of so many meaningful people and places and he will con-

[21] Elizabeth Kubler-Ross, *On Death and Dying* (New York: Macmillan, 1969), 78.

> template his coming end with a certain degree of quiet expectation.[22]

Kubler-Ross insists that acceptance should not be mistaken for a happy stage; rather it is one of peace, almost devoid of feelings. There is less interest in others, a preference for communication through gestures, touching, and meaningful silence.

It is important to notice that constant struggle obviates the coming of acceptance.

> There are a few patients who fight to the end, who struggle and keep a hope that makes it impossible to reach this stage of acceptance. They are the ones who will say one day, "I just cannot make it anymore," the day they stop fighting, the fight is over. In other words, the harder they struggle to avoid the inevitable death, the more they try to deny it, the more difficult it will be for them to reach this final stage with peace and dignity.[23]

So there is a difference between acceptance, on one hand, and militant denial followed by giving up in defeat on the other. This deepens our understanding of the relation of impossibility to the discovery of reversal; letting go is not mere despair but something affirmative. As to those who continue to resist,

> The family and staff may consider these patients tough and strong, they may encourage the fight for life to the end, and they may implicitly communicate that accepting one's end is regarded as a cowardly giving up, as a deceit, or, worse yet, a rejection of the family.[24]

Here the living give the dying the additional burden of having to help them deny their own mortality and the fear of it. The living, not encountering the limit of death so personally and immediately as the dying, have not had to face their feelings about it and have not had to let go of the willful and strident approach to life, and they fear and misunderstand acceptance of death in the dying. In this, they may prevent or interfere with the necessary development of the process of dying in peace.

A complication arises whereby it may happen that one gives up too early, when a fight for life might still help. So family and treatment staff may err on either side, encouraging a too early cessation of effort, or interfering with an appropriate and realistic acceptance.

Dr. Kubler-Ross reports that almost all of her patients who had sufficient time, and support based on understanding the appropriateness

22 *Ibid.*, 99.
23 *Ibid.*, 101.
24 *Ibid.*

and necessity of each stage, reached the point of acceptance. She points out that acceptance is not resignation, for one is accompanied with equanimity and peace, while the other is indignant, embittered and anguished. It was noted above in the examples of spontaneous operations of the reversal of intention that reversal is not quitting, and it does not lead to diminished function but rather to improved functioning. Kubler-Ross has noted the same fact.

> When a patient has accepted the reality of his own finiteness, then he has a much better chance to use all his internal energies to help the physician and the treatment team fight to keep him alive.[25]
>
> Many patients who were able to overcome their fear of death and faced their own finiteness were then able to use all their internal energy and resources in the fight to get well and to get home.[26]

Thus, paradoxically, accepting death may increase chances for survival.

Clearly, in the notion of acceptance, we have empirical evidence of the spontaneous discovery of the value of the reversal of intention through encountering impossibility, an immovable limit. In the case of knowledge of one's own inevitable death, the approach through assertion and effort cannot do anything but fail, but a great value is discovered as soon as all striving ceases.

Two problems to be discussed later arise at this point. One has to do with the question, Is the goal achieved by letting go always the same as the one for which we strove? In the case of stuttering, clearly the answer is yes, but not in the case of death, for one was striving to live, but what we receive in acceptance is not more quantity of life, but a better quality. The question of just what goal is reached through reversal will be taken up in the next chapter.

A second problem raised by the use of the Kubler-Ross discoveries is now encountered for the first time. What is the relation between the operation of letting go of self-effort and one's beliefs? Each traditional text studied offered us a belief-system as the premise of the reversal of effort. Kubler-Ross herself believes in personal conscious survival of death by the human spirit, but she has found the absence of such a belief creates no difficulty for reaching the state of acceptance.

> It does not matter whether your religious belief includes a specific belief in immortality. . . . We have worked with only four genuine, true atheists, and they have died with amazing peace and acceptance, no different from

[25] Elizabeth Kubler-Ross, *Questions and Answers on Death and Dying* (New York: Macmillan, 1974), 38.

[26] *Ibid.*, 156.

> a religious person.[27]

(Kubler-Ross mentions many others in addition to these four who, while they had some kind of notion of survival, such as belief in the immortality of one's influence or in the invincibility of the life-force, did not believe in personal conscious survival of death.) So apparently, reversal of intention is a natural human capability, which makes it possible for us to find "fulfillment despite failure." Kubler-Ross goes on to say religious belief makes the achievement of acceptance easier.[28] Elsewhere, she grants that religious beliefs about afterlife are part of our generalized pattern of denying death.[29] So there is an ambiguity about accepting our finitude while believing our life will be infinite.

Here is the problem. We might say there are two ways of letting go in the face of death. (1) We may let go of life since death is inevitable and clinging is useless and troubling; this is clearly accepting death. (2) Or, we may let go of *this* life because we believe in *another* life after death; this is accepting death on the condition that it is followed by another life. Surely, both include grief over loss and both involve acceptance; but the two are nevertheless quite different. A similar problem arises if we contrast the belief-systems of Gautama and Luther; there is a contrast between "letting go absolutely" and "letting go because God will catch me." This will be a problem in a later chapter.

* * * * *

The question of this chapter has been, How does the idea of the reversal of effort arise? The answer would seem to be that in historical and personal crises, we encounter the impossibility of success through effort. The concept of "limit situations" in the thought of the philosopher Karl Jaspers may be useful here. Certain situations block life as lived by the ethic of attainment, and these cannot be surmounted but only acknowledged.

> I must die, I must suffer, I must struggle, I am subject to chance, I involve myself inexorably in guilt. We call these fundamental situations of our existence ultimate situations.[30]

Impossibility is thus encountered in death, in suffering, in the blocking and frustration of our projects, in our vulnerability to historical calamity, and in guilt. We may fight on and deny the limits, or we may become embittered. Or we may find a way of fulfillment through the reversal of effort.

[27] *Ibid.*, 159.
[28] *Ibid.*
[29] Kubler-Ross, *On Death and Dying*, 14.
[30] Karl Jaspers, *The Way to Wisdom* (New Haven: Yale University Press, 1950), 20.

> To ultimate situations we react either by obfuscation or, if we really apprehend them, by despair and rebirth: we become ourselves by a change in our consciousness of being.[31]

In short, when there is nothing we can do, we may discover that there is nothing we need do in order to find something of great value and importance.

The briefest description of those situations in which letting go is discovered is in the statement, when there is nothing you can do, there is nothing you need do. The value of letting go is discovered when other approaches are impossible. But this phrase may invite misunderstanding, as if the ethic of consolation were mere resignation, hopelessness, and inaction. The ethic of consolation is an affirmation of life and not a negation. But the life which is affirmed is after all one that includes the "limit situations," and therefore affirmation cannot simply be an adolescent rage for life or a sunny optimism which ignores the limits.

[31] *Ibid.*

Chapter 8

TO WHAT PROBLEM IS THE REVERSAL OF INTENTION THE ANSWER? APPROPRIATING THE ENERGY WASTED IN DENIAL

There is no need to struggle to be free; the absence of struggle is itself freedom.

—Chogyam Trungpa
Cutting Through Spiritual Materialism

The reversal of intention occurs in the experience of despair and rebirth; when intention is frustrated so utterly that one abandons it, a value is experienced which could not be achieved through effort. This is the beginning of understanding the paradox of intention. But just what is this value that can only be achieved through giving up the attempt to achieve it? Is giving up a magical way of getting what we want? Some naive approaches to religion promise that if we only give up wanting material things (or pretend to), God will then give them to us. Or, if we do not use reversal to get the goals we normally seek, such as love, wealth, fame, or power, then just what is it that we receive?

Thus a second step toward understanding the paradox of intention begins with the question, "To what problem is the reversal of intention the answer?"

It became clear in the preceding chapter that the idea of reversal always arises in some concrete context; something was sought energetically, and it could not be attained through trying. It is also apparent that the idea of reversal has some specific, short-range applications; it has been used to deal with stuttering, hand-washing compulsions, or impotence. But the four classical texts studied suggest that its significant application is in dealing with what we might call "the religious problem." (Of course, these texts contend the solution to this problem is that there *is* no problem.) That is, the reversal of effort is not a solution to specific problems of the self, although it turns out to have a relevance to them, but to the problem of being a self as such. The distinction between particular fulfillments, satisfactions of particular needs and wants, and the fulfillment of life as a whole is probably not hard to grasp, since the contrast is merely one of scope. But there has been an annoying vagueness throughout our discussion in the term "fulfillment of life." Each text studied presented a different view of this, and it remains to be seen if they are somehow talking about the same thing. What is needed is an understanding of the religious problem that will make clear just what concern is resolved by the reversal of effort.

* * * * *

When we ask, "What is the religious problem? Just what function does religion perform?" We immediately confront the fact that religion has performed many functions and dealt with several distinct problems through its long history. Nothing can be defined or understood as a timeless essence, apart from its historical variation and development. In fact, religion has dealt with the whole range of human problems, from physical survival through social order to life's fulfillment. But there seems to be a gradual shift of concern in its complex history from one end of the hierarchy of human needs to the other.

We can begin with the fact that human existence is precarious; even when life is pleasant and secure, it is in principle at all times subject to a number of specific threats. Frankl had distinguished the three spheres of the biological, the social, and the noetic, "the sphere of meaning," and claimed that they were the special concerns of the three Viennese schools of depth psychology, the Freudian, the Adlerian, and his own. We can use the discrimination of these three spheres to become clear about the threats that beset us. There are threats to our physical or organic security; the threats of disease, hunger, poverty, accident, violence, and death endanger our life and health. Secondly, there are threats to our social self, to our self-esteem and to our sense of belonging to the group; guilt, shame, rejection, ostracism, the loss of status, failure, and the threat of the upwelling of forbidden emotions or drives menace the human as a social being.

And thirdly, there are threats to our sense of meaning; for we are not merely physical and social organisms, but self-conscious beings with a need to find life meaningful. Every belief- system that promises meaning is itself undermined by experiences of life's precariousness. Thus we may fall into a sense of meaninglessness, or *anomie*, due to the disruption of our organic or social well-being; suffering threatens our belief in an orderly, predictable and just world, and must be explained by our belief-system or we lose faith in it.[1] For example, death not only threatens my physical life, but for a meaning-seeking being, it

[1] Peter Berger, *The Sacred Canopy, Elements of a Sociological Theory of Religion* (New York: Doubleday, 1967), 53 ff.

brings into question the meaning of the life that preceded it. This is made clear in the Parable of the Rich Fool (Luke 12. 13-21). A man had spent his whole life gathering great wealth and could scarcely build silos and barns fast enough to contain it. But in a dream he was addressed with the words, "You fool, this very night you must surrender your life; you have made your money — who will get it now?" (Luke 12.20. *N.E.B.*). Here death is not merely the end of life, but an event, awareness of which raises the question of the meaningfulness of the life we have lived. Meaning-systems are also threatened by contact with beliefs different from our own, or by having them subjected to analysis and scrutiny, as for example in books of the sort you are reading.

Threats arise from nature, from other persons and groups of persons, and from hidden or denied parts of ourselves; they are directed to any human interest or value, such as life, health, security, self-esteem, status, growth, integrity, or meaning. These interests which may be threatened are hierarchical; that is, the value of life is basic, for without this the social and spiritual values cannot arise, and, in fact, it is a rare luxury in most societies and possessed only by leisure classes in others to be concerned with problems of meaning in an all-absorbing way. Attention is first directed to biological interests, then later, when these are somewhat in hand, to the social and spiritual.

The theologian Paul Tillich has something like this in mind when he speaks of threats to our self-affirmation as beings, and to our moral and spiritual self-affirmation.

> Non-being threatens man's ontic self-affirmation, relatively in terms of fate, absolutely in terms of death. It threatens man's moral self-affirmation, relatively in terms of guilt, absolutely in terms of condemnation. It threatens man's spiritual self-affirmation, relatively in terms of emptiness, absolutely in terms of meaninglessness.[2]

Our response to specific threats is fear, which leads to action designed to deal with the threat, through some kind of defense, offense, flight or compensation. But the bare fact that we are open to dangers, that our lives are precarious even when specific threats are absent, gives rise to anxiety.

> Fear, as opposed to anxiety has a definite object. . . , which can be faced, analyzed, attacked, endured. . . . Immediately seen, anxiety is the painful feeling of not being able to deal with the threat of a special situation. But a more exact analysis shows that in the anxiety about any special situation

[2] Paul Tillich, *The Courage to Be* (New Haven: Yale University Press, 1952), 41; the order of the three threats in the quotation has been rearranged.

anxiety about the human situation as such is implied.[3]

Crossing Broadway at 122nd Street, I see I have underestimated the speed of a taxi, and I feel fear for a moment at the threat it poses to my physical safety. I trot the rest of the way across the street and a few strides along the sidewalk for good measure. I have acted with competence, and the fear subsides. But as I walk along the street the cold, damp wind coming up from the Hudson River chills me, and I shudder inwardly as a vague, familiar uneasiness sets in. I made it that time, but what about the future? An awareness of the fact that life as such is threatened wells up. This is anxiety, which is objectless; it is not the fear of this or that specific threat, but an awareness of our total precariousness.

Just because anxiety is objectless, our liability to it constitutes evidence concerning the human situation as a whole. It is the novel and insightful claim of existentialists that we must see anxiety not merely as a passing mood to be evaded and forgotten, but as a genuine disclosure of what is involved in being human.

But how can we deal with this feeling that does not intend a particular object? At first, we know no way other than the way of action, the method we use in coping with fears; so we adopt the will-centered approach to life as a whole, putting on armor, building up strength and competence, creating a heroic image through tasks and accomplishments. The root of the ethic of mastery and attainment as a lifestyle is in the anxiety that is inescapably a part of human existence; it is one response, perhaps the most characteristic one, to the fact of our precariousness. In one sense, hyperintention as a posture in life is simply a reflexive reaction to anxiety and not really a choice. Yet, since as we will see it is debilitating, cramping, and destructive to ourselves and others, it is our responsibility to deal with it. Here we have yet another paradox: we are responsible for that which we did not create. It will be my claim that this is the region in which the reversal of effort theme has its most significant application.

The response to both fear and anxiety is activity, the effort to attain. All of culture may be seen as a heroic project of attempting to deal with that which threatens human interests and values.[4] Religion is, whatever else it may be, a human art, an aspect of human culture, and as such it aims at human welfare. Various human arts, such as agriculture or medicine, aim to deal with the precariousness of the human situation by handling specific threats that are manipulable, subject to eventual treatment by human knowledge and skill. Religion differs, according to William Bernhardt, in that it attempts to deal with the

[3] *Ibid.*, 36, 38.

[4] Ernest Becker, *The Denial of Death* (New York: Free Press, 1973), 11 ff.

non-manipulable threats, those which are, given the existing state of knowledge and skill, beyond our ability to control.

> Men will be religious at those points in life where they lack confidence in their ability to achieve and conserve values. Religious behavior will thus be oriented toward those phases of life which are believed to be non-manipulable, that is not subject to objective manipulation or control.
>
> There appears to be a definite relationship between religion, . . . and the growth in knowledge and skill. Where men have confidence in their ability to meet their needs in terms of manipulative control, they do not rely upon religious behavior. Where they lack confidence in their manipulative ability, there they tend to make religious adjustments.[5]

Religion is the attempt to deal positively with the threatening and non-manipulable aspects of experience. (Of course, just which situations are not subject to control depends on the state of development of a culture, and ultimately on personal belief.)

Bernhardt points out there are two kinds of non-manipulable threats. Some threatening aspects of experience are only temporarily non-manipulable due to the limits of existing knowledge and skill; as technology grows through time these matters lose their religious significance for most people. Other threatening aspects of experience seem to be unavoidably and irremediably non-manipulable. These are what Tillich called "absolute threats." We cannot imagine the problems of death, condemnation, or meaninglessness as yielding to increased knowledge and skill. As the first type of non-manipulable threat decreases somewhat through technical progress, this second category increasingly dominates religious concern.

Religion at first attempts to manipulate the non-manipulable by means of ritual magic, which Bernhardt terms "metatechnology." Metatechnology refers to

> all attempts to introduce extra natural or supernatural force or forces into natural technological processes. One may define it more simply, perhaps, as the attempt to utilize supernatural means to achieve technological results.[6]

The prefix *meta-* is used here to mean "beyond;" metatechnology is the attempt to work beyond our present technology. Generally, the more available technology, the less metatechnology. Notice that metatechnology is like technology in that it is an aggressive attempt to manipulate and control the environment.

[5] William H. Bernhardt, *A Functional Philosophy of Religion* (Denver: Criterion Press, 1958), 91-92.
[6] *Ibid.*, 42.

This approach to religion's function is suggested by the studies of Bronislaw Malinowski on the technology and magic of the people of the Trobriand Islands, northeast of New Guinea. When studied, these people relied largely on the results of fishing and gardening. The soil is rich and rainfall plentiful, and yams and taro grow readily. Working only with axes and digging sticks, the Trobrianders clear space for their gardens and plant their crops. They have considerable knowledge of soil types, optimal times for planting, and the effects of weather and pests. But like all human activities, gardening is subject to unforeseen events, and so rites and ceremonies are conducted. After clearing a place for a garden has begun, a three-day *tabu* on work is proclaimed and ceremonies are conducted that lead to burning of the underbrush and clearing of the land. Work is again suspended for ceremonies preceding the planting of yams and at several other times before harvest.

> There is a clear-cut division: there is first the well-known set of conditions, the natural course of growth, as well as the ordinary pests and dangers to be warded off by fencing and weeding. On the other hand there is the domain of the unaccountable and adverse influences, as well as the great un-earned increment of fortunate coincidence. The first conditions are coped with by knowledge and work, the second by magic.[7]

Work and magic are sharply separated, and both are regarded as necessary parts of the technology of growing tubers. The concern of the magical is with the non-manipulable aspects of the situation, both threatening and beneficial.

Bernhardt maintains that Malinowski's studies also show the more risky the enterprise, that is, the less effective the technology, the more magic is used. The Trobrianders procure most of their fish from within their coral lagoons, by poisoning them, and this is a safe and relatively sure means of procuring food. But they also fish in the open sea beyond the reef, and this is dangerous and requires the use of nets and spears, which are much less sure of getting results. While fishing within the lagoon is chancy due to the movements of schools of fish, greater uncertainty arises in fishing in the open sea; there are coral rocks and sandbanks, unpredictable winds and strong currents, and sharks. A much greater use of magic occurs in fishing than in gardening, and more in the open sea fishing than in lagoon fishing. For example, there are three types of canoes, the *kewo'u* which is small and used along the coast within the lagoon, the *kalipoulo* used both within and beyond the reef, and the *masawa* used in great expeditions to

[7] Bronislaw Malinowski, "Magic, Science and Religion," in *Magic, Science and Religion and Other Essays* (Garden City, N.Y.: Doubleday, 1955 [1925]), 29.

other islands. In the construction of the first type of canoe, simple to build and used in safe waters, work proceeds without the use of magic. The second type requires careful selection and use of materials and is used outside the lagoon, and so magic is used. But for the *masawa*, a most elaborate set of rituals and *tabus* is observed. Thus the greater the uncertainty, the more ritual magic occurs.[8]

One might ask why metatechnology is not easily discredited when it fails to procure results. The fact is that when metatechnology fails, people do not abandon it but seek an explanation for its failure based on the magical belief-system. There is a fascinating ancient Hittite divination text which is the record of an inquiry into the failure of a magical ritual. Questions are asked, and lots are cast to yield an answer. Has one of the minor holy days been omitted? Is an image of the god in disrepair? Did ritually impure people enter the sanctuary? Did a dog enter the sanctuary and steal some of the sacred cakes? The questioning goes on at great length.[9] The point is that we will find an explanation of the failure of metatechnology rather than cease to believe in it, simply because to abandon magic we would have to let go of this form of self-effort. We would then have to live in the face of threats without the protection of magic. This reveals that metatechnology has a beneficial effect, which Malinowski noticed; for whether the power of metatechnology to master objective threats is real or imaginary, it produces subjective assurances that are undoubtedly real.

William Tremmel therefore extends Bernhardt's analysis of the function of religion by introducing the concept of "metapsychological changes," by which he means

> those inner psychological changes which are affected by religious beliefs, actions, and experiences — especially those religious responses which go "beyond" normal, expected, psychological responses.[10]

Tremmel mentions the martyr's serenity and ability to forgive his or her tormentors as an example. He points out that these metapsychological changes brought about by religion are of two types. Firstly, *unconscious* metapsychological change is the result of belief in the power of metatechnology; belief in the power of the ritual yields assurance, courage, the loss of inhibition, and thus increased effectiveness in ac-

[8] Bronislaw Malinowski, *Argonauts of the Western Pacific, an Account of Native Enterprises and Adventure in the Archipelagoes of Melanesian New Guinea* (London: George Routledge, 1932), 112, 221.

[9] James B. Pritchard, ed., *Ancient Near Eastern Texts Relating to the Old Testament*, 3rd ed. (Princeton: Princeton University Press, 1969), 497-498.

[10] William C. Tremmel, *Religion, What Is It?* (New York: Holt, Rinehart and Winston, 1976), 43.

tion. It seems likely that the Trobrianders really did fish more proficiently because of their belief that ritual magic went a long way toward handling the unpredictable and otherwise uncontrollable aspects of their venture.

If these metapsychological benefits come to be recognized, they can be sought for themselves, and through time this leads to a greater interest in the second type of metapsychological change. *Conscious* metapsychological change is change required by the religious system. In this, we do not seek so much to change the threatening situation, but instead alter the threatened interest. As knowledge and skill grow in power over the environment and interests toward the physical end of the hierarchy of needs are met, attention in religion more and more shifts toward the metapsychological. George Santayana, as was said of James before, understood all of this quite well; he finds an example in the transformation of sacrifice from "the expression of a profitable dependence" in which we give in order to get, into a more spiritualized act in which the gods no longer ask for a portion of our food, "but for the foolish and inordinate part of our wills."[11]

> When religion reaches this phase it has become thoroughly moral. It has ceased to represent or misrepresent conditions, and has learned to embody spiritual good.[12]

Religious concern thus has shifted through time from the metatechnological securing of physical needs to metapsychological change.

The prayer of Jesus in Gethsemane just before his arrest, in Tremmel's view, represents both metatechnology and metapsychology. "Father, if it be thy will, take this cup away from me. Yet not my will but thine be done." (Luke 22.42, *N.E.B.*) In the movement from the request that the coming suffering may be averted by divine intervention, to the acceptance of whatever comes as divinely sanctioned, religion has ceased to be merely a means of achieving physical security and has become a means of realizing personal values, such as courage, forbearance, patience, or serenity. It no longer merely seeks control over the threatening situation, but an alteration in the self relative to the situation.

Bernhardt uses the example of Paul's attitude toward an ailment, which he calls his "thorn in the flesh." Paul says he prayed about it three times, and the answer he received from God was, "My grace is all you need; power comes to its full strength in weakness." (II Cor. 12.8, *N.E.B.*) Paul did not receive physical healing, but something else. He says,

[11] George Santayana, *Reason in Religion* (New York: Charles Scribner's Sons, 1905), 37.
[12] *Ibid.*

> I shall therefore prefer to find my joy and pride in the very things that are my weakness; and then the power of Christ will come and rest upon me. Hence I am well content, for Christ's sake, with weakness, contempt, persecution, hardship, and frustration; for when I am weak, then I am strong. (II Cor. 12.9-10, *N.E.B.*)

The attempt to appropriate divine power to reach the personal goal of physical well-being is abandoned, and well-being and security of another sort has arisen.

Technology and metatechnology are alike in that they are "control activities" according to Bernhardt, attempts to manipulate the world so that it fulfills human interests and supports human values. All of this belongs to what we have been calling the ethic of attainment, for it seeks the good of human life as the direct result of effort. One seeks fulfillment through control of the external environment, if not through knowledge and skill, then through magic and prayer. But in conscious metapsychological change we have gone beyond the attempt to control the environment to a concern for the reorientation of the mind and emotions. Religion finally approaches the non-manipulable threats in existence by aiding the individual in making subjective adjustments as well as, and in some cases instead of, changes in the objective world.

So we have a picture of religion's function, which is to make possible a positive response to otherwise disorienting and anxiety producing non-manipulable threats to human interests, at first, through metatechnology and then through metapsychology. We see development from concentration on meeting organic or physical needs, to concern for self-esteem and personal growth, and for finding meaning and value in the negative aspects of experience. Metapsychological change as a response to the needs that go beyond the physical is the eventual function of religion, and the reversal of effort is one approach among several to metapsychological change. Progress has been made toward answering the question of this chapter.[13]

Before concluding, it is important to repeat that the approach to metapsychological change through the reversal of intention is not the whole essence or meaning of religion, but merely one approach among others. It must be apparent in the paradoxical nature of the lines quoted by Paul, "power comes to its full strength in weakness," that we are again in the presence of the familiar paradoxical approach to

[13] Tremmel, *Religion*, 52 ff.; Tremmel sometimes uses the term "salvation" for this total reorientation of the self and distinguishes it from metapsychological change, but apparently the difference is merely of degree, and some examples, such as Job, appear under both concepts; in any case, the discussion does not intend to represent Tremmel's views at this point.

fulfillment. Jesus' struggling in the Garden of Gethsemane and his final prayer of "thy will be done" can be compared with the experiences of effort, frustration, despair, and letting be that we found in Gautama and Luther. So reversal is one way to metapsychological change. You will recall from the studies of Paul's letters and Saraha's *Treasury of Songs* that criticisms were made there of the approach to metapsychological change that centers on striving. The heroic approach to life which attempts to triumph over that which is threatening and push through to fulfillment has been extended into the area of metapsychological change. Much of religious life seeks fulfillment of our needs for personal growth and a sense of peace and meaning through the management of the self or God. Self-esteem is sought through moral heroism and peace of mind through self-manipulation in ascetism, meditation, prayer, liturgy, and study. Of course, all of these activities can be approached in a different way, and they need not be attempts to manipulate and control. But when they are, we are trying to extend the manipulative approach to the problem of the self. To take one example, Luther saw that gaining a better self-estimate and higher status by pleasing God and being on the "right side" is an attempt to manipulate divine power by manipulating the self. Thus we must add to what has been drawn from Bernhardt and Tremmel: there are two approaches to metapsychological change, the ethic of attainment and the ethic of consolation.

* * * * *

All forms of the reversal of intention claim to go to the root of the human problem. The precariousness of the human situation calls forth heroic resistance, militant defensiveness, strident assertiveness. This is manifest in both secular culture and in religion, in technology and metatechnology, and in many approaches to metapsychological change and growth. But these defenses and exertions are no remedy, according to the proponents of reversal. In fact, efforts to deal with the anxiety of the human situation intensify it. So our heroic defenses and projects become a secondary problem, for they occupy us in countless forms of the denial of our precariousness and these imprison us and clutter our lives. Religion and ethics have called this problem egoism and selfishness, but this moralism is misleading for it implies something which is reflexive is a moral evil. Psychologists have called it narcissism and have shown its expression in a complicating and debilitating hyperintention. It is precisely this which is remedied by the reversal of effort.

As we noted in the last chapter, the reversal of intention arises through an experience of impossibility. Firstly, we cannot deal with all of our fears and all the specific threats to specific interests and values through skill and knowledge. Some non-manipulable threats are intrinsically such and will not be managed out of existence. This is true of death in spite of the near-comic technological "solution" proposed by cryogenics, freezing individuals immediately upon death until a cure is found for their disease. And so, impossibility will be encountered here. Secondly, our problem as self-conscious beings is not just fears, but anxiety, not merely specific threats but awareness of our inescapable precariousness. The attempt to handle the generalized, objectless anxiety generated by the human situation through effort and action cannot succeed. There is simply no single threat to ward off, no single interest to be satisfied. This becomes evident when we recall Luther's experience in the monastery; he attempted to handle condemnation, the generalized sense of alienation from God, by dealing with specific sins and specific commandments. As Tillich has said, we always attempt to transform anxiety into fear, for then our distress can be imagined to have a cause and a cure. But however many threats we succeed in overcoming and however many values we succeed in satisfying, we have not escaped our precarious situation.

To put it more technically, an intentional approach cannot be taken toward a problem, awareness of which is non-intentional. That is, anxiety is non-intentional in the sense that it intends no specific object, and thus the intentional or will-centered, problem-solving approach to it cannot be fruitful. The self-defensive, self-assertive response to anxiety must lead to frustration, and for some, to the discovery that our anxiety about the precariousness of our situation can be resolved or lived with only through letting go.

The reversal of intention is offered by those who represent it as the solution to the problem of anxiety about the precariousness of our existence, and to the secondary problem of the burdensome defensiveness and heroic exertions evoked by this anxiety. It represents what Alan Watts called "the wisdom of insecurity."[14] Our existence is inescapably insecure, and our lives are cramped and cut-off from the fullness of experience by our efforts to deny and escape this. We cannot free ourselves from the underlying anxiety about this precariousness by fighting for security. We may learn to deal with anxiety by giving up efforts and accepting our insecurity. When there is nothing we can do, there is nothing we need do. Gabriel Marcel, the existentialist Catholic, speaks of making the transition from self-preoccupation to disposability.[15] This is what the reversal of effort accomplishes.

This applies to our anxiety about threats both to our physical being and to our social being or self-esteem. The Buddha was at first dis-

[14] Watts, *Wisdom of Insecurity*, 13 ff.

[15] Gabriel Marcel, *Being and Having* (New York: Harper and Row, 1965), 73.

tressed over the bare vulnerability of life to suffering and death; this was anxiety and not fear of some specific and present threat. He found peace in treating his physical being as disposable, relinquishable, released, yielded up. He was free of or able to cope with anxiety, and he was free of all those exertions aimed at denial and escape that added to his distress. Luther seems to have been concerned with threats to his self-esteem, perhaps centering in conflicts over his father's expectations for him, and he found peace in treating his self-worth as disposable; he relinquished his concern for it, and yielded himself up to divine mercy. He was freed from the pain of guilt, and from all of those efforts which robbed him of peace and subtly reinforced his sense of unworthiness. He accepted his unworthiness as the Buddha accepted his insecurity.

The acceptance of inescapable insecurity is expressed in Gautama's teaching through the *anatta* doctrine. There is "no *atman*," no personal, individual soul-substance, and thus it is pointless to cling to the separate self and seek to preserve personal existence apart from and against the larger whole to which we belong. In the teaching of the nothingness of the separate self, the precariousness of our physical being is accepted. Similarly, in the doctrine of the "total depravity of human nature," Luther accepts threats to our self-esteem as unavoidable and irremediable through self-effort. As sinners we are unable to help ourselves and must therefore rely wholly on divine grace. Both doctrines involve accepting our insecurity in different aspects of our existence and letting go of fruitless and counterproductive striving. But the Buddha did not, in fact, escape from being insecure, and Luther did not, in his belief, cease to be unworthy. Rather, in accepting either insecurity or guilt, they were freed from both anxiety and the feverish efforts to deal with it.

Moving from self-preoccupation to disposability, from hyperintention to yieldedness, comes from accepting our insecurity; it is liberating. It may free some from anxiety; more likely, it frees us from the debilitating effects of anxiety and enables us to live with it. Luther was beset with periodic depressions in which he felt tempted to doubt divine forgiveness, but was able to live with this. It frees us from all of those necessarily fruitless efforts to escape the inescapable and ward off the inevitable. The benefits of being freed from the effort to deny and escape our insecurity require comment.

Firstly, Frankl showed that action based on anticipatory anxiety brings about what it fears. The idea we are examining is that most of our life-effort is based on such an anxiety. If I recognize that much of my time is spent in flight and avoidance, then my anxiety is increased rather than escaped. When we recognize the effort spent in escape and defense, the painful realization comes to us, if I'm running so hard, something fearful must be pursuing me. This can best be made clear in that form of denial of threats to our self-esteem called "having something to prove." Having to prove ourselves simply reinforces the underlying problem of self-doubt. If your underlying assumption is that you are unworthy, then all attempts to prove yourself become evidence that something is wrong. Energetic attempts to make people like us cause the underlying discontent to grow. It's as if I say to myself, "If I weren't working so hard at being likable and charming, and they knew me as I am, they wouldn't like me at all." We seem to notice ourselves working hard to prove ourselves, and part of us isn't fooled. This part reaches the obvious conclusion: "If I have to work so hard to prove myself, something is really wrong."

Perhaps we are rarely aware of how trapped and isolated we are behind our defenses, and how much energy is wasted in denial and flight. Thus secondly, in addition to increasing our anxiety, our denial cuts us off from reality. We develop selective attention so as to be unaware of experiences that would remind us of our precariousness. For example, because they confront us with death, suffering, and chance, we isolate the sick, dying, troubled, and defective, only to be put away by others if our turn comes. Or again, we dread to know ourselves, hiding from our dreams and impulses for fear the unacceptable will become public and we'll lose a sense of social worth. Indeed, the two fears, death and loss of self-esteem, interlock in a strange way in our culture, because admitting to anxiety about death and suffering leads to fear of loss of self-esteem, since it is not acceptable to admit to this emotion. The general pattern manifest in hundreds of specific acts of avoidance and denial of our insecurity is stated by Henry Nelson Wieman: "We reduce to a feeble flicker of appreciation what would give us greatest joy if we did not dim our vision to conceal the lurking evil."[16] Our awareness is intentionally dimmed less it prove evidence of threat, and we are to that extent less alive, as if our precariousness would go away if we refuse to look at it.

Thirdly, energy is diverted from life to defense and escape, and we become trapped within the defenses and obligated to our heroic projects. We must be a great people and establish an eternal empire to defend ourselves from a sense of smallness and mortality, and war and domination follow. Our efforts to prove and protect our sense of self-worth lead to treating life as a performance and other persons as either the audience to acclaim us or competitors who might upstage us.

In short, anxiety about threats to our organic security and to our

[16] Henry Nelson Wieman, *Man's Ultimate Commitment* (Carbondale, Ill.: Southern Illinois University Press, 1958), 61.

self-esteem leads us to the "fight or flight reflex," and we become prisoners of our defenses. It is the problem of anxiety and the secondary problem of entrapment by futile defenses to which letting go is the solution. The one problem has no remedy, and to be free of the other requires only that you cease the struggle to be free. The reversal of intention is thus an end of our defensive isolation and an opening outward; in accepting our insecurity, we are able to reappropriate the energy wasted in denial.

It should now be apparent that the reversal of effort is not a way of getting our goal, as much as it is a redefinition of the goal. Letting go *is* the goal. Thus the law of the reversal of effort is not really a logical paradox. You do not really get the goal by giving up the attempt to get it, because there is no goal beside the cessation of effort. Letting go did not make the Buddha secure from death and suffering, nor did it make Luther really righteous; but then, anxious effort could not do this either. Reversal of intention is not a way of achieving our old goals of security from threat or the fulfillment of our wishes. It is a redefinition of the goal, a total reorientation of the self. The claim is that peace cannot arise by our becoming secure and satisfied through our own efforts; rather, these very efforts destroy whatever peace and satisfaction is really possible. Therefore, we needn't do something right, but only stop doing the wrong thing, the hyperintention of security in a situation irremediably precarious.

There is a sense in which reversal does nevertheless apply to specific problems and short-range goals. Of course, it applies to anxiety about our total situation, and not to specific fears and their causes, which presumably we will handle in the normal way; reversal is an answer to an ultimate problem, the problem of how to respond to our precariousness. But when you respond by letting go of useless defenses and tasks and denials, an attitude arises that may lead to more appropriate and effective action toward proximate problems. The previous chapter mentioned examples of this including the observation of Dr. Kubler-Ross that after accepting death and ceasing to deny and resist, patients are better able to use their remaining resources to live well and even to survive. Or again, often action is marred by the fact that we are dealing with two things at once, the immediate activity and our overall insecurity. Action would then become more effective when our insecurity is accepted as irremediable. If in running we seek not only to perfect the art of motion and to enjoy the experience of the functioning of our bodies, but also to master our anxieties through an impressive victory, we become tense and we fight our own movements; we run better when it is just a matter of running and not also a means of achieving ultimate security. When the problem of the self has been taken care of, or rather, let go of, then one can simply play at everyday things, incidentally and indirectly becoming more effective. When I am disposable, I am at my own disposal.

There appears to be a form of the reversal of intention idea to which the last two paragraphs do not apply. In these beliefs, we *can* get specific goods and need not really renounce the quest for security and satisfaction. That is, in some belief-systems, letting go is seen as a kind of magic or metatechnology. "If I let go, God will reward my dependence by being the wished for parent and give me all I want." This is the attempt to control one's situation by dependence and disability; my helplessness and need are a demand that forces others or God to take care of me. Preachers of this approach promise, "Give everything up and you get it all back." One would be a fool not to, if this were the way it worked. The appeal here is merely to self-interest; this message addresses the old self and promises the old goals. It is not letting go of control activities and of the attempt to manipulate; it is not a total reorientation of the self. We have only to compare this approach with the passages above regarding Jesus and Paul to see this. So letting go is not as easy as it might have seemed, since there are subtle counterfeits and ways of holding back that masquerade as the real thing. So difficult is it, and so great the burden of self-knowledge regarding the many ways we fight against and counterfeit surrender, that there is a saying among Buddhist monks, "Better not to begin; once you begin, better to finish it."[17]

This leads to a related problem. Threats to our physical organism and to our self-esteem may well be handled by accepting our insecurity. I can't overcome death, make everyone love me, or become righteous before God by my own efforts. But each classical instance of the reversal of intention contained a justification for letting go through a set of beliefs about the nature of reality. These beliefs are subject to the threat of doubt. And so again the problem of a later chapter is encountered. Is letting go possible only if we believe that reality will meet us with a supportive response? If the answer is yes, then is the reversal of intention authentic? For the counterfeit of letting go noted above was false precisely because it was conditional, saying, "I'll give it up *if* I get it back."

[17] Chogyam Trungpa, *Cutting Through Spiritual Materialism* (Berkeley: Shambhala Publications, 1973), 47.

Chapter 9

IS LETTING GO DROPPING OUT? ACTING WITHOUT ATTACHMENT TO THE RESULTS OF ACTION

> It is not possible for the embodied to relinquish actions entirely; but he who relinquishes the fruits of action is called a (true) relinquisher.
>
> —*Bhagavad-Gita*, 18.11

The greatest part of most people's effort is a reflexive and automatic response of resistance, denial, and compensation, evoked by that anxiety which is an inescapable part of the human situation. The various forms of the paradox of intention offer ways to become unburdened from the cramping and numbing effects of these efforts which deny the precariousness of our situation. They accomplish this by pointing out that it is impossible to escape our precariousness anyway, and when we accept this fact, the energy wasted in denial is released for life. The next set of questions that must be answered if the reversal of effort is to be understood is, "What kind of action follows from letting go? If the experience of impossibility blocks the will and we let go of self-effort, then do we simply drop out of all forms of human activity? If so, isn't the reversal of intention world- and life-denying? If not, what kind of activity would not include the effort to attain?"

This complex of questions can be focused by considering the examples of artistic creativity and acts of caring for and helping others. If all culture and action is a heroic project aimed at the denial of existential anxiety, and if letting go is a rejection of this, then doesn't it lead to an end of creative and caring action? Isn't letting go irresponsible? Would we have had a Bach or a Schweitzer if they had simply let go and dropped out? The response to this question will sharpen our understanding of the criticism of effort in the ethic of reversal. For it will become clear that what is rejected is not action itself, but a certain way of undertaking it. When we act to deal with anxiety, we do not fully enter into the act itself; when we are doing two things at once, creating or helping on one hand, and proving our worth or establishing our reality on the other, our action is spoiled. Wouldn't the conscious intention to create "great" music and to achieve a kind of immortality in this way have had the same effect on Bach or Mozart that thinking about walking with a hundred legs had on the centipede? Wouldn't the intention to prove his or her worth in acts of compassion have made Mother Teresa or Schweitzer a self-preoccupied and self-congratulating Pharisee rather than a saint? Great music is not written for the sake of greatness, nor are genuine acts of self-giving done to enhance self-esteem. So our question is, Just what is the character of action that is free and not part of the heroic denial of death? As we gain an answer to this, it will become evident that dropping out is a choice which some people make, but it is not necessary to nor does it follow from letting go.

* * * * *

The most direct approach to the question of action that does not seek to attain that we can find within the classical literature of philosophy and religion occurs in the ancient Hindu text called the *Bhagavad-Gita*, or "The Lord's Song." As it now stands, the *Bhagavad-Gita* is an interlude within the immense epic, the *Mahabharata*. It was composed sometime in the two centuries before the beginning of the Christian era, and it seems intended to unite and synthesize a number of different strands in Indian philosophy and religion. Because relating diverse systems of belief and practice is relevant to the problem of a later chapter, some attention will be given to this, as well as to the *Gita's* approach to the problem of action.

From the Upanishadic scriptures the *Gita* draws the ideas of Brahman as the divine reality including and undergirding all seemingly separate things, and of *maya* as the mysterious fact that there appears to be a world of separate objects which prevents us from seeing the divine unity. The inner being of every person and thing is identical with Brahman, and in the state of blessedness or enlightenment, we come to realize this. From the early forms of the Samkhya school of thought, the *Gita* takes the account of the created world as consisting of *purusha*, "person or self", discrete living souls, and the independent and antithetical *prakriti*, "lifeless matter or nature." In this view, *prakriti*, or nature, is differentiated into a variety of things and persons through the combination of the three *gunas*, "basic qualities of matter." There is a tension between this view of each soul as separate and the Upanishadic idea that all souls are one. From the popular cult of the God Vishnu comes the idea of salvation through the grace of the personal God and also the notion of the periodic appearance of an *avatar* or "incarnation of God." There is thus a second tension in the *Gita*, between the picture of God as transcendent of the creature and the Upanishadic idea of God as immanent in each soul. The *Gita* may even integrate elements of Buddhism, which officially stood outside orthodox Hindu tradition; these may include the idea of salvation as open to any caste, and the moderate or "middle way" approach to the practice of meditation and religious discipline.

Looked at in another way, the *Gita* accepts and relates three very different approaches to the fulfillment of life that were current in the Hindu world, three different yogas, or disciplines leading to salvation. First there was *karma yoga*, "the way of works or deeds," which consisted in the scrupulous observance of one's caste duty in both its social and ritual aspects. According to the law of karma, each deed in life causes a corresponding reward or punishment in an after life of heavens and hells, and in one's subsequent reincarnation in a new earthly life. One function of the concept of karma was to justify the existing allocation of power and privilege by rank and race, for one's position in life is the result of the karma or causal power of past deeds. Through fulfillment of caste duty, one will eventually be incarnated as a brahmin, "a priest-scholar" who is capable of escape from *samsara*, "the cycle of repeated incarnation." For as much as some Westerners may find the idea of reincarnation appealing as a solution to the problem of death, to the sensitive Hindu it represents the problem for which a solution must be found.

Secondly, life might be fulfilled through *jnana yoga* or the way of wisdom. Here one escapes from ignorance through inward discrimination of a truth that sets one free from the tiresome, painful cycle of reincarnation. In the tradition stemming from the Upanishadic scriptures, one learned to see that the personal soul is not a discrete entity, but is identical with the divine, all-inclusive Brahman; you must come to recognize within yourself the changeless element, and you must know this as identical with the inner essence of all things. When you realize that "the *atman* is the Brahman," that your soul is identical with the soul of all things, you cease to react to the everyday world with desire and fear. In this state of consciousness one consumes all karma remaining from past deeds and accumulates no more; thus one is freed from the cycle of rebirth to enjoy an eternity of bliss. But such a realization is open only to the *sannyasin*, a holy one who has renounced the world and found the liberating insight through meditation and the practice of austerities. This way of wisdom was placed within the way of deeds by the practice of postponing one's quest for liberation until after a point in life when one's duties as a householder and parent had been performed.

Lastly, there is *bhakti yoga* or the way of devotion to a particular god in love and thankfulness. At the time the *Gita* arose, many were finding that regardless of caste, worship of a personal god leads to the same surrender of self as does the elite way of wisdom. The *Gita* in its present form begins with this insight and seeks to integrate with it the way of deeds and the way of knowledge; it seeks to relate the doctrines of the *Upanishads* to the view of God as personal and transcendent.

* * * * *

The *Gita* is relevant to the question of this chapter, having let go of the effort to attain, does one continue to act? It is relevant to the question of a later chapter on the relation of discordant belief systems to the idea of reversal. The problem of action arises in the *Gita* in relation to the story of the *Mahabharata* of which it is a part. The usurping Kauravas are opposed in a righteous war by the Pandavas; the two clans are blood relations and have come to the plain of Kurukshetra for a battle to settle their conflicting claims to rule. As the opposing armies stand ready to begin battle, Arjuna, hero of the Pandavas, expresses his dismay and perplexity to his charioteer, who is Krishna, an *avatar* of God. Arjuna can see in the opposing battalions his own kinsmen and has no heart for strife and killing. Yet it is his duty as a member of the *kshatriya*, or "warrior caste," to uphold the right with force. The ostensible problem is thus, how can one do one's caste duty when it seems wrong?

The Lord Krishna offers a preliminary answer to the dilemma. Each person lives many lives and exactly when this present one ends can be of no great importance; our separate lives are unreal, while that which is real within them all cannot cease to exist.

> Know that to be indestructible by which all is pervaded. No one is ever able to destroy that Immutable. These bodies are perishable, but the dwellers in these bodies are eternal, indestructible and impenetrable. Therefore, fight! . . . He who considers this (Self) as a slayer or he who thinks that this (Self) is slain, neither of these knows the truth. For It does not slay, nor is It slain. (2.17-19)[1]

The Self is changeless and eternal and puts on lives like garments. There is really no such thing as killing and being killed. Since there is nothing higher for a *kshatriya* than a righteous war, Arjuna must fight.

This answer comes from the way of wisdom. Those who know what is real and what is mere appearance do not take deeds with the same intensity as the unwise. But Krishna continues with an answer that integrates the way of deeds with this. When you act out your caste duty, you must act without attachment to the fruits of action.

> To work alone thou hast the right, but never to the fruits thereof. Be thou

[1] "The Blessed Lord's Song" (*Srimad-Bhagavad-Gita*), trans. Swami Paramananda, in ed. Lin Yu-Tang, *The Wisdom of China and India*, (New York: Random House, 1942), 57-114. All quotations from the *Gita* are from this source, and are identified by chapter and verse. Occasionally, capitalization has been removed.

> neither actuated by the fruits of action, nor be thou attached to inaction. . . . Abandoning attachment and regarding success and failure alike, be steadfast in *yoga* and perform thy duties. . . . Work (with desire for results) is far inferior to work with understanding. . . . Wretched indeed are those who work for results. (2.47-49)

Action in this mode accords with the way of wisdom, for when we identify with the Self we know that we do not act; we act without acting. *Karma yoga* and *jnana yoga* are thus the same in result, both leading to release from karma and rebirth; however, the way of works must be practiced without desire for the results of action in order to have this effect. Arjuna must not delight in killing nor may he aim at power, wealth, victory, or even a better reincarnation; rather, he must act without regard to the outcome. This leads to oneness with Brahman just as does the way of wisdom. While caste duty in the normal mode leads to a better rebirth, duty done without attachment to its fruits is deliverance from the cycle of rebirth.

We might have thought that *jnana yoga* was a higher way, and that those with insight would abandon all action. But it is impossible to refrain from action entirely.

> A man does not attain to freedom from action by non-performance of action, nor does he attain to perfection merely by giving up action. No one can ever rest even for an instant without performing action. Do thou therefore perform right and obligatory actions, for action is superior to inaction. Without work, even the bare maintenance of thy body would not be possible. Therefore, do thou perform action without attachment. (3.4-9)

The attempt of the extremists of renunciation and discipline to attain to non-action would be an end to this life, but not a means to liberation from the round of rebirths. Since action is inevitable, one must act without aiming at a benefit as the outcome.

While to attempt to be still is impossible, and those who try do violence to themselves, action without attachment does manifest a kind of stillness.

> He who sees inaction in action and action in inaction, he is intelligent among men; he is a man of established wisdom and a true performer of all actions. Him the sages call wise whose undertakings are devoid of desire for results and of plans, whose actions are burned by the fire of wisdom. Having abandoned attachment for the fruits of action, ever content and dependent on none, though engaged in action, yet he does nothing. Being freed from longing, with self under control, and giving up all sense of possession, he is not tainted by sin merely by performing bodily action. Content with whatever comes without effort, undisturbed by the pairs of

> opposites (pleasure and pain, heat and cold), free from envy, even-minded in success and failure, through acting (he) is not bound. (4.18-22)

In action without attachment to its outcome, one has discovered a still center within. The way of wisdom explains this as discovering the center as God. This approach to *karma yoga* in a sense erases the distinction between action and inaction.

When we act without being concerned with fears and wants, we are acting without being moved. This kind of action, this approach to *karma yoga*, is congruent with the truths of *jnana yoga*, that our real identity, the Self, is not moved and does not act. Being already identical with the Self, one already possesses everything; thus we need not seek anything nor fear anything.

> That man, who is devoted to the Self, is satisfied with the Self and is content in the Self alone, for him there is nothing to do. (3.17)

When we cease acting out of passion and attachment, in the ensuing calm we are able to see our real identity, the Brahman.

> Surrendering all action to Me and fixing the mind on the Self, devoid of hope and egoism, and free from the fever (of grief), fight, O Arjuna. (3.30)

Thus the ways of wisdom and deeds intermingle.

The way of wisdom as represented in the *Gita* knows that Brahman is the inclusive reality. And unlike more philosophical texts, the *Gita*, which is close to popular religion, is sure the divine oneness pervading all is a personal God incarnate as Krishna, and not merely the impersonal All-Soul.

> There is naught else (existing) higher than I. Like pearls on a thread, all this (universe) is strung in Me. . . . I am the sapidity in waters and the radiance in sun and moon, I am *Om* in all the Vedas, sound in ether, self-consciousness in mankind. I am the sacred fragrance in earth and brilliance in fire; I am the life in all beings and austerity in ascetics. Know me . . . as the eternal seed of all beings. I am the intellect of the intelligent and the prowess of the powerful. . . . Of the strong I am the strength, devoid of desire and attachment. (7.7-11)

One is to see God in all and all in God. All things are said to be in Brahman as objects are in space. The wisdom way transcends everyday knowledge in seeing this underlying divine unity.

> By my unmanifested form all this world is pervaded; all beings dwell in Me, but I do not dwell in them. (9.4)

The supreme Brahman alone exists, devoid of qualities and thus not easily perceived, sustaining the world that is known to common sense. On an Upanishadic reading of the *Gita* based on passages like the above, we should know that our soul is really not a discrete entity, but one with the divine Brahman. Since this is our true identity, we can be unattached to the events that seem to befall us in the world. There is nothing we lack and nothing apart from us that could threaten us; the world of common sense is a mysterious appearance which is ultimately unreal.

The wisdom teaching of the *Gita* goes on to give an account of the world known to everyday consciousness which draws on ideas from the Samkhya system. *Purusha*, "the multitude of living souls", and *prakriti*, "matter," are mysteriously generated by God, giving rise to *maya*, "that which is made, the created world." Here it is harder to maintain the Upanishadic reading, for the Supreme Self seems to be separate from the Self of each person.

> There are two kinds of beings in the world: the perishable and the imperishable; all beings are perishable, but the *purusha* (Self) is imperishable. But there is another, the Highest Being, called the Supreme Self who is the Immutable Lord, pervading the three worlds and supporting them. (15.16-17)

Yet even if we see each soul as separate, we may know that our real identity is unmoved by action and event, and so we may look on pleasure and pain, praise and blame as alike. For nothing can touch or destroy the discrete but eternal Self within each person. This interpretation requires a new reading of some of the passages quoted above, with special attention to the meaning of "Self." But in either interpretation of wisdom, the way of wisdom unites with the way of deeds. For in both views, the truth about reality is that our real identity, whether the Self as the Brahman or the Self as the separate soul, is unmoved and untouched; and when we are unattached to the outcomes of our acts, we embody this in our lives.

In any case, in creating the world, God remains unmoved; all action within the world flows from the nature of *prakriti*; it does not come from the Brahman and it does not come from your own soul. Therefore, the real remains unmoved by action and is unattached; when we regard our actions without attachment to their results, we act in accord with reality. We are then doing the truth.

> The Supreme Lord abides in all beings equally; (He is) undying in the dying; He who sees (thus) sees truly. . . . And he who sees that all actions are being performed by *prakriti* (nature) alone and that the Self is not acting, he sees truly. When he sees the separate existence of all beings estab-

> lished in One, and their expansion from that One alone, then he becomes Brahman. (13.27, 29-30)

That which delivers from the cycle of birth and rebirth, according to the wisdom way, is the realization that all things flow forth from the divine One, and differentiation and action belong to the realm of nature only. In this Upanishadic reading, our real identity is the Brahman and thus we do not really act.

It follows that both the wise and those who act without attachment reach the same goal, realization of their unity with Brahman. The truth is, our real identity is the One, and the One is unmoved and does not act. When I act, saying, "I do nothing at all," I act truly (5.8). When action occurs, it is not my real self that acts, not the divine Brahman, but *prakriti*. The actor who knows this is unattached to the fruits of action and earns no karma toward future rebirths.

> He who performs actions, surrendering them to Brahman and abandoning all attachment, is not polluted by sin, as a lotus-leaf by water. (5.10)

As the pure and delicate lotus is not defiled by the pond in which it grows, so is the one who acts without attachment and the desire to earn merit free from the karmic value of the act. If we act with attachment, seeking to ward off what we hate and grasp what we want, even if we do our caste duty in order to rise higher in the next life, our acts earn karma and we will be reincarnated until it is consumed. Acting without attachment to the fruits of action is thus identical with enlightenment in which we see our oneness with Brahman. *Karma yoga* and *jnana yoga* are one, when seen in this way.

The meaning of unattached action as enlightenment is also seen in the way Krishna, as the incarnation of God, acts. Surely Krishna has no need to attain to anything through his acts. Yet he does act from time to time to give the world a saving example. His incarnation and activity within the world are thus embodiments of action without attachment.

> Actions pollute Me not, nor have I any desire for the fruits of action. He who knows Me thus, is not bound by action. (4.14)

To really understand the action of the incarnate one would be to see the truth.

The unmanifested form of Brahman is known in the wisdom way, but in the view of the *Gita*, this occurs only with great difficulty. Far easier is the way of worshipful devotion to the God revealed in Krishna.

> Greater is their difficulty whose minds are set on the Unmanifested for the goal of the Unmanifested is very arduous for the embodied to attain. But those who, surrendering all actions to Me and regarding Me as the Supreme Goal, worship Me with single-hearted devotion, for them whose hearts are thus fixed on Me . . . I become ere long the Savior from the ocean of mortal *samsara* (birth and death). (12.5-7)

Bhakti yoga leads to the same result as *jnana yoga* and as *karma yoga* when practiced with detachment. For in the ecstasy of worship we experience oneness with God, and *bhakti* is identical with the wisdom way.

> I am the Origin of all, everything evolves from Me. Knowing this the wise worship Me with living ecstasy. (10.8)

In selfless devotion to God, one acts with detachment from results, and so *bhakti* is one with way of deeds.

> He who neither rejoices, nor hates, nor sorrows, nor desires and who has renounced good and evil, he who is thus full of devotion is dear to Me. (12.17)

In the notion of surrendering all action to God and acting with God as the supreme goal, devotionalism encourages action unattached to its fruits; in acting for the sake of God, one does not seek gain or merit, but simply glorifies God.

The *Gita* clearly prefers the way of devotion, and seems to argue for the value of this way of salvation against the claims of precedence made by the wisdom way.

> Those who, fixing their minds on Me, worship Me with perpetual devotion, endowed with supreme faith, to My mind they are the best knowers of *yoga*. (12.2)

All castes may come to God through *bhakti*-devotionalism.

> Fill thy mind with Me, be thou My devotee, worship Me and bow down to Me; thus, steadfastly uniting thy heart with Me alone and regarding Me as thy Supreme Goal, thou shalt come unto Me. (9.34)

The *Gita* unites the three ways of salvation as one in their effect. Union with Brahman and the transcending of attachment to the little self and its wants and fears comes about through *knowledge* of the One reality pervading the world, through *action* in the world which is not attached to results, and through selfless *devotion* to the personal God revealed in Krishna.

Krishna's final answer to Arjuna's question about action requires a brief statement of the way in which the three *gunas*, or qualities manifested by *prakriti*, affect human behavior. Here it is shown that the *Gita's* approach is a middle way between despair of effort and hyperintention of effort.

Everything in *prakriti*, or material nature, manifests the three *gunas*, or basic qualities, in different ratios of combination. *Sattwa* contributes order to material nature, *rajas* contributes life and motion, and *tamas* inertia. Since the human body and mind are part of *prakriti*, human character can be described in terms of the dominance of one or another of the *gunas*. *Sattwa* is transparent, free, good, and true; when it dominates, the person is calm, unattached, and thus transparent, and so the underlying Self can be perceived and enlightenment attained. *Rajas* is turgid, passionate, and lusts after pleasure, power, and spiritual enlightenment; but just because the *rajas* person is intent on attainment, spiritual insight is impossible. In the contrast between the transparent *sattwa* and the turgid *rajas*, Hindu psychology has given an account of why effort in the spiritual life is self-defeating and why the goal of religious life can only be attained by giving up the attempt. *Tamas* is dark, ignorant, and inert, and those in whom it dominates are deluded and slothful. The allotment of these characters is the result of karma, and the ratio of the *gunas* present at death determines the nature of our new incarnation.

The three temperaments approach worship and religious discipline in characteristically different ways. The *sattwic* person performs sacrifice without desire for benefit, simply because it is the right thing to do. The *rajasic* person performs sacrifice to gain the favor of the gods and a reputation for holiness, while the *tamasic* person either omits sacrifice or performs it in an improper and defiling way.

> That sacrifice is *sattwica* which is performed by men desiring no fruit, as it is enjoined by the Scriptural laws, with the mind fixed on the sacrifice alone, just for its own sake. But . . . that which is performed with the desire for fruits and for ostentation, know that to be *rajasica* sacrifice. (17.11-12)

The same contrast between those unattached to the fruits of action and those acting to attain arises in the practice of religious discipline.

> When . . . austerity is practiced, by men of steadfast devotion, with great faith, without desiring fruits, it is said to be *sattwica*. When this austerity is performed with the object of gaining welcome, honor and worship, or from ostentation, it is said to be *rajasica*, unstable and fleeting. The austerity which is performed with deluded understanding, by self-torture or for the purpose of injuring another, that is said to be *tamasica*. (17.17-19)

Notice that the self-destructive extreme in austerities is associated with ignorance rather than hyperintention to attain. The *sattwic* way is the middle path between doing too much with too much intensity and doing nothing or the wrong thing.

In worship and discipline, it is the *sattwic* person who acts without that intensity about outcomes which spoils action. The *sattwic* person is clear it is not they who act and thus they can approach action with an inner calm. The opposite of this is the deluded person who does not know who he or she is, and thus says, "I am the doer" (18.17). But it is not the Brahman who acts, but *prakriti* and the *gunas*, and we cannot say *we* act. According to the *Gita*, those without understanding say,

> This has been gained by me today and this desire I shall obtain, this is mine and this wealth also shall be mine. That enemy has been slain by me, others also shall I slay. I am the lord, I am the enjoyer, I am successful, powerful and happy. I am rich and well-born; who is equal to me? (16.13-15)

But Arjuna must know he is not the doer, and that even in slaying in battle "he neither slays nor is bound (by action)" (18.17). Arjuna is moved by his own *prakriti*-nature, his place in the physical universe as a *kshatriya*-warrior, to enter the battle on the plain of Kurukshetra. Arjuna is compelled by his situation to fight, but he must not fight in a *rajas*-like way to gain power and fame or to earn merit for a future life; he must act in the middle way, between despondent inaction and passionate action. For in both of these extremes egoism is manifested.

> If, actuated by egoism, thou thinkest: "I will not fight," in vain is this thy resolve. Thine own nature will impel thee. O son of Kunti, being bound by thine own karma, born of thine own nature, thou shalt be helplessly led to do that which from delusion thou desirest not to do. (18.59-60)

Both *tamasic* inertia and *rajasic* assertion are based on an egoistic misunderstanding of who we are. But Arjuna, knowing he is really one with the eternal Brahman, can act, but with non-attachment to the outcome. Since his ultimate security is in hand, he need not seek any benefit through his action.

* * * * *

Since more time has been devoted to the exposition of the belief-system of the *Gita* than to that of some of the traditional texts encountered previously, it should be pointed out that our study is of the reversal of intention itself, and not of any set of beliefs or practices some have thought necessary to it. The answer to the question of this chapter drawn from the *Gita* is not that when you act it is not really you but your body responding to its world, since you are really the isolated, untouched Self beyond all this. The question of belief-systems is for a later chapter. All that is of interest at present is the notion of acting without attachment to the fruits of action, as a middle way between paralysis and self-defeating intensity. The alternative to the ethic of attainment is not the renunciation of action and life, but a new kind of acting and willing that is not crippled by the hyperintention of the outcome.

This brings us back to belief-systems. For in the *Gita*, the intense approach to action can be relinquished precisely because the underlying existential anxiety at its root has been dealt with in the discovery of the divine Self as our true identity. The Self is eternal and untouched by emotion and eventfulness, beyond death and failure; since this is you, imagined threats to your organic existence and to your self-esteem are literally nothing. Having discovered a still center within, it is not necessary to stop the wheel of action to attain peace; having attained this peace, action itself is free and spontaneous, and more likely to reach its goal.

Before developing a fuller statement of this view of will and action, it will be helpful to turn back to previous statements, which bear on our question, especially the Pauline-Lutheran approach to works. You will recall that when I was spinning wildly in a centrifuge in an amusement park, letting go of the pointless attempt to escape or control my anxiety was a release that made a playful and active approach to the experience possible. Similarly, letting go of the pretension of omnipotence as a teacher created an atmosphere in which action was less tense and more flowing, responsive, and effective. Of greater weight is the observation of Kubler-Ross that patients who have let go of their denial and resistance to death are actually better able to live and even recover if this is possible. In these occasions, energy consumed in denying or attempting to escape or overcome the inevitable is released for life. This commonplace discovery was raised to the level of a metaphysical mystery in the *Tao Teh Ching*. For when we act in a non-interfering way, we are following the *Tao* of our lives, and the *teh*, "the power and fulfillment" appropriate to us, is bestowed. *Wu-wei*, recall, was not non-action, but action which is not forced or contrived. Letting go is not necessarily dropping out, unless you want it to be; it is instead a release of vitality.

The whole question can be seen from a new perspective if we look at the Pauline-Lutheran approach to works of righteousness. It was clear in the sketch of Luther's experience in the monastery that the threat which evoked a crippling intensity of defensive effort in Luther was directed against his self-esteem; the problem is not that of the Buddha, death, disease, and old-age, but the sense of sinfulness before a righteous God. It is surely incorrect to attribute just this psychological experience to Paul, although Protestants often mistakenly read back into the letters the experience of Brother Martin in the Augustinian order. Nevertheless, Luther discovered in the letters of Paul the good news that salvation is a free gift and not an attainment. Does it follow, then, that we may do as we please, and that works of obedience and thankfulness to God, caring for others, and building up the community of faith are not necessary? Does letting go of the effort of self-salvation lead to a slackened effort to grow into full humanity?

Just this question seems to have arisen in Paul's own churches. In Romans Paul asks this question rhetorically.

> What are we to say, then? Shall we persist in sin, so that there may be all the more grace? No, No! We died to sin, how can we live in it any longer? (Rom. 6.1-2, *N.E.B.*)

Elsewhere he deals directly with a misunderstanding of his message in his church at Corinth.

> "I am free to do anything," you say, Yes, but not everything is for my good. No doubt I am free to do anything, but I for one will not let anything make free with me. (I Cor. 6.12, *N.E.B.*; cf. Rom. 3.8)

As this passage continues (I Cor. 6.9-20), Paul insists that the unjust cannot possess the Kingdom of God, and that having been justified by God's grace, the Christian will now manifest a new life as the dwelling-place of God's spirit and part of the body of Christ. The outcome of faith is a new moral life manifest most fully in love.

Paul regards this new life as the work of God's spirit within the faithful but he also exhorts his followers to exert complementary efforts in this direction out of thankfulness to God. This is clear in Romans, chapters 12 and 13. In response to God's self-giving, the Christian must offer the self as a sacrifice acceptable to God. There follows a list of ethical requirements of the Christian life: loath evil, cling to the good, give to the needy, be hospitable, bless your enemies, comfort those who mourn, do not be haughty, never return evil for evil, submit to authority, pay tax and toll. All of this is seen as both the work of God's spirit in the Christian and the result of effort. "With unflagging energy, in ardour of the spirit, serve the Lord." (Rom. 12.11, *N.E.B.*) Paul concludes with the need of the Christian to keep the spirit of the Mosaic commandments, which are summarized in love to the neighbor.

> He who loves his neighbor has satisfied every claim of the law. For the commandments, "Thou shalt not commit adultery, thou shalt not kill, thou

> shalt not steal, thou shalt not covet," and any other commandment there may be, are all summed up in the one rule, "Love your neighbor as yourself." Love cannot wrong a neighbor; therefore the whole law is summed up in love. (Rom. 13.8-10, *N.E.B.*)

Apparently, understanding salvation from sin as a gift and not an achievement does not lead to relaxation of efforts after goodness, although it surely puts them in a different light.

Accepting oneself as a sinner does not lead to self-excuse and contentment, in Paul's view. Indeed, paradoxically, Paul is maintaining that as soon as we accept ourselves as we are, then we begin to change. When we trust in divine grace, God's spirit transforms us into new creatures who manifest ethical traits and spiritual powers that human effort could not achieve; these are the gifts of God's spirit. When we have experienced divine forgiveness, we are freed from sin, the essence of which is self-concern and self-reliance, and thus we are able to move toward concern for others, which as Paul stated above, is the center of ethical life.

These ideas can be stated in a way relevant to the question of the chapter, drawing on the thought of the theologian Paul Tillich and the psychologist Carl Rogers.[2] In brief, Paul says we can love because we have received love. That is, being accepted by God's love, we can accept ourselves, and having accepted ourselves, we can accept others. If I can accept myself, I need no longer pretend to others, I need no longer compete with them to prove my worth, I need no longer defend myself from another's knowledge and judgment. Defensiveness, competitiveness, and self-absorption that bind us when our self-esteem is weak and threatened begin to lift, and a new ethical life is possible. So paradoxically, when we accept ourselves as we are, we begin to change, and in the Pauline theology, this self-acceptance is possible because of God's acceptance of us.

To go on, in Paul's view, forgiveness frees moral effort from that self-defeating character it previously had. Prior to the birth of faith, efforts at personal renewal were part of the self-reliant attempt to prove oneself righteous, and as such they were self-seeking. As Frankl said, if one seeks a good conscience, one is already a hypocrite. If one's goodness is an attempt to raise one's sense of self-worth, it is for that very reason not goodness, but self-interest, and every success in such efforts is accompanied with the sin of pride. If becoming acceptable is my achievement, then I take the credit. Thus we have an account of

[2] Tillich, *Courage to Be*, 163 ff.; Carl Rogers, *Client-Centered Therapy, Its Current Practice, Implications and Theory* (Boston: Houghton Mifflin, 1951), 138, 194, 513-514; *On Becoming a Person, a Therapists's View of Psychotherapy* (Boston: Houghton Mifflin, 1961), 51, 62-64, 66, 207, 237.

why it is that when we accept ourselves as we are, we then begin to change. When the problem of the self and its worth has been settled by divine acceptance of us as we are, we are freed of the necessity to prove ourselves in our acts. Now we must act rightly and with love and justice, but such action is freed from self-concern. Acts which might benefit another person are nevertheless selfish when they are part of an attempt to prove our worth. When we accept ourselves as we are because God accepts us, then such acts can be genuinely centered on the other. Moral effort is no longer the anxious attempt to prove something, or the resentful and laborious task of earning merit. Now our moral efforts are free and spontaneous, not grudging and anxious, because they are not attempts to win acceptance, to prove ourselves, to overcome underlying feelings of self-contempt. This problem has already been taken care of. Now moral action is free to be just what it is, an attempt to do what we can, an occasion to grow toward fuller responsiveness to others. It is not burdened and cramped by the additional self-centered concern to prove yourself. As in the *Gita*, when the problem of existential anxiety in any of its forms is dealt with and the sense of the still center arises, a new kind of action follows.

While Luther and Paul are not simply identical, the Pauline idea that the right relation to God cannot be the outcome of effort, but that nevertheless moral effort is necessary, is clearly found in Luther. His rather monastic way of stating this is as follows.

> Since by faith the soul is cleansed and made to love God, it desires that all things, and especially its own body, shall be purified so that all things may join with it in loving and praising God. Hence a man cannot be idle, for the need of his body drives him and he is compelled to do many good works to reduce it to subjection. Nevertheless the works themselves do not justify him before God, but he does the works out of spontaneous love in obedience to God[3]

Good works do not justify us, but are necessary. From this it follows that when we do them, we expect nothing from them; we are unattached to their results. Luther expresses this by saying the person of faith does good works as Adam and Eve did.

> We should think of the works of a Christian who is justified and saved by faith because of the pure and free mercy of God, just as we would think of the works which Adam and Eve did in Paradise, and all their children would have done if they had not sinned.[4]

[3] Martin Luther, "The Freedom of a Christian," trans. W. A. Lambert and H. J. Grimm, in *Three Treatises* (Philadelphia: Fortress Press, 1970), 295.
[4] *Ibid.*, 296.

Created righteous, Adam and Eve had no need for justification by works, and yet they performed the task of tilling and keeping the Garden.

> This task would truly have been the freest of works, done only to please God and not to obtain righteousness, which Adam already had in full measure.[5]

This "freest of works" is work done without attachment to its outcome; it is work done without an eye to gain.

What renders an act righteous, to Luther, is precisely this lack of self-interest and self-reliance, which is the same as to say, a total reliance on God's mercy. Luther uses the example of the great saints of his tradition.

> For the saints, to whom these works were counted for righteousness, certainly did not do them in order to be regarded as righteous; indeed, they did not know whether God would behold them. But they did what they could in humble faith, always with the prayer that their works might be acceptable to God according to his mercy. And so they were first reckoned as righteous on account of the yearning of their faith, and only afterward also their works were accepted and approved. But foolish perverter that you are you commence with the works that were accepted and you leave aside the inner yearning by which you, too, could first be reckoned as righteous just as they were.[6]

What makes one righteous in Luther's view is reliance on God's mercy, that is, faith; works are not a means of earning merit, but simply doing what we can in humble faith. Here in Pauline-Lutheran terms is the message of the *Gita*, letting go of self-effort is not inaction, but right action, action that does not seek benefit from its results.

Just as in the *Gita*, the reversal of intention does not lead to an end of intention, but to a new kind of intentionality. Action is spoiled when we are doing two things at once; trying to deal with anxiety about our finitude or our guilt prevents us from entering fully and freely into the action at hand. When the underlying anxiety is accepted and dealt with, action can be just what it is, and we can move toward genuine involvement in the reality of the moment, its feelings, relationships, and tasks. This still center from which a new, freer, more spontaneous action flows is discovered in the *Gita* through knowing the true identity of the self, and in Paul and Luther through experiencing divine forgiveness for sin.

5 *Ibid.*

6 Martin Luther, *Lectures on Romans*, trans. Wilhelm Pauck (Philadelphia: Westminster Press, 1961), 131.

* * * * *

By now it is clear that the reversal of intention is not an end of intentionality, but only of the hyperintentional approach to life. In the *Gita's* terms, it is a movement from the *rajasic* mode to the *sattwic*, from contrived action focused on attainment as a way of overcoming our existential precariousness to spontaneous and flowing action which expresses our nature and our situation with an absence of tenseness about the outcome. It is not a matter of willing or not willing, but of the wrong and right kinds of will; it is not a matter of choosing between action and passivity, but of finding their appropriate combination.

A step toward greater clarity regarding the right and wrong kinds of willing and doing might be taken if we recall Frankl's ideas of wrong passivity and wrong activity. By wrong passivity he meant withdrawal from anxiety producing situations, as in the life dominated by fears. The reversal of intention claims not to be a form of flight, but a way of engaging and coming to accept the painful and the negative. Wrong activity was characterized by the psychologist as the fight against awareness of obsessions and compulsions, as well as the fight for pleasure and performance. Moving beyond the realm of neurotic problems, these may also be taken to represent patterns of negative response to existential anxiety, despairing flight, and activist resistance or compensation. The whole heroic project of achieving security and self-esteem is, according to the great statements of the reversal of effort theme, the wrong kind of activity.

The approach to the religious problem, coming to terms with our precariousness, through the path of achievement cannot succeed because it is based on negation; it rests on our negating, ignoring, or denying something about ourselves or something about our world. If I approach artistic achievement as a means of grasping immortality, I deny the fact of death; and incidentally, this wrong kind of intentionality destroys the openness and flowingness creativity requires. "Writer's block" and "over writing" show this in different degrees, as does the attempt to control the flow of water-colors, which spoils the painting. If I approach an act of affirming another person as a way of building up my self-esteem, I hide from the underlying lack of it; and in the process, I fail to embody genuine caring, and my insincerity offends and drives the other away. The psychotherapist Rollo May gives this reason for the failure of "Victorian will power" to achieve authentic character; in his view, Freud showed that change and development through will power were a sham because of the denial and ignorance of the needs and drives considered unacceptable to the Victorian mind. You cannot force yourself to do or abstain from doing while you ignore your hidden motives which pull in the opposite direction[7] On a larger scale, the assertive approach to life similarly denies the truth revealed in the limit situations: our existence is precarious, our lives and our sense of self-worth are vulnerable to threats from within and without. Therefore, it follows that a kind of passivity is an element in the right kind of activity or willing, that passivity which accepts our insecurity. This would be the beginning of a new approach to willing: let it not be based on negation and denial.

Accepting insecurity is not passive in the despairing sense. For when we accept our situation as it is, we come to have greater control over it. This is seen in the psychological sphere, the realm in which self-esteem is threatened from within. When we accept ourselves as we are, including unacceptable and troubling elements, we come to have greater authority over ourselves; self-acceptance does not lead to stagnation, but change. The psychologist Carl Rogers uses this example.

> I am driving my car on an icy pavement. I am controlling its direction (as the self feels itself to be in control of the organism). I desire to swing left to follow the curve of the road. At this point the car (analogous to the physical organism) responds to physical laws (analogous to physiological tensions) of which I am not aware, and skids, moving in a straight line rather than rounding the curve. The tension and panic I feel are not unlike the tension of the person who finds that "I am doing things which are not myself, which I cannot control." The therapy is likewise similar. If I am aware of, and willing to accept all my sensory experiences, I sense the car's momentum forward, I do not deny it, I swing the wheel 'with the skid,' rather than around the curve, until the car is again under control. Then I am able to turn left, more slowly. In other words I do not immediately gain my conscious objective, but by accepting all the evidence of experience and organizing them into one integrated perceptual system, I acquire the control by which reasonable conscious objectives can be achieved.[8]

Here Rogers illustrates the paradox that when we accept ourselves just as we are, then we can begin to change, whereas will power based on a denial of and attempt to overcome hidden aspects of the self was fruitless. Will power based on evasion and resistance could not achieve the desired result, but letting go of denial, in spite of its seemingly passive and accepting approach, actually leads to change. The insight of the psychologist can be generalized. Accepting our existential precariousness may be the prelude to a new, more fruitful kind of action.

When the fear that always lurks just beyond the edge of awareness

[7] Rollo May, *Love and Will* (New York: W. W. Norton, 1969), 235, 239.

[8] Rogers, *Client-Centered Therapy*, 514.

is faced, it turns out to be merely what it is. It is merely death, or it is only a feeling of self-condemnation, and not nearly the formidable monster we had expected. In this moment, for it must be an experience and not an idea, we are released from the efforts of denial and compensation; a new energy is available, and a new level of awareness is possible. The still center arises, out of which a new kind of willing and acting may come. The really life-affirming response to the limit situations and the resulting anxiety is not heroic resistance but acceptance. This is simply Frankl's paradoxical intention, the right kind of passivity, which accepts, affirms, wills that which is feared and integrates it into the self and one's concept of reality.

The result of accepting our situation as threatened is a new kind of intentionality centering on responsiveness to the present moment, person, or task. Normally, we are doing two things at once, for each task must be both itself and also proof of our worth or a means to our ultimate security. Most action is spoiled by this weight, for no accomplishment can render our lives ultimately secure or prove our value once we doubt it. In that action which follows letting go and the acceptance of our insecurity, action is just itself rather than a heroic project of overcoming the limits of our existence. Here we act, but we are without attachment to the outcome, with nothing to prove; paradoxically, more is accomplished.

The *Gita* depicted this as "going with *prakriti*," acting in the way that embodies an uncontrived response to our nature and our situation; the Taoist called it non-interfering harmony with *Tao*, the natural course by which things become themselves. Rollo May says willing is listening, and he calls this kind of intention "willing by participation."[9] Here the tension has left intention, and the will expresses the whole self responding to the whole situation, rather than one part denying and negating another.[10] Thomas Hora has called this "reverent responsiveness to whatever is real, moment by moment." Willing by participation, responsiveness to the moment, is a kind of acting, and yet it includes elements of what we usually call passivity, in that one participates in a situation and responds to it. The assertive form of willing that masters its fate and captains its soul acts as if it were in a vacuum; it lacks that acceptance, participation, and responsiveness which characterize action that affirms and is unattached to its fruits.

It should be apparent by now that we are in quest of a concept which goes beyond the active-passive dichotomy. What is the nature of that way of being which is neither active nor passive? To explore this area that is obscured by our black-and-white thinking, Thomas

[9] May, *Love and Will*, 246.
[10] *Ibid.*, 217.

Hora uses the example of the birth process. On the surface of things, it appears we must be either active or passive, self-sufficient or helpless, dominant or submissive, masculine or feminine. We either assert our will in taking charge of our lives, or we surrender our will and allow our lives to be shaped by external forces. But there is a third modality that is neither only active nor only passive, which Hora has called responsive.

> One of the most meaningful examples of this is childbirth. Clearly, childbirth is an event in which a woman is required to respond lovingly, reverently and wholeheartedly to that which is from moment to moment. She can neither assert her will nor remain passive or resistant without hampering the process and suffering painful consequences.[11]

In childbirth the woman is called upon to be neither active in the assertive, coercive, manipulative sense, nor merely passive, but rather, responsive, participative.

This way of being is not inaction, but is clearly a form of "doing." This doing is responsiveness to a situation, it is participating with other factors. We can act in this way only if we have listened to the situation and have not insisted on being the only actor in it, dominating all its elements and pushing through to achieve our conception of the desired result. If we insist, and attempt to manage the birth process, we must fail, for no one knows how it is done anymore than we know how to swallow; if we listen and respond, participating in the process, nothing will be left undone. In order to be responsive, the situation must be approached with something like reverence, for in treating that which is with reverence, we accept its right to be. Reverence for life is free of that negation and denial implied in either passive avoidance or active domination.

Hora uses a second example, that of floating, to lead us beyond thinking dominated by the active-passive dichotomy.

> Now the question arises, is floating passive? Is it correct to say that we surrender ourselves to the water when we float? If we were to surrender ourselves to the water, we would drown. What is required in order to float? What kind of activity is required in floating? Attention. Floating is an activity occurring in consciousness. Floating is not passive, floating is not surrendering to the water, floating is not relaxing. It is the quality of consciousness which is alert, attentive and responsive to that *invisible power* present in the water which is called buoyancy. If we judge by appearances, floating may seem passive.[12]

[11] Thomas Hora, "Responsibility" (an unpublished lecture, Dec. 19, 1961); *Existential Metapsychiatry* (New York: Seabury Press, 1977), 69.
[12] Hora, *Existential Metapsychiatry*, 60.

Floating is actually not surrender to the situation, nor is it the active domination of the situation; it is attentiveness or responsiveness to it, participation within it. In both pure activity and pure passivity we center on the needs and moods of the self in isolation from the field or context of which it is a function. It is either "I'll get what I want through management and control!" or "I'm weak and tired, and if I'm helpless, they'll have to take care of me." In responsiveness we reverently affirm being that surrounds us and in which we are embedded, along with ourselves.

I believe this is the way we should understand "going with *prakriti*" in the *Gita*, although it is a very difficult and complex text. Arjuna is not to push through to a bloody triumph to gain honor and wealth, nor is he to insist on his scruples about warfare and subside into passivity; he is to act as what he is, in the situation in which he finds himself. To understand this example, of course, you must believe in the rightness of his cause and of his caste duty, which the original readers of the Gita did. Going with *prakriti* is action, not inaction; it is action by participation, the doing being called forth by the context. It is neither *tamasic* omission and denial of action nor *rajasic* ambitious and assertive action; it is *sattwic* action, which is, however, unattached with regard to its own outcome.

Every path of fulfillment has its dangers and distortions. In this approach, the danger is what Sartre calls "bad faith." "One way of defining bad faith is to say that it replaces choice with fictitious necessities."[13] We are free, responsive persons, but we often seek to evade the responsibility of this freedom by treating ourselves as things. We excuse ourselves by saying, "With my character or background, you can't really expect anything of *me*. This is just the way I am." Or, "You can't expect me to help you. It isn't my job." Through reference to our temperament, conditioning, disabilities, or role, we give ourselves a fixed definition which covers over the fact that we are free to decide and respond; in this we excuse ourselves for doing what we find least troublesome. Now it is clear that one could say, "I am not responsible because I am responding to the situation, going with *prakriti*. It is not I, but my karma." In doing this, responsiveness is distorted into a way of becoming less human rather than more. If the tightly controlled, emotionless manipulator so valued in our culture is dehumanized, so is the glazed-eyed drop-out of the counter culture who merely "goes with the flow." Responsiveness is response-ability and not evasion. Properly understood, willing by participation is a way of undertaking the burden of being a deciding self and not a way of escaping it.

13 Berger, *Sacred Canopy*, 93; cf. Jean-Paul Sartre, *The Philosophy of Jean-Paul Sartre*, ed. Robert D. Cumming (New York: Random House, 1966), 137 ff.

It is a middle way between inaction and contrived, inappropriate action. In this problem of the misuse of "going with *prakriti*" as an excuse and an evasion, we have entered upon the subject of the next chapter.

To summarize, responsiveness means my task is not to manage the outcome, but to participate. To act in this way one must be detached from the results of action. This is possible only when we have accepted that our lives and our self-esteem are radically vulnerable, so that we will not have to insist that the outcome of our acts bolster our sense of self-worth or make our lives totally secure. When the center is still, and the problem of our precariousness has been confronted, action need no longer be entangled with this problem and may become responsive. Thus for the center to be still, it is not necessary that the wheel of action stop.

* * * * *

Being free of the necessity of making each act a way of proving oneself, and no longer approaching the self as a problem to be managed, one would be free to play. Paradoxically, in playfulness action often acquires a capacity it could not have had before.

Robert Neale has suggested a definition of work and play that may help clarify this and make the idea of letting go more available to our will-dominated mentality. He defines work as any activity undertaken to resolve conflict; while as a writer of psychology, he is concerned with work as dealing with inner conflict, in the terms of our discussion, we can expand the concept by saying work is the attempt to deal with any aspect of our precariousness.

> From a psychological perspective, *work is the attempt to resolve inner conflict*. . . . Psychic energy is already engaged in warfare, and there is not enough left over for normal activity. . . . All that the individual does is done for the sake of minimizing the battle. . . . The work self created by continual conflict has been deceptive enough to receive great honor among men.[14]

Note that *any* activity which is rooted in conflict is work; much that we normally call "play" is work, and the mark of this is that our recreation does not re-create, but leaves us exhausted because we are operating out of conflict, and it leaves us in need of increasing doses because the underlying conflict remains just as it was.

Play would then be action that is not burdened with the necessity of making our physical being secure in the ultimate sense, enlarging

[14] Robert Neale, *In Praise of Play, Toward a Psychology of Religion* (New York: Harper and Row, 1969), 23-24.

our self-esteem, or making life meaningful. Again Neale focuses on the psychological area of conflict.

> Play is psychologically defined as *any activity not motivated by the need to resolve inner conflict.* . . . The individual does not need to be an achiever, because he has already arrived.[15]

The point made earlier in our study, that letting go is not mere passivity, can now be examined in terms of work and play.

> It should be realized that [play] is not the cessation of activity, but the absence of conflicted activity. . . . The peace of play is peaceful action. The perversion of this attitude is the "peace" of inaction.[16]

The distinction between work and play is not between action and inaction, but has to do with the way action is taken up. Much that we normally call "work," action that is productive or for which we are paid, is really play because it is not part of the denial of our precariousness.

Since work is any action that seeks to deny, escape, overcome, or compensate for our vulnerability, the freedom to play would arise from accepting our precariousness. Then it might well be that many of the same activities would be undertaken, but in a different way. Of course genuine and notable achievements do occur through intensity, and the reversal of effort does not point to the only way of being human. But the way of willful attainment is brittle, vulnerable to being undermined by experiences of impossibility, because it is founded on avoidance and denial of the limits. This denial is the root of that fundamental tension which impedes and handicaps action.

The criticism of various forms of the ethic of attainment in the classical texts was no doubt polemical and at times unfair; when properly understood, it is directed not at action and attainment, but at the way they are approached. The ethic of reversal claims in effect that the way to attain is to free effort from the impossible task of abolishing the fundamental threats to our existence, and this occurs when we accept our insecurity and practice yieldedness toward ourselves and our deeds.

The ethic of attainment is a formalized religious or philosophical expression of an underlying attitude that seeks either to ignore or to overcome our precariousness; the ethic of consolation begins in accepting the impossibility of either willful ignorance or victory through a frontal attack on being. According to the common sensical ethic of attainment, those who preach there is "but one thing needful" in life

15 *Ibid.*, 24.
16 *Ibid.*, 45, 72.

are guilty of a dreadful over-simplification. No one decision or remedy can cover all of life's complexity. There is not just one thing needful, for each situation presents its own unique tasks, materials, and choices. The ethic of consolation is not understood rightly if it seems to deny this. Rather, accepting the unique demands of each situation, there is nevertheless one thing needful in every circumstance, and that is letting go of hyperintention. This will be found to raise the level of all of our action.

How this is so is suggested by the story of the instructions for the assembly of a Japanese motorcycle, which begin, "Before assembling motorcycle, obtain peace of mind."[17] When the center is still, the wheel spins more truly. Letting go of efforts to deny our precariousness, we may well do many of the same things that the compulsive attainer does, but in a different way. Therefore, the point of our argument is not about what you do, although from an ethical point of view this is important, but it is about how. Do we act from the still center or from hyperintention? Action which is yielded with respect to its consequences is play, and therefore it is more effective. Thomas Hora makes clear how action freed from the work of establishing our security is more flowing and capable.

> It is interesting to consider the fact that some people swim with great effort, while others swim effortlessly for hours on end without getting tired; they don't even get winded. The difference lies in the quality of awareness. If we believe that we have to do our own swimming, it will then be a very strenuous, exhausting exercise and we will be poor swimmers. But if we understand that there is a sustaining power present, then it becomes easier and easier.[18]

In the terms of our study, action taken as if all depended on my effort, action designed to deal with the ultimate threats to our being in some way, is exhausting and ineffectual, but that action which participates within the situation and is attentive to it achieves. The prerequisite of this success is that one has let go of the need for it. The way to do is simply to be.

[17] Thomas Hora, *Dialogues in Metapsychiatry* (New York: Seabury Press, 1977), 99.
[18] Hora, *Existential Metapsychiatry*, 61.

Chapter 10

IS THE INVERSION OF INTENTION REGRESSIVE AND MASOCHISTIC? THE END OF THE STRIDENT SELF IS NOT THE END OF THE SELF

Renunciation is the cornerstone of wisdom, the condition of all genuine achievement.

—George Santayana
Reason in Religion

Every step so downward, is a step upward. The man who renounces himself, comes to himself.

—Ralph Waldo Emerson
"Divinity School Address"

From the first moment the idea of getting a goal by giving up the attempt to get it is encountered, many have a feeling of offense and opposition, sometimes of surprising force. The idea seems to embody weakness and failure of nerve, to invite quitting in the face of difficulties and the abdication of our powers. Others respond at first more positively, finding in the notion of reversal of intention an appealing peacefulness and gentleness, or a liberating release from some tension or effort of which they were only partially aware. It is as if the idea expressed something they had known intuitively or longed for unconsciously for a long time. But these same people may gradually come to feel that this sense of affinity for the idea of reversal arises precisely because it appeals to a part of their temperament which they do not want to emphasize, now that they are aware of it. The suspicion that the idea of letting go appeals to tendencies in ourselves we do not admire or admit can evoke rejection of the idea, and even fear and anger.

If the answer to the question of the last chapter was that letting go need not be dropping out, it is hard to ignore the fact that this is just what it is for many. Many things which can and should be done to benefit ourselves and others are irresponsibly omitted when we make our goal peace of mind rather than attainment. Perhaps the whole idea of reversal is based on the timid counsel of safety that says, "Don't seek to attain and you never risk defeat." It may be that Luther entered the monastery for fear of failing to satisfy his father's expectations and ambitions for him; and in that case, the "salvation by faith alone" doctrine simply reflects a pattern in Luther's character of avoiding failure rather than seeking success. Perhaps the maneuver of reversal of effort purchases peace at too great a price, the loss of the self and its powers, and the loss of the world and relatedness to it. If peace means passivity and apathy, we do not want it. After all, what have the great texts of the reversal of effort given us more than Aesop's fable of the fox who couldn't reach the grapes, and so concluded they must be sour. If the reversal of effort amounts to no more than the gambit of making a virtue out of a necessity, perhaps our original sense that the paradoxical must be profound was mistaken.

It may be that these criticisms have already been answered. Letting go is not a "wretched contentment," but the beginning of change and growth; it is not passivity and apathy, but responsiveness. Salvation by faith would be "cheap grace" if it did not lead to works. In the *Gita*, Arjuna is advised to find the middle way between omission of duty and the hyperintensive use of action to prove himself. Or again, seeing the Innate Buddha in yourself, you cannot rest content with withdrawal, but must feel compassion for others who likewise embody the Innate but suffer without this knowledge. All of this has been said and more, and yet the criticisms of the ethic of consolation must now be stated and heard with more force, compelling the conclusion that the idea of reversal has indeed been used in regressive and masochistic ways. The question to be confronted in this chapter is, "Is the the idea of reversal regression to a state of dependency? Is it masochistic, a self-destroying throwing away of our powers and their possible fruits? Is it irresponsible, accepting as unavoidable things that really could be changed?" If the previous chapter suggests that a negative response to these questions is possible, and yet we know reversal has, in fact, functioned to encourage evasion, we must also ask, "If letting go can have a role in fulfilling life, how is this use distinguished from its life-denying or escapist form?"

These questions can be clarified, and the foundation laid for a later response, if we sketch a definite meaning for the terms regression and masochism. Many myths of our beginnings speak of an original oneness with nature and of the loss of this paradise. This may reflect our earliest awareness as infants of being one with the mother and of enjoying a state of consciousness in which we did not distinguish ourselves and others as separate objects within the ocean of experience. In speaking of the myth of the Garden of Eden as a reflection of this consciousness, Paul Tillich refers to it as "dreaming innocence;" one is innocent of a sense of the self, its powers and relations. As in the myth of the Fall of Adam and Eve, self-awareness begins with an assertion of the will, with the positing of a "No!" Awareness of ourselves as separate from the mothering environment arises as a Fall from the state of union. A primal oneness is followed by a sense of differentiation of the self due to the action of will as negation; the movement is from oneness to what is at times a strident individualism.[1]

The myths differ as to what evaluation is to be placed upon this change. To call it a Fall is to express distrust for the emerging assertive ego and a nostalgia for the peace and nurturance of the original unity. All of the values of the developing self are made possible by this transition, which is inevitable in any case, and so some are quite clear that the Fall is "up." The religious tradition portrays this in the belief that through the Fall the Kingdom of God is made possible as the result of God's dealing with sin; in the Kingdom, a community of love and worship arises, constituted by self-responsible and fully realized persons, and their state surpasses in perfection the dreaming innocence of the Garden. In its mythic images, the tradition suggests the ambiguity involved in separation.

The question before us in this chapter is simply whether letting go is falling back into primal oneness, an attempt to renounce the emergent ego and its powers, to be unburdened of the task of growth and responsiveness, and to escape the loneliness of being a separate self. When Paul speaks of sin as self-reliance and salvation as letting go and trusting God's love, and when Saraha speaks of our oneness with the essence of all things, which is discovered when we cease to assert ourselves as distinct from the other, aren't they expressing a longing for the lost oneness of the first few months of life? (Of course, the two have different views of reality, Paul seeing the self as distinct from God, and Saraha seeing them as one; but perhaps both express a fatigue at having to maintain the ego apart from the nurturance we once knew.) A provisional answer to this question might be: *if* there are only two possibilities, regression to primal oneness and strident individualism, then the ethic of consolation does appear regressive, while the ethic of attainment seems on the side of development.

In what follows, we will examine three thinkers who are in different ways critical of the ethic of consolation, the sociologist Peter Berger, the philosopher Friedrich Nietzsche, and Joseph Campbell, a student of myth and symbolism. Berger's description of "masochistic

[1] Erich Fromm, *Man for Himself, an Inquiry into the Psychology of Ethics* (New York: Holt, Rinehart and Winston, 1947), 40-50; May, *Love and Will*, 284; Paul Tillich, *Systematic Theology, vol. 2, Existence and the Christ* (Chicago: University of Chicago Press, 1957), 33-36.

liberation" and Nietzsche's ideas of "slave morality" and "*ressentiment*" will clarify the way in which reversal may indeed be regressive; Campbell's analysis will raise the question of just what it is that proponents of letting go let go of. This will help us separate two forms of reversal.

* * * * *

Berger states that one way of dealing with our vulnerability is masochism; life as a social being requires a degree of self-denial, and this is intensified in masochism in order to achieve a kind of safety. He defines masochism as "the attitude in which the individual reduces himself to an inert and thinglike object *vis-a-vis* his fellowmen."[2] Here we encounter Sartre's idea of "bad faith," or reification, the attempt to become invulnerable by ceasing to be a separate person with needs, demands, responsibilities, and will, through becoming a thing. This leads to "the intoxication of surrender," a sense of release and of having transcended the normal situation and its tensions.

> "I am nothing — He is everything — and therein lies my ultimate bliss" — in this formula lies the essence of the masochistic attitude. It transforms the self into nothingness, the other into absolute reality. Its ecstasy consists precisely in this double metamorphosis, which is profoundly liberating in that it seems to cut all at once through the ambiguities and anguish of separate, individual subjectivity confronting the subjectivities of others.[3]

The masochistic attitude becomes a way of dealing both with the loneliness of the self that has emerged from primal oneness, and with the meaninglessness which threatens the self now that it knows it is exposed to suffering and death. Both loneliness and vulnerability to suffering and death are escaped in masochism through absorption in the other.

> Not being able to stand aloneness, man denies his separateness, and not being able to stand meaninglessness, he finds paradoxical meaning in self-annihilation. "I am nothing — and therefore nothing can hurt me." or even more sharply: "I have died — and therefore I shall not die," and then: "Come, sweet pain; come sweet death" — these are the formulas of masochistic liberation.[4]

In this life-position, pain is welcomed as ratifying the posture of self-denial; pain proves that surrender is real.

The masochistic attitude arises in personal relationships, but it may

[2] Berger, *Sacred Canopy*, 55.
[3] *Ibid.*, 56.
[4] *Ibid.*

be lived out in relation to a group or nation; or in philosophical and religious beliefs, the other may become God, ultimate reality or the cosmos as a whole. This is not to say that all belief-systems are masochistic. In Berger's view, many belief-systems merely seek meaning in the suffering and loneliness to which we are subject, a way of accepting them and living with them; a person's system is masochistic if it seeks happiness in pain through self-negation. The important difference is whether one's religious posture is designed to nullify and escape or to accept and bear up under the limit situations. Thus masochism is like the negative will described in the previous chapter, based on denial of something about ourselves and our situation.

Some of the expressions of the ethic of consolation that we have encountered have undergirded the notion of reversal with a mystical belief-system, emphasizing the believers' union with a sacred force or being, compared to which the fate of the little self is nothing. Berger feels mysticism is often masochistic.

> It is safe to say that a strong masochistic element is present in nearly all varieties of mysticism, as evidenced by the cross-cultural recurrence of ascetic self-mortification and self-torture in connection with mystical phenomena.[5]

Both in the story of the Buddha's enlightenment and in the *Gita*, we have encountered a rejection of this pattern; so apparently there are forms of mysticism that are masochistic and approaches to it which are not. But this distinction does not, in my view, enable us to put some texts and traditions on one side, and others on the other; for one and the same religious system can be approached by different individuals, or by one individual at different times, masochistically or otherwise.

Other expressions of the ethic of consolation we have encountered contain belief-systems centering on the relationship of the self to God or ultimate reality, rather than on union. It is Berger's belief that the most acute form of religious masochism is found in the theistic religions, those focused on a transcendent, personal God. For if we believe in a single God who is the source of the universe, and who is wholly righteous and good, then suffering and evil must either be attributed to humanity's sin or be interpreted as somehow for our own good and a sign of divine concern. Those who have worked out security-systems based on "He is everything, I am nothing" can thus readily continue this pattern in relation to the personal God, and peace in the face of life's negativities is found. The price of this is the destruction of our being as responsible selves, and many in these same theistic religions see the self as God-given, the result of men and women being

[5] *Ibid.*, 64.

created in the image of God, and thus not to be thrown away, even if suffering and loneliness sometimes accompany it. And so, just as in mysticism, Berger makes possible a distinction between life-fulfilling and life-denying forms of belief and practice. The question remains as to whether the operation we have been calling the inversion of intention is always masochistic, or whether it may be one way in which life is affirmed. Since the ethic of consolation centers on giving up the effort to attain, perhaps it belongs exclusively to the masochistic and regressive side of religious life; the likeness of Berger's statements about the formulas of masochism to the paradoxes encountered in the great texts of the ethic of consolation is striking. But before this questions can be confronted directly, the role of will in life-affirmation and life-denial must be clarified, and for this we turn to Nietzsche.

* * * * *

Friedrich Nietzsche (1844-1900) had a great antipathy for Luther, and in order to make possible a comparison of the two men, something should be said of his life. Nietzsche was born in Saxony as the son of a Lutheran pastor; his mother's father and grandfather had also been Lutheran pastors. His father died when Friedrich was five, and except for a brother who died in the first year of life, he lived in an exclusively female environment with his mother, sister, grandmother, and two aunts. Due to his serious and withdrawn character as a child, he was known as "the little pastor." In 1864 he entered the University of Bonn and the next year followed his teacher, the classicist Ritschl, to Leipzig. In 1869 on Ritschl's recommendation, Nietzsche, without having the doctoral degree, was appointed to the chair in philology at the University of Basle. He resigned in 1879 due to ill health and discontent with academic life. He increasingly wrote in the style of a prophetic critic of middle-class morality and religion, expressing amazement and outrage at the easy talk about Christ-like self-renunciation on the part of the comfortable, the complacent, and the acquisitive. He became increasingly isolated, and from 1889 until his death he was incapacitated by an organically caused insanity and cared for by his mother and sister.

In Nietzsche's view, human character is shaped by the way we respond to and use the raw emotional energy derived from our physical organism that strives toward gratification. We may call this "the will to life and power." As animals, desire moves us to act and to achieve, and as humans, we are free to decide how this vitality is to be used; the uniquely human response is the channeling of this emotional energy into works of creative self-expression in which both physical and spiritual delight coincide. The life-will in humans is thus not merely the drive toward the satisfaction of biological urges, but the source of beauty, truth, goodness, and all forms of human greatness.

The will to life is for this same reason a troubler of the soul. It sets before us the task of self-control so that our action is not destructive of self and others, and it poses for us projects and achievements that might give it human form. Our vitality is a responsibility and a task. There are therefore those whose response is to seek peace through the negation of the will to life. This "nihilism," the renunciation of the will to power and life, seeks to avoid pain rather than to achieve fulfillment. But it is not an easy way, and only a few great individuals have been able to sincerely and consistently subdue the life-force within them; these include, according to Nietzsche, Jesus, the Buddha, and some of the early Hindu and Taoist masters. Thus while Nietzsche utterly rejects this denial of what we are, he admires the immense achievement it involves, even if it is an achievement against life.

However, it would be an error to view this achievement as heroism, for heroism seeks obstacles to overcome and deeds to accomplish, whereas the nihilists reach peace precisely by abandoning the will to resist and achieve. Speaking of the evangel or good news of Jesus, Nietzsche says,

> But if anything is unevangelical it is the concept of the hero. Just the opposite of all wrestling, of all feeling-oneself-in-a-struggle, has here become instinct: the incapacity for resistance become morality here ("resist not evil" — the most profound word of the Gospels, their key in a certain sense), blessedness in peace, in gentleness, in not *being able* to be an enemy. What are the "glad tidings?" True life, eternal life, has been found — it is not promised, it is here, it is *in you*: as a living in love, in love without subtraction and exclusion, without regard for station.[6]

In Nietzsche's view, the message of Jesus is that one can have peace now, not after death, through renunciation of the will to life and power; if we cease to resist evil, we are already within the kingdom of God and it is in us. Here, we should set aside the question of what the historical Jesus actually said and did, and ask only, what psychological type is Nietzsche describing? What response to the life-will is he trying to clarify? The key for Nietzsche is "non-resistance to evil," which implies a relinquishing of will and a marvelous peace and openness; when all clinging to life ceases, all troublesome striving and defending end. For Nietzsche, this must be based on an "instinctive hatred of reality." The renouncer is then free of all antipathy and ignorant of all divisions and barriers separating persons. However, for Nietzsche this

[6] Friedrich Nietzsche, *The Antichrist* (1888), in *The Portable Nietzsche*, trans. Walter Kaufmann (New York: Viking Press, 1954), 585-586.

attitude would be the end of all culture and of all attainments of truth and beauty.

Nietzsche delights in making contrasts between this evangel and the message of the early church. To him, Jesus' way offers blessedness now, not after death or at the end of the world. It is not a new belief, but a new life. It is open to everyone who will renounce themselves, without any requirement of belief in a dying and rising savior; for Nietzsche, Jesus' death was not a sacrifice for sin, but an example of how to live out non-resistance to evil and renunciation of self.

> This "bringer of glad tidings" died as he had lived, as he had taught — *not* to "redeem men" but to show how one must live. . . . He does not resist, he does not defend his right, he takes no step which might ward off the worst; on the contrary he *provokes* it. And he begs, he suffers, he loves *with* those, *in* those, who do him evil. *Not* to resist, *not* to be angry, *not* to hold responsible — but to resist not even the evil one — to *love* him.[7]

Nietzsche feels that the apocalyptic element in Jesus' message, the prediction of the end of the world and destruction for the enemies of the Kingdom of God was, like the idea of his death as a sacrifice for other people's sins, a churchly addition. Here the church shows its desire for revenge against its enemies and its total misunderstanding of "resist not evil." In this matter of Jesus' apocalyptic teachings, Nietzsche is historically mistaken according to the best critical scholarship, but we are merely interested here in the psychological type he is sketching.

One response to the will to life and power within us is to deny it and in this way to find peace, indifference to external fortunes, and openness and love toward all. A second response is that of "the Overman," who through self-mastery sublimates the life-energy into great achievements. This is the essentially human response to the will to life, and it is the great achievers and creators who justify the species. The Overman does not seek peace through renunciation of life, nor does the Overman let raw vital energy rule life by living for power and pleasure as ends in themselves. Overman conquers and controls the will to life by directing it to great historical and artistic achievements; Overman's will to power is manifest in power over oneself. Both the desire for peace, which would lead us to renounce life, and the desire for self-indulgent satisfaction of the will to life must be overcome so that there may arise achievements of a spiritual and cultural sort through heroic exertions. The ideal is not Don Juan or Napoleon, but Goethe.

[7] *Ibid.*, 608-609.

Overman must have self-discipline and willingness to undertake great tasks.

> The most spiritual men, as the *strongest*, find their happiness where others would find their destruction: in the labyrinth, in hardness against themselves and others, in experiments; their joy is self-conquest; asceticism becomes in them nature, need, and instinct. Difficult tasks are a privilege to them; to play with burdens which crush others, a recreation. Knowledge — a form of asceticism. They are the most venerable kind of man; that does not preclude their being the most cheerful and the kindliest. They rule not because they want to but because they *are*; they are not free to be second.[8]

Due to a prevalent misunderstanding, it must be emphasized that the Overman is not bent on the rule and use of others, but on self-rule for the sake of creating new values in art, science, law, and morality that benefit humanity. Those manifesting potential for making a contribution to history are harsh and demanding on themselves and others of like quality, but kindly with persons of lesser potential.

> When the exceptional human being treats the mediocre more tenderly than himself and his peers, this is not mere politeness of the heart — it is simply his *duty*.[9]

Nietzsche knew this ethic of attainment meant a return to the values of ancient Greece and to the "great-souled man" of Aristotle's ethics. Of course this would involve a "revaluation of all values" within modern European civilization, which gives lip service to the ethic of renunciation. In Nietzsche's sketch of the Overman, the ethic of attainment is seen to be undeniably the source of great values in human life; it is the final contention of this and the preceding chapter that a creativity may also result from the ethic of reversal.

A third form of response to the question of how to deal with our will to power is adopted by mediocre persons who have not the courage, self-discipline, or ability genuinely to achieve. These are the ones who give outward approval to the hard way of nihilism, but do not live it; their commitment to the way of renunciation is merely verbal, and it is motivated by their desire to reject and devalue the life and ability of the great-souled achievers. This way is based on resentment of the Overman and is an insincere form of the way of Jesus and the Buddha. This brings us to "slave morality" and "*ressentiment.*"

Good in ancient Greece was defined by reference to the qualities of free and noble persons, according to Nietzsche; it meant noble, aristo-

[8] *Ibid.*, 645-646.
[9] *Ibid.*, 647.

cratic, privileged, powerful, well-developed, cultured, and beautiful. This is the natural, life-affirming meaning of the term good; the knightly-aristocratic ideal is one of self-development and -expression. But this is not what the weak and impotent admire; it is what they hate and resent. Nietzsche felt that among the Jews after the loss of their kingship, aristocracy, and political independence, a priestly caste developed an ethic which rejected the natural values of their conquerors and redefined the good as weakness and failure. This slave morality expressed the resentment of the conquered and the inept against their rulers and was literally making a virtue out of a necessity. Again, we are not concerned with Nietzsche's historical accuracy about ancient Judaism (indeed, he seems really to have meant bourgeois Protestant Germany); we are concerned with the psychological type.

> All that has been done on earth against "the noble," "the powerful," "the masters," "the rulers," fades into nothing compared with what the *Jews* have done against them; the Jews, that priestly people, who in opposing their enemies and conquerors were ultimately satisfied with nothing less than a radical revaluation of their enemies' values, that is to say, an act of the *most spiritual revenge*. For this alone was appropriate to a priestly people, the people embodying the most deeply repressed priestly vengefulness. It was the Jews who, with awe-inspiring consistency, dared to invert the aristocratic value-equation (good = noble = powerful = beautiful = happy = beloved of God) and to hang on to this inversion with their teeth, the teeth of the most abysmal hatred (the hatred of impotence), saying "the wretched alone are the good; the poor, impotent, lowly alone are the good; the suffering, deprived, sick, ugly alone are pious, alone are blessed by God, blessedness is for them alone — and you, the powerful and noble, are on the contrary the evil, the cruel, the lustful, the insatiable, the godless to all eternity; and you shall be in all eternity the unblessed, accursed, and damned!"[10]

Nietzsche was not anti-semitic and, in fact, was strongly opposed to this aspect of German culture. His point is merely that slave morality reverses the natural order of values due to its hatred of excellence and its desire for revenge. In his view, this revaluation triumphs in Christianity.

The reversal of the natural order of values thus expresses "the vengefulness of the impotent."

> The slave revolt in morality begins when *ressentiment* itself becomes creative and gives birth to values: the *ressentiment* of natures that are denied the true reaction, that of deeds, and compensate themselves with an imag-

[10] Friedrich Nietzsche, *The Genealogy of Morals* (1887) in *Basic Writings of Nietzsche*, trans. Walter Kaufmann (New York: Random House, 1966), 469-470.

inary revenge.[11]

Nietzsche uses the French term *ressentiment* for resentment or rancor, perhaps because it also has the meaning of "the return of a feeling," as in the slight recurrence of a pain; thus *ressentiment* is "re-sentiment," the return of a denied and repressed anger. In this case, hate returns as the reversal of values in which the despised excellences are devalued. The revaluing of the noble idea of goodness is seen in these lines.

> How different these words "bad" and "evil" are, although they are both apparently the opposite of the same concept "good." But it is *not* the same concept "good:" one should ask rather precisely *who* is "evil" in the sense of the morality of *ressentiment*. The answer, in all strictness, is: *precisely* the "good man" of the other morality, precisely the noble, powerful man, the ruler, but dyed in another color, interpreted in another fashion, seen in another way by the venomous eye of *ressentiment*.[12]

What the weak and oppressed cannot avoid, they make a value; making a virtue out of a necessity is the essence of the slave morality.

> When the oppressed, downtrodden, outraged exhort one another with the vengeful cunning of impotence: "let us be different from the evil, namely good! And he is good who does not outrage, who harms nobody, who does not attack, who does not requite, who leaves revenge to God, who keeps himself hidden as we do, who avoids evil and desires little from life, like us, the patient, humble, and just; — this, listened to calmly and without previous bias, really amounts to no more than: "we weak ones are, after all weak; it would be good if we did nothing *for which we are not strong enough*;" but this dry matter of fact, this prudence of the lowest order which even insects possess (posing as dead, when in danger, so as not to do "too much"), has, thanks to the counterfeit and self-deception of impotence, clad itself in the ostentatious garb of the virtue of the quiet, calm resignation, just as if the weakness of the weak — that is to say, their *essence*, their effects, their sole ineluctable, irremovable reality — were a voluntary achievement, willed, chosen a *deed*, a *meritorious* act.[13]

Just because the values of submissiveness and humility are expressions of resentment of the capable and the strong, slave morality is an insincere counterfeit of the way of renunciation adopted by Jesus. Those incapable of both the way of renunciation and the way of achievement make a virtue of a necessity and exalt weakness and failure as good. Here we see what Nietzsche calls the shrewdness of slave

[11] *Ibid.*, 472.
[12] *Ibid.*, 476.
[13] *Ibid.*, 482.

morality. It does not really abdicate the will to power, but seeks to excel over the excellent by redefining goodness; the "rat race" is not abandoned, only its direction is changed. Now the way to be first is to be last.

To Nietzsche, the great examples of *ressentiment* ethics are Paul and Luther. Unable to follow Jesus in the immense task of renunciation, Paul preaches the message of salvation by faith in Christ's death and resurrection, which Nietzsche understands as meaning "by belief" rather than as total trust and personal transformation. Again we have to question Nietzsche's accuracy about history, but our interest is in Nietzsche as psychologist.

> The very word "Christianity" is a misunderstanding: in truth, there was only *one* Christian, and he died on the cross. The "evangel" *died* on the cross. What has been called "evangel" from that moment was actually the opposite of that which *he* had lived: "ill tidings," a *dysangel*. It is false to the point of nonsense to find the mark of the Christian in a "faith," for instance, in the faith in redemption through Christ: only Christian *practice*, a life such as he *lived* who died on the cross, is Christian.[14]

To Nietzsche, Christianity does not imitate Christ's renunciation of self, but hopes to get a reward without this effort, just through belief and some relatively painless outward concessions. If this is not fair to Paul, it is surely accurate as a description of much of popular Christianity, as already noted in the description in chapter eight of that type of renunciation that gives up possessions in order to get them back with interest. Faith of this sort is indeed merely a kind of shrewdness.

In Nietzsche's view, faith in salvation by Christ's atoning death rose from the need of the disciples to explain Jesus' death. They interpreted it as a deed of the Jewish leaders, whom they as outcasts resented; God allowed Jesus' enemies to crucify him, they concluded, because his death is a blood sacrifice for *our* sins. The heavenly Christ will soon return (Paul believed within his own lifetime) to avenge himself on the church's enemies. In this, Nietzsche feels, the church transformed the one who resisted no evil into a projection of its own resentment.

The church looks for future blessedness through faith, whereas Jesus offered it in the present by the harder path of renunciation. Nietzsche felt that the idea of immortality undercut any sincere effort to better human life in the present; if blessedness is a gift in the hereafter in exchange for identifying with Christian belief, then any effort after self-conquest and moral excellence is superfluous. For Nietzsche, this is a resentful rejection of the natural moral order.

[14] Nietzsche, *The Antichrist*, 612.

> If one wants to be "chosen by God" — or a "temple of God" or a "judge of the angels" — then any other principle of selection — for example, according to integrity, spirit, virility and pride, beauty and freedom of the heart — is merely "world," *evil in itself*.[15]
>
> At the bottom of Christianity is the rancor of the sick, instinct directed *against* the healthy, *against* health itself. Everything that has turned out well, everything that is proud and prankish, beauty above all, hurts its ears and eyes. Once more I recall the inestimable words of Paul: "The *weak* things of the world, the *foolish* things of the world, the *base* and *despised* things of the world hath God chosen." This was the formula; *in hoc signo* decadence triumphed.[16]
>
> "Whatever makes sick is *good*; whatever comes out of fullness, out of superabundance, out of power, is *evil*" — thus feels the believer.[17]

In this view, salvation by faith sets aside the natural idea of excellence as achieved, thus expressing the resentment of those who cannot achieve.

Nietzsche maintains that not only does the easy path of salvation by faith undercut and devalue genuine moral excellence, but it also falsifies the quest for truth. Paul had said in effect that the paradox of salvation by faith instead of works confounds the world's wisdom, but that beside this truth the world's wisdom is foolishness. Not only are the normal order of effort and achievement reversed, but so is the normal relation of inquiry and truth. To Nietzsche, Paul's idea of faith devalues patient research and experiment in which one's hopes and wishes are rigorously held in check, and it gives a shortcut to truth, the mark of which is that it is just what we want to hear. The comfort found in a belief is no proof of its truth; indeed, to Nietzsche, intellectual honesty is the willingness to come to conclusions one does not like. Therefore, he concludes, the strong are skeptical and free, foregoing the comfort of having all the answers and able to live with ambiguity and mystery.

> Great spirits are skeptics. . . . Strength, freedom which is born of the strength and overstrength of the spirit proves itself by skepticism. . . . A spirit who wants great things, who also wants the means to them, is necessarily a skeptic. Freedom from all kinds of convictions, to be able to see freely, is part of strength. . . . Conversely: the need for faith, for some kind of unconditional Yes and No, this Carlylism, if one will forgive me this word, is a need born of *weakness*. The man of faith, the "believer" of every kind, is necessarily a dependent man — one who cannot posit *himself* as an end, one who cannot posit any end at all by himself. The "believer" does not belong to *himself*, he can only be a means, he must be

[15] *Ibid.*, 626.
[16] *Ibid.*, 634. The quotation from Paul the Apostle is from I Cor. 1.20.
[17] *Ibid.*, 635.

> *used up*, he requires somebody to use him up. His instinct gives the highest honor to a morality of self-abnegation, of self-alienation. If one considers how necessary most people find something regulatory, which will bind them from without and tie them down; how compulsion, *slavery* in a higher sense, is the sole and ultimate condition under which the weak-willed human being, woman in particular, can prosper — then one will understand conviction, "faith."[18]

In these powerful lines we see the characteristic emphasis on strength, which resists anything that might seem the easy way; and we see the association of weakness and surrender with a betrayal of the human cause, as alienation from our true being as living, striving embodiments of the life-will. For the first time we see surrender associated with women; we must return to this later.

Just as the comfort derived from faith is no sign of its truth to Nietzsche, so the sincerity and determination of the believer is irrelevant. Nietzsche says martyrs harm the quest for truth because they create the illusion that if they are willing to die for their faith, it must be true. For Nietzsche, religious conviction leads to self-deception, the inability to see contrary evidence; his example is the way in which the early church saw countless allusions to the Christ in the Hebrew scriptures, many of which are specious in the view of biblical scholars.

As a subversion of the effort to achieve both moral excellence and truth, the idea of faith in Paul and Luther is, in Nietzsche's criticism, a crime against the will to life.

Nietzsche's ideal of the Overman clearly represents an assertion of the ethic of attainment. What can we suppose he would say about the ethic of consolation, and the idea that the goal is reached by giving up the attempt to achieve it? Firstly, Nietzsche says when this is sincere, it is nihilistic and life-denying; but it is rarely sincere. Secondly, in its insincere form in mass religion, it is merely making a virtue out of a necessity on the part of those who are weak-willed and cannot achieve. Jesus and Gautama were sincere renouncers, splendid in their self-abnegation, but ultimately betrayers of the will to life. Paul and Luther were insincere in their talk about letting go of self-effort; being unable to attain either genuine self-mastery or consistent self-renunciation, they invented the notion that we needn't bother. In either its sincere or its insincere forms, giving up the effort to attain is surrender of our real destiny; it is either self-negation or resentment. These are the hard sayings of Nietzsche about the ethic of consolation.

* * * * *

Although the ego emerges from the consciousness we have called

[18] *Ibid.*, 638-639.

primal oneness through the assertion of negative will, a no-saying to the nurturing, enfolding world of mother, it never escapes a nostalgia for the past. The loneliness, vulnerability, responsibility, and fatigue of being a self-actualizing person may draw us back, and the joy of exercising our powers and the exultation in simply being may dim, especially when we encounter frustration, impossibility, and limit situations. Perhaps all that the paradox of intention represents is a failure to sustain our individuation and a life-denying negation of our being as persons.

Peter Berger's idea of masochistic liberation clearly applies to forms of the ethic of reversal, although he also seemed to allow for the possibility of authentic, non-regressive forms. Our interpretation of Nietzsche suggests he would dismiss all forms of reversal of intention as regressive; if sincere, it represents self-annihilation, and if insincere, a kind of paralyzed resentment that cannot really live and yet fears to renounce life. So powerful is this critique, so true to what we know about ourselves and see about us, that we cannot deny that the ethic of consolation may often be lived out in life-denying and insincere ways. The question remains as to whether it may not have an authentic form.

To push on toward this possibility, the thought of Joseph Campbell will prove helpful. In looking at his thought, bear in mind this question: when the ethic of consolation calls us to let go, just what is it that is renounced? Is it being a self which we renounce? Or is it some *way* of being? If the first, then we are being asked to harm ourselves and regress to an earlier level of adjustment. As yet we are unclear about what the second possibility could mean.

Whereas Nietzsche was involved in an attack on the Pauline-Lutheran tradition, Campbell has been more interested in separating the authentic and inauthentic in the ethics of Hindu mysticism.

Campbell warns that the Western concept of the mature self worked out with great difficulty in Greek and biblical experience must not be hastily abandoned on first contact with Indian wisdom. Greek tragedy and epic, and biblical story are concerned with the unique individual, born but once, distinct from all other persons. In much of oriental thought, the self is not this embodied ego, which belongs to the realm of illusion and is ephemeral and transitory; it is an impersonal, undifferentiated eternal substance, the common factor in countless incarnations. The you who reads and understands this sentence would not recognize the real self, which thousands of previous lives have in common. If the real self is not the self you know, but an immaterial transmigrant underlying a series of countless such selves, then the ideas of the matured ego, free will, the realization of your unique potential, and responsible action are all implicitly rejected as false and unnatural. Thus a choice must be made as to how we are to understand ourselves.

In discussing the background of the *Gita*, it was pointed out that the way of merit by performance of caste duty was integrated with the way of immediate enlightenment and release from the cycle of rebirth, through the postponing of the quest for release until after performing the duties of a householder. To expand this idea, we may describe the "four permissible goals of life" in ancient India. In this way of seeing things, there are four goals natural to the human, each of which is worthy and sought after by honorable people; yet they represent a hierarchy of ascending value. First, there is *kama*, which is "pleasure," especially through sexuality. This goal is commendable if pursued well and in a way which is within the bounds of accepted practice. The *Kama Sutra* of Vatsyayana gives instruction in the artful pursuit of *kama*. Second, there is *artha*, "power and possession." This too is a worthy goal, and various *Artha Sutras* give advice on how to succeed, as do the animal fables with their practical wisdom, found in the *Panchatantra*. *Kama* and *artha* represent natural goals of the human prompted by our physical organism, and Indian thought typically accepts these "lower" strivings within its social ethics, without seeking to deny or repress them.

If the first two goals represent the physical self, the third represents the social self. The third acceptable goal is *dharma*, "morality," especially in the sense of the responsible householder doing caste duty. The *Code of Manu* describes in great detail just how this is to be done. *Dharma* is thought to be more commendable and satisfying than the above because it transcends the egoistic desire for pleasure, power, and wealth. Yet, like the first two goals, the satisfaction provided by the fulfillment of caste duty is less than ultimate because it does not lead to release from reincarnation. This discontent leads to the quest for the fourth goal, *moksha*, "liberation," which is complete release from bondage to the ego and its illusory goods; this would lead to an escape from the cycle of reincarnation and an eternity of pure consciousness, consciousness that is brilliantly aware but has no content. Since the first three goals correspond to Frankl's notion of the physical and the social, we suspect that *moksha* should correspond to the noetic. Yet what we have in the fourth goal is not the fulfillment of the ego whose physical and social needs were the focus of the first three, but its extinction in the discovery that you are not really this ego at all, but an eternal undifferentiated or non-individuated consciousness. *Moksha* might seem like falling back into primal oneness rather than the fulfillment of the self; it all depends on how we define the self, whether as "the unique, concrete individual" or as "the immaterial transmigrant common to thousands of past lives."

Campbell makes use of a description of the four goals similar to this, suggesting there is a choice to be made between these two views of the self, and if we choose that found in Greek and biblical thought, we must be selective in what we learn from the Hindu tradition. We will then be less interested in the extinction of the ego than in its full development, and we will draw on Hindu materials only insofar as they contribute to this.

Campbell suggests that the idea of the highest goal of life is conceived differently in the West; he contrasts the goal of ego-maturation with *moksha*. Campbell takes the thought of psychologist Carl Jung as an example of the Western concept of the fourth goal. Jung describes the fulfillment of human life as "individuation," which is becoming a whole self through the integration of conscious and unconscious, active and passive aspects of the self. It is an ideal of being a unique individual in wholeness, which involves seeing your socially defined and learned roles as only part of your full potential. This is a striking contrast to the Hindu ethic, which seems to say, we are to fully identify with our social roles, but finding this unfulfilling, we then seek to slip like raindrops into the sea of being. There is an alternative to this pattern of finding life lived solely on the basis of the public ego unsatisfying and then seeking to escape it, and that would be ego-maturation. Discontent with the development of the self that social conditions have so far permitted is a sign that the process of individuation must be intentionally undertaken. In the early years of life, we develop those social and vocational skills that make for competence and success, but then in the middle years we may well feel that the specialized and structured self is a prison. Out of the wealth of unconscious potential, we have selected certain aspects for development, and we mistakenly identify the so far developed conscious portion of the self with the whole; the result is that our lives are cramped and impoverished. In the process of individuation, the task of the second-half of life, the ego is expanded by being brought into fruitful and energizing relation with its unconscious sources. Since this involves meeting and accepting hidden and denied aspects of the self, it can be painful and difficult. Yet through this process of growth, a larger portion of the self is brought into relation with a wider and fuller range of experience, and the stymied feeling of the "householder" is overcome. The goal here is not to escape from the concrete self, but to fully realize its unique individuality.

Since the point is not to substitute some particular psychology for the Eastern, but to broadly contrast the Eastern and the Western, Campbell also uses the thought of the psychiatrist Sigmund Freud. In Freudian terms, *kama* and *artha*, the first two goals, each express the "id," the biological drive toward satisfaction. The ego dominated by these drives is the infantile ego, which lives on the level of "I want!" *Dharma*, the third goal, corresponds with the "superego;" this is roughly conscience conceived as the learned values and inhibitions that control the biological urges. This internalized will of the parent says in effect, "Thou shalt!" Campbell maintains that the perception of the journey of the self contained in the Hindu notion of the four goals is " 'Thou shalt!' against 'I want!' and then 'Extinction!' "[19] The life urges are frustrated by social inhibition, and in this stymied position the ego seeks only extinction; freedom here means release from the will to live. The ego is conceived merely as the infantile ego, and the alternative to extinction, represented by maturation of the ego, is absent.

> There is no provision or allowance whatsoever for what in the West would be thought of as ego-maturation. And as a result — to put it plainly and simply — the Orient has never distinguished ego from id.[20]

The conflicts of the infantile ego are escaped by letting go of the ego rather than by growing up.

> The word "I" (in Sanskrit, *aham*) suggests to the Oriental philosopher only wishing, wanting, desiring, fearing, and possessing, i.e., the impulses of what Freud has termed the id operating under pressure of the pleasure principle. Ego, on the other hand (again as Freud defines it), is that psychological faculty which relates us *objectively* to external, empirical "reality:" i.e., to the fact-world, here and now, and in its present possibilities, objectively observed, recognized, judged, and evaluated; and to ourselves, so likewise known and judged, within it. A considered act initiated by a knowledgeable, responsible ego is thus something very different from the action of an avaricious, untamed id; different, too, from performances governed by unquestioning obedience to a long-inherited code — which can only be inappropriate to contemporary life or even to any unforeseen social or personal contingency.[21]

Since the possibilities of the ego are exhausted by the infantile ego and its conflicts in the view under examination, extinction of the ego is substituted for its maturation.

The answer to the question raised at the beginning of the discussion of Campbell's thought is that the Hindu ethic of renunciation is really concerned to renounce not what we would call the mature ego, but the infantile ego. If this is done in the absence of any concept of the mature ego, it will appear to those of us committed to the Western concept of the self as regressive. Seeking for *moksha* is masochistic

[19] Joseph Campbell, *Myths to Live By* (New York: Viking Press, 1972), 72.
[20] *Ibid.*, 73.
[21] *Ibid.*

and regressive, if one seeks to escape all conflicts, snuff out the ego altogether, and fall back into oceanic oneness.

But Campbell's analysis makes possible a selective use of Hindu thought. It is surely also possible to practice renunciation as the letting go of the infantile ego for the sake of ego maturation. If this is what we let go of in the reversal of intention, then letting go may be a step forward rather than a step backward; surrender would then be a way of coming to oneself, a means of fulfillment.

We cannot judge all forms of the ethic of consolation as either fulfilling or annihilating the self, but we must ask in each case, just what is it that is being renounced, selfish clinging or the self. Berger, Nietzsche, and Campbell make clear that some letting go is masochistic, an escapist regression. But some of the proponents of letting go seem already to have known this. Even though the Deer Park Sermon speaks of the goal as nirvana, "snuffing-out," it offers the way of enlightenment not as extinction of the will as such, but as a middle way between infantile, grasping will and no will. What is to be extinguished is, you will remember, only *tanha*, "craving," which we might call the id-dominated ego.

* * * * *

Then let us say there are two ways of living out the idea of the reversal of intention, one of which is falling back into nothingness and the other of which is moving beyond the strident, combative will of the emerging infantile ego into willing by participation. In the previous chapter, participative willing or responsiveness was described as a union of active and passive elements, and now it is clearer what this means. Primal oneness is passive, open to the nurturance of the world, but barren of those values that arise through the emergence of the ego. The infantile ego that arises in saying no to passivity and dependence establishes a new value. Precisely because it is so exclusively active, strident, manipulative, discordant, and individualistic, it cannot draw support from its milieu, and it lives only by combat and conquest, through which it grasps what it needs. Thus it falls into fatigue and loneliness and it meets ultimate limits of what can be attained. In letting go of infantile will, the strident self and not the self as such, a third stage is reached that adds to the activity of the infantile will, the letting be of primal oneness. One does not cease to act, but acts with responsiveness; the ego does not cease to be, but comes to itself.

Of course the choice is always ours to live out reversal in the regressive and masochistic way. So we might ask, how can the two ways of seeing surrender be discriminated. The point, of course, is not to separate different texts or belief-systems or people, some of whom espouse fulfillment while others are masochistic. The point is rather to discriminate attitudes and motives within ourselves. It may well be that every text or person representing the ethic of consolation includes both.

Perhaps the mark of the regressive use of renunciation is that it seeks total invulnerability; it wants entire freedom from the negative aspects of being a self. This can only be gained through ceasing to be a self. But if what is renounced is the strident self and not the self as such, one accepts one's precariousness and does not escape it.

The difference between the masochistic and escapist use of reversal and its authentic, life-fulfilling form is this. In masochism, one still seeks to be in control and uses the paradox of intention *magically* to achieve ends. The maxim of this approach is, therefore, "Victory through defeat!"[22] For it is some sort of triumph and power that is sought, as Nietzsche knew. The word "through" shows defeat is a magical means to power. The authentic occurrence of reversal is not a control activity; it is the acceptance of the inescapable. Its maxim is "Fulfillment despite failure."[23] The word "despite" shows failure is not sought and used, but accepted when it is found inevitable, and in this it is transcended, but not escaped.

A certain view of the self has been taken as normative here and throughout this chapter. From this point of view, the idea of the diamond-hard self immune to pleasure and pain seems dehumanized. Passages in the *Gita* or the *Manual of Epictetus* fail to evoke a sense of recognition in some of us. When the Stoic said, "It is silly to want your children and your wife and your friends to live forever . . . " (14) we were puzzled; does he mean we should so long for peace and freedom from troubling emotion that we do not care? For while some painful emotion is due to our infantile demands, much is simply part of being human. Are we to seek invulnerability at the price of dehumanization? Or is something else meant? Is the point not to feel, or to feel and accept?

Perhaps part of our difficulty derives from our insistence on black-and-white thinking. We assume that if we are not attached to others we are detached and aloof. In the last chapter we set aside the two-valued active-passive dichotomy and substituted the scheme active-responsive-passive. Similarly, we should not assume that we either cling to others in a grasping and fearful way or neglect them and become detached in a quest for personal peace and invulnerability. Perhaps the possibilities are not exhausted in the dichotomy of attachment-detachment, and there is some form or meaning of responsiveness as a third possibility. Using the language of the *Gita*, we may pose the

[22] Theodore Reik, *Masochism in Sex and Society* (New York: Grove Press, 1962 [1941]), 429.

[23] Frankl, *Will to Meaning*, 76.

three-valued distinction "attachment-non-attachment-detachment."[24] Just as responsiveness is not passive merely because it is not activist, so non-attachment is not detached and uncaring merely because it is not clinging attachment. Just as responsiveness accomplishes tasks, so non-attachment as an expression of responsiveness in relationships cherishes persons; it does so without insisting that the other meet my needs, fulfill my expectations, and become a permanent and invulnerable part of my security-system.

Letting go is a process of learning non-attachment to persons and things, but non-attachment is not detachment or withdrawal; the relevant image is touching, without clinging. Kubler-Ross described grief in the dying as a process of letting go of attachments, and she pointed out how those close to the dying may misinterpret this as rejection and detachment. This helps us understand what seems like inhumanity in Epictetus: he advises us to make that movement from attachment to non-attachment which occurs in grieving. This expression of letting go is, of course, a shifting from the denial of vulnerability to acceptance. Attachment which clings is a denial of our precariousness and that of those we love; it is part of the defensive and resistant attempt to become totally secure. Being based on denial, it leads to unnecessary pain. At the other extreme, detachment from relationships also seeks invulnerability and is therefore a denial of our situation. Non-attachment would then be a way of being with others without using and possessing them, a way that lets them be. As a form of responsiveness, it derives from accepting our insecurity as well as that of others.

At least this is the interpretation of the *Gita* and of Epictetus, which is consistent with the views emerging from our study. If they mean something else, that we are or can become invulnerable and unmoved, we simply reject this. Surely, many expressions of the ethic of consolation in their concern for serenity and peace of mind do represent a failure to care and to risk in relationships; they aim at safety through detachment, rather than at non-attached, responsive relationship. And in this, they are regressive.

* * * * *

While one form of letting go is regressive, escaping back into primal oneness, another is a step in maturation, a step beyond will as negation to will as participation. As a synthesis of passive and active, responsiveness arises by letting go of the infantile phase of the ego, the strident self, but not so as to regress to egoless bliss and pure passivity. This maturation of the self does not arise through doing, as an accom-

[24] Hora, *Existential Metapsychiatry*, 121-123, 207-209.

plishment, but by a cessation of the wrong kind of doing, through letting go.

It is interesting to note that masochistic styles are much like the strident, infantile ego, described in the previous chapter as negative will. For both are based on denial of something about ourselves or our situation. Masochism denies the vulnerability involved in being a separate self and defines the real self as invulnerable. The strident way of being a self likewise denies our precariousness and imagines that all of the limits can be transcended and made over by our willing. Responsiveness as a way of being begins in letting go of this strident denial of the limits and accepts our precariousness.

There is room for this third possibility in the criticisms of Berger and Campbell, but not in Nietzsche. We must thus ask, why cannot Nietzsche admit the possibility of reversal as one way to self-fulfillment? It will turn out that this is not so much a question about the man Nietzsche as about the psychological type represented by the extreme of the ethic of attainment.

We can move toward an answer by observing the irony in the contrast of Luther and Nietzsche. Luther seems dominated by his father's expectations of achievement. It is as if he received from his father a "conditional love" that says, "I love you, *if* you please me." His picture of God was at first like this; God will love us *if* we make ourselves worthy. But love with conditions isn't love, and those who withhold their acceptance and set conditions are often incapable of accepting us as we are, and all of our efforts to please them do not change them. So the attempt to earn love must fail. The solution of Luther's dilemma was simply the idea of unconditional acceptance, what folk-wisdom calls the love of a mother. The irony is simply that the father-dominated discovers mother-love. On the other hand, Nietzsche, raised exclusively among women, represents the most strident expression of fulfillment through will and effort. Luther, dominated by his father's expectations, discovers unqualified, maternal love as the answer to his self-contempt, his failure to measure up; while Nietzsche, raised among five women, fears "equal love for all" as undermining the heroic will necessary to real achievement.

Nietzsche seems to represent a form of vigorously individualistic will that fears surrender. Letting go can only be perceived by such a person as regression; there is only letting go and fighting on. Surrender means defeat of the heroic will, and it cannot be conceived that it could be a paradoxical means to victory. It is associated in such personalities with images of night, death, and the enveloping mother, all of which threaten to swallow the ego. This fear corresponds with a stage in the emergence of the ego from primal oneness, according to Erich Neumann.

> During the phase when consciousness begins to turn into self-consciousness, that is, to recognize and discriminate itself as a separate individual ego, the maternal overshadows it like a dark and tragic fate. Feelings of transitoriness and mortality, impotence and isolation, now color the ego's picture of the . . . [maternal] in absolute contrast to the original situation of contentment.[25]

The maternal may thus come to symbolize a devouring threat to identity. A rigid, intensely individualistic will-centered approach to life that cannot let go and let be may be a reaction to the fear of the loss of the ego to the smothering, enveloping primal oneness associated with the maternal. "If I let go, I will be overwhelmed, I will lose my identity; to be I must assert, strive and master." Nietzsche did, in fact, fall back into this oceanic oneness in the decade of his insanity.

Thus as there can be a compulsive desire for the loss of self, there can be an equally compulsive fear of letting go. Just as the father's demands for attainment may have led Luther to discover maternal or unconditional love, perhaps the oppressive presence of the maternal led Nietzsche to fear surrender and to see fulfillment as the outcome of the individualistic will alone. Whatever may be the case, Nietzsche cannot see the possibility of transcending the active-passive dichotomy; for him, if one is not active, one is passive, if one is not striving for victory, one has conceded defeat.

The reversal of intention may be a part of the fulfillment of the self or its annihilation. When impossibility blocks the will, we may let go of the self, or of the stridency of the self. In the latter case, the brittle, manipulative, coercive will is transcended in participative willing. This "step forward" is taken, paradoxically, by letting go.

[25] Er,ch Neumann, *The Origins and History of Consciousness*, vol. 1, trans. R. F. C. Hull (New York: Harper and Bros., 1954), 45.

Chapter 11

DOES LETTING GO DEPEND ON A BELIEF-SYSTEM? TWO STORIES WITH THE SAME EFFECT ARE THE SAME STORY

> The theories which Religion generates, being thus variable, are secondary; and if you wish to grasp her essence, you must look to the feelings and the conduct as being the more constant elements.
>
> —William James
> *The Varieties of Religious Experience*

> It is no longer the creed that guides us, but moral earnestness and serious commitment, undertaken in uncertainty, without outside guarantees.
>
> —Karl Jaspers
> "Myth and Religion"

You and I are subject to threats to our physical self, that is, to our life and health; to our social self, our sense of self-worth and our place in the human group; and to the noetic self, the meanings, values, and beliefs by which we orient ourselves in life and give reason for living in the face of threats. This three-fold precariousness was observed several chapters ago, but in subsequent discussions consideration was given only to threats to life and to self-esteem. Thus Gautama and Luther were described as coming to terms with the threats of death, disease, and old-age in one case and guilt and condemnation in the other by accepting their insecurity. No attention has yet been given to the threat to the belief- and value-systems by which we live. In a sense, this was our strategy toward spinach as children, leaving the worst until last.

The present is a time of acculturation, much like the Hellenistic crisis or the period immediately prior to the Reformation. Due to the intercommunication of diverse cultures, and due to the conflict within European-American culture between modernity and tradition, many people experience doubt and uneasiness toward inherited belief-systems and are selective in what they accept from them. Periodic revivals of the more rigid and authoritarian aspects of traditional religious belief do not count against this observation. Rather, in the very fact that these revivals cultivate a style of faith that is tense, defensive, rigid, outwardly cock-sure, fearful of criticism and dissent, and in need of constantly larger doses of emotional uplift to maintain itself, we see confirmation of a loss of confidence in the tradition; for fanaticism is simply one form of response to the fear of the loss of meaning. The same loss of confidence is indicated by the equally compulsive rush after new gods and new assurances in popularized oriental religions and in new Western technologies of self-development. To point to this crisis of belief is not to imply that belief in any of its traditional forms is irrelevant or impossible, but that belief is a problem; we live in a time and place in which the threat to the sense of meaning is real for many.

The crisis over beliefs is intimately related to the idea of the inversion of intention, because in each of the ancient texts consulted, letting go was undergirded by a set of beliefs about reality. Each document substantiated its claim that fulfillment cannot be achieved through effort on the basis of a certain understanding of reality. The Stoic claimed the world of events is ruled by a divine natural law and cannot be affected by our efforts. Paul says the essence of sin, the very root of our alienation from God, is our prideful self-reliance, our unwillingness to submit to being creatures; thus, the right relation to God cannot be the result of self-reliant efforts at being righteous. The *Tao Teh Ching* contained the vision of all things as fulfilled by effortless being, and since this is the way of nature, the effort to improve on nature through contrivance and manipulation must fail. Saraha saw all self-effort, even the effort after Buddhist enlightenment, as keeping alive the mistaken idea of the separate self, therefore leading only to suffering and dismay.

More importantly, each text justified its injunction to renounce self-effort on the basis of its beliefs. We were assured that, common sense expectations to the contrary, letting go of effort would lead not to disaster but to fulfillment because of the way things are. The Stoic claims that while the world is a determined system in which human will is powerless to affect outcomes, we can control our desires and our responses; one is asked to believe both this view of the world and this view of the self. Paul's assurance that the goal can be reached by giving up the attempt is based on his belief in the personal God, transcendent of the world, who has proposed to do for us what we cannot do for ourselves through the offer of forgiveness in the death and resurrection of the God-man Jesus Christ. Faith is entire trust in this offer and the total renunciation of self-effort and includes belief that certain things are true. The *Tao Teh Ching* believes the power or fulfillment appropriate to each thing comes to it when it is a non-obstructive channel of *Tao*; non-interfering action fulfills because reality is like that. Saraha's assurances depend on the monistic, all-is-one vision of reality. It is as if each text invites us to let go of the edge of the pool and float, and each offers us some form of Archimedes' Principle to assure us that we won't sink.

Now the problem of this chapter arises when we notice that each of these belief-systems is open to doubt; they are not patently false, but each asserts something to be the case, and therefore may be questioned. Here we encounter a form of the threat to the noetic self.

For example, each belief-system grew up in particular times and places in response to particular problems and conditions, and knowing their relativity to time and culture as we now do may make wholehearted belief difficult. To take a single case, some become hesitant to accept the uniqueness of Paul's story when they learn of the dying and rising saviors and incarnate gods and their sacraments of initiation and communion so prevalent in the Hellenistic world; or when they confront the claims of the biblical scholars about the way in which the Jesus tradition was transformed in the telling by the ancient church in such a way that Jesus' human characteristics are progressively de-emphasized in favor of his God-like attributes, as is seen when we read the Gospels in the order of their composition.

Further, the belief-systems we have encountered conflict with each other, and thus cannot all be true. If God is the natural law structure of the universe that assigns fates to men and women without caring for the individual, then God is not a person whose eye is on the sparrow, who numbers even the hairs of our heads, and cares for even the lilies of the field. If God is the personal being, of whom it is correct to say "He," the One who exists beyond and before the world, caring for each unique individual child, then "He" is not the Innate, the one individual, apparently impersonal, beside whom there is no other, identical with and not apart from all reality. If God created things and beheld them as good, it is not an illusion that they exist, and if the fulfillment of life is union with the immanent divine, then it is not a personal relationship with the transcendent God. If we possess naturally, just as we are, the power and divinity that completes our lives, then we are not alienated from God and in need of grace from beyond ourselves. And on it continues. At important points the belief-systems conflict, and they can't all be true if taken on their own terms, if believed the way they each ask to be believed.

Not only do they conflict, but the glaring eyes of Nietzsche make us uneasy, and we recall that each belief-system assures us, after all, of precisely what we wish to believe anyway. Of course, each accuses us in one way or another of having arrested our development at an infantile stage in which grasping, clinging, demanding, and denying are what we do best. But each does offer us something suspiciously corresponding to our wishes for peace and security. For we are surely not disappointed to hear that God loves us just as we are, or that we are already one with the divine essence of all things, or that for some other reason we already possess what we seek. This correspondence plants a suspicion, perhaps wholly unfounded, that the wish begat the belief.

We may at least ask if clinging to belief-systems may not itself be the last form of clinging to be renounced. If accepting our insecurity is the meaning of letting go, then perhaps belief as a security system must also be abandoned. This question was first encountered in discussing the acceptance of death. Has death been accepted when we believe it is the transition to continued life or to an eternity of bliss?

Knowledge of the historical and cultural relativity of belief-systems, the conflicts between rival belief-systems, and their correspondence with our wishes all raise doubts and questions about beliefs. Although this is not historically unprecedented, it is a typically modern problem; for it arises from our contact with other cultures that contain alternatives to our way of being human, and from our new practice of subjecting all beliefs to critical scrutiny. The point is not that these observations end our belief, but that they raise the question of the truth of the belief-systems underlying the idea of reversal. Beyond the question of their truth is the question of whether one has really let go if one clings to beliefs. Thus the question of this chapter is simply about the relation of reversal to belief systems. "Must one believe something to let go? Is some particular belief about reality necessary to reversal and to responsiveness? If so, is this really letting go, or do assurances appeal to the infantile rather than the maturing within us? Would authentic letting go mean the end of belief-systems? But is this possible or advisable? Is there a way of relating to our beliefs about reality that is not clinging?"

* * * * *

Firstly, let's consider the possibility of letting go absolutely, of letting go without a particular belief-system and its assurances, of letting go *of* beliefs. Surely, if some belief-system is known to be true, this is a false and needlessly difficult approach. But for some it is temperamentally necessary, and examples exist in abundance of the reality and possibility of this stark and austere way. We already know from studies of the dying that letting go is a universal and recurrent human response to impossibility quite independent of any belief-system. We are about to discover that this possibility of letting go without a belief-system has been consciously affirmed and elaborated.

While one might be forced to explore this way by one's doubts, by the inability to enter whole-heartedly into any belief-system, it is important to understand that some choose this path out of conviction and not deficiency. That is, some recognize you have not let go until you cease clinging to beliefs; sincerity and honesty therefore require this last austerity.

In this view, assurances appeal to the infantile ego and bolster its dominance. We have not let go when we have merely responded to the call "Let go and I'll catch you!" It is not until we let go utterly, without outside guarantees, that we have gone beyond the point of demanding that reality be as we would like it to be. Reversal of effort is not genuine when it is conditional, "I'll let go *if* you catch me." It is only authentic, in this view, if we have fully accepted our insecurity, including our inability to capture ultimate reality in a belief-system. As severe as this may sound, we are assured by those who practice this way by choice and who have little lingering nostalgia for familiar but lost beliefs, that peace, freedom, and even happiness result from it.

Those who are skillful in detecting insincere or self-deceiving talk about renunciation and letting go point out that the problem with beliefs is that when you cling to them you think you've let go when you haven't. If the belief-system says the mark of surrender is firm belief, then the one who is really clinging to beliefs for the security they give is misled into thinking surrender is complete. The conditional nature of surrender within a belief-system, "I'll stop struggling for security *if* God or Something Else will take over the job," reveals that one has let go everything *except* belief, and the clinging, grasping potential of the self is still in command.

An example of an individual who chooses letting go without outside guarantees is the French novelist, playwright, and essayist Albert Camus. You recall that Gautama was sensitive to threats to our physical being and found peace through accepting his vulnerability. In the *anatta* doctrine he proclaimed the nothingness of the separate self. That peace which could not be achieved by defending the self against threats arose for him when he let go of the self. Similarly, Luther was deeply troubled over the threat to his sense of self-worth, and yet he transcended this through accepting his insecurity. In the doctrine of "original sin" he portrayed each self as without a claim to acceptance by the righteous God. And as with the Buddha, that peace which could not be achieved by efforts to become righteous followed for Luther when he abandoned the effort after righteousness through works and accepted God's mercy. In a very similar way, Camus deals with threats to the beliefs and values that are supposed to give meaning to life. Camus accepts the nothingness of the conventional meaning-systems; in his concept of "the absurd," he accepts that no meaning is to be found in life. Yet paradoxically, in the courage and honesty which accepts the absurd, Camus finds a humanly created meaning. While life is meaningless in itself, a meaning can be created in the way this is faced. This is precisely what Frankl meant by attitudinal values, the giving of meaning to a hopeless situation through suffering it well. Thus that sense of meaning which cannot be achieved through the effort to maintain what are for Camus the conventional lies, is found when we let go of this effort and accept meaninglessness.

We normally accept beliefs, if not religious then secular, that assure us of the meaningfulness of the life we lead, that there is a reason why things should be as they are and we should continue as we do. Our social roles are vaguely accepted as necessary and right, and playing these parts structures our lives. Yet, according to Camus, these beliefs and roles are an evasion, and that painful realization which they seek to ward off may yet break through. The feeling of the absurdity, of the bare givenness, facticity, arbitrariness of things may jump out at us at any time; we then realize there is no reason why things must be as they are, either in the physical or the social worlds. At this point, "the void becomes eloquent, . . . and the hold of everydayness is broken."[1] The question of "Why?" has arisen, and no justifying belief or routine appears as anything more than stage scenery; having seen the sets totter and wobble, it is hard to believe any more in their reality. This has occurred to most of us, but we have always fled back to the evasion that we call normalcy; Camus instead accepts it and explores its significance.

All week at work, I look forward to the weekend; then bored with the unstructured time of the weekend, I anticipate the unselfconsciousness of the week's routine. Each blankness, the week and the weekend, borrows by anticipation a sense of meaning from the other. When I catch myself doing this, when I realize that both the week and the weekend are empty, the sense of the absurd may arise.

The sense of the absurd, the unjustified givenness of life, is evoked especially by the realization of death, according to Camus. Life is not just as we would wish it, but no matter, surely tomorrow or someday it will be. When I admit that I do not have an endless supply of "somedays," and that one of the tomorrows for which I live contains my death, the pointlessness of the life lived for tomorrow wells up. Death in its arbitrary finality does not come when you are finished, when you have completed your intentions, but just when it comes, either long before or long after life is "complete."

In short, in some way we may awaken to the realization that the world has no unifying, over-arching reason or meaning, such as is supposed to be provided by belief in God or progress or duty. Reason is able to understand parts of the world, thus raising the hope of a full

[1] Albert Camus, *The Myth of Sisyphus and Other Essays*, trans. Justin O'Brien (New York: Vintage Books, 1955 [1942]), 10.

understanding, but reason in the end can find no unified, meaningful vision of the world as a whole. "There are truths, but no Truth."[2] To insist that behind it all is the mystery called "God" is, according to Camus, simply to give a name to the absurd, with the dishonest hope that some of the connotations of familiarity and rationality which go with this well-known word may take away the sense of meaninglessness.

Camus maintains that most of our efforts are expended in living within a conventionally defined life so as to bolster up the sense that life is meaningful; we thus evade the recognition of the fact that the world and our routines are arbitrary, and that there is no reason to live. This realization lurks on the edges of our mind, and to evade it we exert increasing efforts. When we awaken to this we are suddenly freed from all of the efforts of denial, all of the exertions and dishonesties by which we sought to make our role seem necessary and our beliefs true. When the absurd is faced it is seen to be, after all, only a fact. Whereas only a precarious sense of the meaning of life was possible before, always haunted by our suspicion that there is no reason for it, when we accept the meaninglessness of life, we begin, according to Camus, to move toward a kind of meaning that is secure, based only on ourselves, and not founded on illusions or wishes.

Meanwhile, the energy wasted in fortifying conventional beliefs and pouring life into conventional roles is freed for living. In the terms of earlier discussions, accepting meaninglessness releases the energy wasted in denial. One result of giving up the pretense that life is meaningful and accepting the absurd is freedom. We once feared to step outside the definition that roles and beliefs gave us for fear of the absurd; but we are now free from the artificiality and confinement accompanying conventional beliefs in the meaningfulness of life. This need not mean that we abandon roles and drop out; it might mean that we play within them, acting less compulsively, more freely, seeing through them and not being taken in by them.

Camus continues, we are liberated from anxiety over the future, since all ends in death. Recall that the threat with which Camus is dealing is not that posed by death to our physical being, but that posed by death to our sense of the meaningfulness of the life which precedes it. We have evaded awareness of death to flee from the shadow of meaninglessness it casts back over life. Having accepted the absurd, we now can accept death, and we are freed from the debilitating effects of denial. None of us is getting out of this alive anyway, the worst we feared will in fact occur, and so our timidity, reserve, and elaborate precautions are to no purpose. This is a form of "the wisdom of insecu-

[2] *Ibid.*, 15.

rity;" we become free from our hiding in meaning-giving roles and free from our life-cramping efforts to avoid death when we recognize there is no meaning and death is the end.

Related to this result of accepting absurdity for Camus is passion. Accepting the finality of death gives a new sense of the preciousness of the moment and inspires a quest for quantity of life through increased awareness rather than through endless duration. Thus contrary to a popular misunderstanding of "accepting the absurdity of life," it is not negative and despairing but exuberant and life-affirming. By accepting impossibility, Camus transcends it, and the energy dissipated in denial is channeled into life; in short, the matter stands just as it did with the believing practitioners of reversal.

Not only is the energy wasted in denial released for life, but a meaning is found, paradoxically, in accepting meaninglessness. The example Camus gives of one who accepts the absence of meaning in life and thus finds meaning is the myth of Sisyphus. Because of his obstreperous love for life, Sisyphus was condemned by the gods to ceaselessly roll a rock to the top of a mountain, only to watch it roll to the bottom again. For the meaning-seeking being, no punishment could be worse than hopeless labor. Camus portrays Sisyphus as surmounting his fate by accepting it; he raises his absurd fate to the level of tragedy by consciously accepting its lack of meaning. "Crushing truths perish from being acknowledged."[3] He is able to say, like Sophocles' Oedipus, "Despite so many ordeals, my advanced age and the nobility of my soul make me conclude that all is well."[4] In accepting his fate in its absurdity, in ceasing to evade with illusory beliefs showing that it is really rational and for a purpose, Sisyphus creates his own meaning, which is the heroic way in which he suffers his fate.

> The absurd man says yes and his effort will henceforth be unceasing. For the rest, he knows himself to be the master of his days. At that subtle moment when man glances backward over his life, Sisyphus returning toward his rock, in that slight pivoting he contemplates that series of unrelated actions which becomes his fate, created by him, combined under his memory's eye and soon sealed by his death. Thus, convinced of the wholly human origins of all that is human, a blind man eager to see who knows that the night has no end, he is still on the go. The rock is still rolling. I leave Sisyphus at the foot of the mountain! One always finds one's burden again. But Sisyphus teaches the higher fidelity that negates the gods and raises rocks. He too concludes that all is well. This universe henceforth without a master seems to him neither sterile nor futile. . . .
> The struggle itself toward the heights is enough to fill a man's heart. One

[3] *Ibid.*, 90.
[4] *Ibid.*

must imagine Sisyphus happy.[5]

Life is affirmed, not because it is meaningful in itself, but because a meaning is found in accepting this absurdity.

Thus for Camus, meaning is found in the way meaninglessness is borne. Here we have a way of getting the goal by giving up the attempt to get it, one which is not predicated on a belief-system; for the goal is precisely a sense of life as meaningful in the absence of any beliefs that portray it as such. Meaninglessness can be transcended by accepting it, just as death and guilt were by Gautama and Luther. Yet Camus makes clear that acceptance need not be acquiescence, for he does not see Sisyphus as ceasing to look for light even though he knows the night of the absurd has no end. If he had despaired of meaning, he would not have found that meaning which rests in is own perseverance. Acceptance is not submission and suicide, the erasure of the ego, but its fulfillment under the direst of circumstances.

* * * * *

In the affirmation of Camus that life can be good even if it has no reason rooted in the nature of things, we see the way of reversal which lets go even of beliefs. In a second example, the thought of the German existentialist philosopher Martin Heidegger, we see the classical pattern of the great statements of the reversal theme even more clearly. The familiar critique of the will-centered ethic of attainment is found in Heidegger's description of "calculative thinking," and his idea that meaningfulness arises in the mode of thought called "waiting" will be seen to embody the paradox of intention.

Heidegger's point of departure is the question of how modern people are to find meaning in life. What kind of thinking is required to disclose meaningfulness? Due to the revolution in the relation of humanity to its world represented by science and technology, calculative thinking is pervasive, and, in fact, we are on the verge of concluding that it is the only valid form of thought. But the problem is that calculative thinking is unable to provide a sense of meaning in life; to borrow from Camus, calculative thinking gives us truths, but no Truth.

While the dominance of calculative thinking is typically modern, as one approach beside others, it has always been a part of human life and has its role to play in the maintenance of the human community. Calculative thinking is problem-solving; it operates to serve some definite purpose, to achieve some chosen end. Just because it serves some specific human need and aim and seeks a foreknown result, it cannot really hear what the world is saying to us. When an object, whether a

[5] *Ibid.*, 91.

person or a forest, is approached with an interest in its usefulness in meeting our need or solving our problem, we never know it directly. Calculative thinking never stops, never collects itself, and therefore never hears "the meaning which reigns in everything that is."[6]

Beside calculative thinking there has always been meditative thinking; both are needed and justified, and neither is appropriate in seeking the goals of the other. Meditative thinking is useless in carrying out practical affairs, and calculative thinking fails in giving rise to a sense of the meaningfulness of life. Since we are losing touch with the nature of meditative thinking and tend to identify thought itself with its active, manipulative form, we are falling deeper into a sense of the meaninglessness of the world; if the world is nothing but what it appears to be in calculative thinking, a collection of dead and meaningless objects, it is empty and hollow for the meaning-seeking being.

> The world now appears as an object open to the attacks of calculative thought, attacks that nothing is believed able any longer to resist. Nature becomes a gigantic gasoline station, an energy source for modern technology and industry.[7]

Operating on the basis of calculation, we find nothing but means in the world and nothing that is an end in itself. Such a world is lacking in meaning, for each achievement is merely a means to some further achievement and nothing is savored as an end in itself, and so the whole series of problem-solving operations is pointless.

According to Heidegger, we are losing the ability to approach the world with the respect which knows it has its own being apart from the way it figures in our plans. It is therefore crucial that meditative thinking be kept alive as a possibility. If we could understand the world through meditative thought as well as through calculative, then the latter would be put in perspective. Then it would be possible to use technological devices and yet remain free of them, able to set them aside at any time, and able to know the world as more than it appears when mediated to us through our tools.

> We can use technological devices as they ought to be used, and also let them alone as something which does not affect our inner and real core. We can affirm the unavoidable use of technological devices, and also deny them the right to dominate us, and so to warp, confuse, and lay waste our nature.[8]

[6] Martin Heidegger, *Discourse on Thinking*, trans. J. M. Anderson and E. H. Freund (New York: Harper and Row, 1966 [1959]), 46. The German title of the book is *Gelassenheit*.

[7] *Ibid.*, 50.

[8] *Ibid.*, 54.

Thus the first result of revived awareness of meditative thinking, deep thinking that goes beyond the surface of things revealed in calculation and manipulation is a loosening of our possessive grip on things, which in turn lets them be just what they are in their fullness. "I would call this comportment toward technology which expresses 'yes' and at the same time 'no,' by an old word, releasement toward things."[9] The word is indeed old, for *Gelassenheit*, now usually meaning "calmness or unconcern," was the term used since Eckhart by German mystics and pietists for "yieldedness, letting go of self-concern." One is tempted to say that something like "action which is unattached to its fruits" is intended; the "yes" to technology assures us that we are not talking about abandonment of action, and the "no" reminds us to let things be themselves and not to regard them merely as means to our predetermined ends.

The second result of restored awareness of the meditative approach to the world will be "openness to the mystery," a readiness to sense within the one world, the world handled in technology, a hidden richness pervading it that can be a source of a sense of meaning.

> *The meaning pervading technology hides itself.* But if we explicitly and continuously heed the fact that such a hidden meaning touches us everywhere in the world of technology, we stand at once within the realm of that which hides itself from us, and hides itself just in approaching us. That which shows itself and at the same time withdraws is the essential trait of what we call the mystery. I call the comportment which enables us to keep open to the meaning hidden in technology, *openness to the mystery.*[10]

The use of the term "mystery" together with my comments on "yieldedness" may invite a certain misunderstanding of Heidegger, especially on the part of those whose traditional religious or mystical persuasion will not allow them to conceive real disagreements in deep matters, and therefore are not secure until they imagine everyone is saying just what they themselves have always believed. The mystery here is not another realm beyond the world disclosed in technology, but precisely the fullness of this one world. To approach the mystery imagining you know pretty well what it is, and even what to call it, is the religious form of calculative thinking; for when we impose our needs, purposes, and beliefs, we fail to listen and to let being be just what it is.

Calculative thinking succeeds in its sphere, but it cannot disclose the world as meaningful; the active, coercive, manipulative approach

[9] *Ibid.*
[10] *Ibid.*, 55.

may have considerable success in making our physical existence secure, but it cannot "solve the noetic problem" and render life meaningful. This is because the meaningfulness of life cannot be evoked as a solution to a problem; the problem-solving approach must fail in this sphere. Here we find the familiar criticism directed against the ethic of attainment. The threat to our sense of meaningfulness cannot be overcome by activist and assertive forms of thinking. Rather, following the logic of the ethic of reversal, a sense of meaningfulness will arise precisely when we abandon the effort to grasp it. For meditative thinking, with its "releasement toward things" and its "openness to the mystery," is a kind of listening that does not impose and insist; through it a sense of meaning arises that could not be found in any other way. The goal of meaning is reached by giving up the attempt to reach it.

But it is not yet clear what meditative thinking is. As we proceed with Heidegger's description of it, an observation made in a previous chapter regarding other embodiments of the reversal of intention will become clearer; letting go is not the means to some end, but is itself the end. Meditative thinking is not the way to arrive at some idea or belief which will show life as meaningful; it is itself the meaning.

Heidegger's exploration of meditative thinking is well represented in a philosophical dialogue between a scientist, a scholar, and a teacher, which is called "Conversations on a Country Path about Thinking." We know we are beginning a discussion of the paradox of intention when we encounter at the very beginning of the dialogue a paradox: thinking can only be understood by looking away from it, or, in other words, by not thinking about it.

> If thinking is what distinguishes man's nature, then surely the essence of this nature, namely the nature of thinking, can be seen only by looking away from thinking.[11]

That is, meditative thinking cannot be understood through calculative thinking about it, but only through itself; meditative thinking is not so much doing as being. Calculative thinking is a kind of willing, through which we represent to ourselves the world of experience, structuring and arranging it according to our interests, purposes, and mental categories; the resulting mental picture *re*-presents the world, that is, it "presents the world again," mentally. Representation is a mental map of reality; but the map is not the terrain. Meditative thinking is not this willful reordering of experience in the mind; it is non-willing, and thus it is able to listen to what the world has to say.

Heidegger faces a problem we will touch on in the next chapter,

[11] *Ibid.*, 58.

namely, the question of whether the reversal of intention is itself an intention, whether letting go is an act of will. He says that non-willing is itself a kind of willing, the willing to cease willing, but, on the other hand, as a state it is entirely apart from willing.

> Non-willing, for one thing, means a willing in such a way as to involve negation, be it even in the sense of a negation which is directed at willing and renounces it. Non-willing means therefore: willingly to renounce willing. And the term non-willing means, further, what remains absolutely outside any kind of will.[12]

The notion we are seeking is beyond willing and non-willing, beyond the distinction of active and passive.

As we cannot will a thinking that is not willing, we simply seek to be released to it, in Heidegger's words. "So far as we can wean ourselves from willing, we contribute to the awakening of releasement."[13] Again we encounter the word *Gelassenheit*, releasement or yieldedness. Being released to meditative thinking is not our doing, but is, so to speak, produced from somewhere else; it is "not effected, but let in."[14] Here we have a counterpart to the familiar idea of divine grace, but it must be understood that no idea of God is posited by Heidegger. As will be seen, releasement to meditative thinking is possible because of the openness of being to it.

It might seem that if meditative thinking is not active, then it is mere passivity. As we found in earlier investigations, letting go is not inaction, but in a sense a higher form of action. The three participants in Heidegger's dialogue express this as follows.

> You speak without letup of a letting be and give the impression that what is meant is a kind of passivity. All the same, I think I understand that it is in no way a matter of weakly allowing things to slide and drift along.
>
> Perhaps a higher acting is concealed in releasement than is found in all the actions within the world and the machinations of all mankind
>
> . . . which higher acting is yet no activity. Then releasement lies — if we may use the word lie — beyond the distinction between activity and passivity . . . because releasement does *not* belong to the domain of the will.[15]

Being beyond the active-passive dichotomy, releasement would seem to be identical with what we earlier called responsiveness or participation.

Heidegger is quick to point out that the traditional religious use of

[12] *Ibid.*, 59.
[13] *Ibid.*, 60.
[14] *Ibid.*, 61.
[15] *Ibid.*

Gelassenheit, as in the sermons of the Christian mystic Meister Eckhart, is not what he intends; releasement is not the casting off of "sinful selfishness" and the substituting of divine will for self-will. Perhaps Heidegger insists on this because such a religious interpretation would be "conditional releasement," letting go being predicated on being caught; but if we claim to know in advance what the mystery must be, that it is like our concept "God," then we are not really open to it. As mentioned earlier, the situation may be distorted by moralizing about our selfishness; we become operators and manipulators because we are stressed and threatened, not because we are wicked. Reflections such as these may or may not be behind Heidegger's wish to dissociate himself from the religious use of *Gelassenheit*.

If at this point we become impatient and ask for a clearer concept of meditative thinking, we show that we have slipped back into calculative thinking, and want a representation. The mind trained in the ways of calculation and manipulation wants a clear concept that may serve as a plan of action. If we now ask, "What in the world am I to do?" the answer can only be, "We are to do nothing but wait."[16] Here we are as close to a concept or a plan of meditative thinking as we will get; it is waiting.

Why is it that waiting will lead to the goal of a sense of meaningfulness in life, while calculative thinking will not? To make progress here we must use some of Heidegger's unusual but strangely effective terminology. When we look about us, our visual field forms a horizon; there is a definite limit, in the distance and to each side, of what can be seen. Yet as we move willfully forward into the field or turn to each side, the horizon recedes. Thus we are aware that our horizon moves within a larger region of what there is to be seen; there is always more to be seen beyond our present horizon. This fact is not due to our looking; rather, the region "comes out to meet us." The horizon within which we see is formed by our willful decision and it moves as we move; but seeing is possible because of the being of that region within which our horizon occurs. What representing, our active, structuring, organizing thought sees is the "side facing us of an openness which surrounds us."[17] If we had no fear of cumbersome terms, as Heidegger surely does not, we might speak of this active presence or openness which manifests itself to us in our seeing as "that which regions." To repeat, we perceive a horizon of sight formed by our activity as placed within a larger region, the being of which makes sight possible; it is this that comes to meet us, it is this which is the openness that surrounds us. When we speak of the region within which we form

[16] *Ibid.*, 62.
[17] *Ibid.*, 64.

our horizon as manifesting "that which regions," we portray that reality within which we function as actively meeting us and opening to us; if we remember Heidegger's intention in choosing this term, we can translate it simply as being. Here we have the mystery of being hidden within the world of technology. Knowing is possible because of the surrounding activity, presence and openness of being.

Heidegger is reminding us that we are embedded within being. We humans who wish to know what being is, already stand within it; while we inquire after being, we are being. We are implicated in being, and therefore cannot understand being as an object apart from ourselves. This is the very good reason why calculative thinking cannot grasp being; it always seeks an object to know and use, some thing apart from ourselves to represent or manipulate. But the knowers and users are themselves also beings, they are in the process of being themselves, they are within being, and therefore they cannot grasp being as some thing. We can only think about being, "that which regions," meditatively, that is, by waiting.

For this same reason, waiting is not awaiting. It is not some concrete thing or idea for which we wait, but the sense of being in us and around us as the presence and activity partially manifest in calculative thought. Heidegger's dialogue therefore contains this interchange.

> Waiting, all right; but never awaiting, for awaiting already links itself with re-presenting and what is re-presented.
>
> Waiting, however, lets go of that, or rather I should say that waiting lets re-presenting entirely alone. It really has no object.
>
> Yet if we wait we always wait for something.
>
> Certainly, but as soon as we re-present to ourselves and fix upon that for which we wait, we really wait no longer. In waiting we leave open what we are waiting for.[18]

Rather than representing reality to ourselves and relating to the world through the mediation of this mental picture, in waiting we enjoy an immediate relation to being. Calculative thinking seeks something corresponding to a human interest or idea and always operates in terms of specific things it selects from within the fullness of experience, but meditative thinking lets being be and waits for a sense of that fullness. Waiting does not preconceive what this sense of the fullness of being must be, and so specific beliefs and conceptions, especially those generated by religion and philosophy, destroy genuine waiting.

Waiting is possible, Heidegger says, because of the openness of being. Calculative thinking can actively select objects for attention and

[18] *Ibid.*, 68.

form a horizon out of the surrounding region because being is there (with apologies) "regioning." Meditative thought can simply wait for a sense of the richness beyond and beneath what calculative thought discovers because being is this fuller reality. Waiting is thus not doing, but letting be; "everything is in the best order only if it has been no one's doing."[19] In this frame of mind, we are open to being, and it manifests itself to us; but of course it is not manifest as something particular.

This awareness of being is a sense of meaningfulness, though it is not *a* meaning. We cannot form a concept of an awareness or a sense of presence which is not mediated through concepts. In the moment of awareness, we cease to live through the abstractions formed by the representing of calculative thought and we are in an immediate relation to being; the distance between ourselves and being which is created by the mediation of concepts is wiped out. We encounter the terrain and not the map. Being which surrounds and permeates us is now felt not as this or that, but as itself.

> The relation to that which regions is waiting. And waiting means: to release oneself into the openness of that which regions.[20]

If we remember the simple meaning of the unusual phrase "that which regions," the openness and activity of being which is a fuller and deeper reality beyond the horizon of specific things formed by mental activity, we see that it is preferable in some ways to the term being; for we are in the habit of objectifying and mystifying this word which simply means "that which is." When we speak of "the being which surrounds us" we may well be thinking of *a* being, God, or of some particular characterization of being such as Brahman or the Innate Buddha; this is to humanize and to particularize "that which regions," and therefore it is an intrusion into genuine waiting. That which arises in meditative thinking is not *a* meaning, but a sense of meaningfulness, not the security of being undergirded by benevolent and supportive everlasting arms, but the authenticity and genuineness of touching the real.

Through meditative thinking a sense of meaningfulness in life arises, though not a specific idea or belief. In the words of another existentialist philosopher, "We have felt release, but not discovered a solution."[21] In meditative thinking, the artificiality and sense of dis-

[19] *Ibid.*, 71.

[20] *Ibid.*, 72.

[21] Martin Buber, *I and Thou*, 2nd ed., trans. Ronald Gregor Smith (New York: Charles Scribner's Sons, 1958), 111. In the translation of Walter Kaufmann (New York: Charles Scribner's Sons, 1970), 160, this passage appears in a more literal form as "We have felt salvation but no solution."

tance and abstractness which arise when we live only in and through the concepts constructed by calculative thought are escaped, and we come to an authentic and immediate awareness of being. According to Heidegger, the problem of boredom and meaninglessness is not due to the absence of beliefs which show life as meaningful; it is the result of living only on the surface of things which never yields a sense of engagement and involvement with anything real. Calculative thinking, useful in its way, operates at the surface, and it therefore must be supplemented with deep thinking or waiting. In this we have an immediate relation to being not mediated by tools and concepts; it is this sense of the presence of being and not some theory of being which gives meaning to life. This awareness is itself received from being, which is in us and around us, on the condition that we do not assert and represent.

Put in terms of earlier discussions, our problem is that we seek meaning in life and do not find it in the active, manipulative mode. Confronted with this failure, we let go of that effort and fall into waiting. Waiting is that intent listening to being which does not insist on what it is to hear; it is thus not inquiry, which seeks the answer to a human question or the solution to a human problem. Waiting receives as a response a sense of the fullness of being which is the meaningfulness we sought. Thus the goal of a sense of meaning in the face of the death of traditional systems of belief is received by giving up the attempt to grasp it; that sense of engagement with the real, which could not arise through the efforts of calculative thought, is received as a gift when this effort is relinquished. Though passive in a sense, waiting is also actively attentive; thus we have here a form of responsiveness, that way of being which is neither merely active nor passive. In this kind of thinking a meaning arises which could not be found in any other way, and the meaning is precisely this waiting. This very attitude toward experience which listens attentively and does not demand an answer in its own terms is itself the meaningful life.

* * * * *

While the teachings of Gautama the Buddha do not represent a thorough rejection of belief-systems, they are based on a self-conscious awareness of the possibility that belief-systems may simply be something more to cling to and thus serve as a barrier to letting go. All of his teachings seem calculated to lead to letting go of selfish craving, and questions not directly pertinent to this are ignored and turned aside as idle and misleading.

Considerable attention is given to the reductive analysis of the self; it is as if this teaching is skillfully designed to loosen our grip, finger by clinging finger, by showing us there is nothing in the self to which to cling. According to the doctrine of "dependent origination," whatever now is, is derived from something which is prior, and this will in turn perish in giving rise to something new.

> Here the learned and noble disciple, O priests, attentively considers dependent origination — Behold, this exists when that exists, this originates from the origination of the other; this does not exist when that does not exist, this ceases from the cessation of the other.[22]

According to another text, "the elements of being join one another in serial succession: one element perishes, another arises, succeeding each other as it were instantaneously."[23] The green bud perishes in giving rise to the early pink blossom, which perishes in giving rise to the full crimson flower, which perishes in giving rise to the brown seed pod, and so on with both objects and states of consciousness; all reality is flux, and no namable object abides as itself. Yet for all this, the whole process of change itself always continues to be; thus the Buddhist teaching of dependent origination is a "middle doctrine" between two extremes.

> That things have being . . . constitutes one extreme of doctrine; that things have no being is the other extreme. These extremes . . . have been avoided by [the Buddha], and it is a middle doctrine he teaches.[24]

On one side is nihilism which says nothing is real, and on the other side is realism which says there is some substance, the essence of the object, the soul, the divine, which is changeless amidst all change. The middle view is that nothing remains self-identical through time, but the process of change is itself real, and thus while each thing perishes, something will always be. To characterize this abidingness of the flux itself, as say the eternal Brahman, would be to give the little self which fears to let go something to cling to. Thus we cannot discriminate any eternal substance behind change, neither the individual soul nor an eternal divine being; to use the terms of the Upanishadic scriptures of Hinduism to make a point quite different from theirs, there is no *atman* and no *Brahman*.

Our idea of an abiding object or self is simply a name for a composite of successively perishing parts. Therefore, a Buddhist teacher introduces himself to King Milinda in this way.

> Your majesty, I am called Nagasena; my fellow priests, your majesty, address me as Nagasena: but whether parents give one the name of

[22] *Samyutta-Nikaya*, 12.62.1, in Warren, *Buddhism in Translation*, 151.
[23] *Milindapanha*, 40.1, in Warren, *Buddhism*, 149.
[24] *Samyutta-Nikaya*, 22.90.16, in Warren, *Buddhism*, 166.

> Nagasena, or Surasena, or Virasena, or Sihasena, it is, nevertheless, your majesty, but a way of counting, a term, an appellation, a convenient designation, a mere name, this Nagasena; for there is no ego here to be found.[25]

The self is merely a name for a combination of parts which will eventually dissolve, the parts finding a new order and other forms. When this idea of the nothingness of the self was mentioned last it was to show the way in which the Buddha transcended his insecurity by accepting it. Now it can also be seen that the skillful teacher finds in this doctrine a way of provoking the experience of letting go; since there is nothing to cling to, there is nothing to do but let go.

When the idea of dependent origination is applied to the problem of human suffering, it is shown that this can be traced back to ignorance, which mistakenly takes the separate self as real and clings to it, seeking happiness through its satisfaction and defense.

> On ignorance depends karma; on karma depends consciousness; on consciousness depend name and form; on name and form depend the six organs of sense; on the six organs of sense depends contact; on contact depends sensation; on sensation depends desire; on desire depends attachment; on attachment depends existence; on existence depends birth; on birth depend old age and death, sorrow, lamentation, misery, grief and despair. Thus does the entire aggregation of misery arise.[26]

Ignorance takes namable objects like the self as abiding; however, to take what is dependent and perishing as abiding is to make oneself vulnerable to unnecessary suffering, for if we wish that which perishes to last and we make our happiness dependent on this, we must be disappointed. There is no substantial self which abides through all changes; the self is merely a temporary composite, and so there is nothing to which to cling.

The awareness of the Buddha that any more developed belief-system would provide something to which to cling is clear in the teaching usually called Questions which Edify Not. There is much beyond the minimal doctrine given above that the inquisitive intellect would like to know, and Malunkyaputta is said to have brought a list of such matters to Gautama: Is the world eternal or not? Is it infinite or not? Are the soul and the body one? Or is the soul separate and immortal? Do the enlightened exist self-consciously after death or not? Or do they somehow both exist and not exist? According to the tradition, the Buddha refused to go beyond those minimal teachings necessary to pro-

[25] *Milindapanha*, 25.1, in Warren, *Buddhism*, 129.

[26] *Samyutta-Nikaya*, 22.90.16, in Warren, *Buddhism*, 166.

voke letting go, nor would he provide a belief-system with ideas of eternal substances to which we might cling.

> It is as if, Malunkyaputta, a man had been wounded by an arrow thickly smeared with poison, and his friends and companions, his relatives and kinsfolk, were to procure for him a physician or surgeon; and the sick man were to say, "I will not have this arrow taken out until I have learnt whether the man who wounded me belonged to the warrior caste, or to the Brahmin caste, or to the agricultural caste, or to the menial caste." . . . In exactly the same way, Malunkyaputta, any one who should say, "I will not lead the religious life under the Blessed One until the Blessed One shall elucidate to me either that the world is eternal, or that the world is not eternal, . . . or that the saint neither exists nor does not exist after death;" — that person would die, Malunkyaputta, before [the Buddha] had ever elucidated this to him.
>
> The religious life, Malunkyaputta, does not depend on the dogma that the world is eternal, nor does the religious life, Malunkyaputta, depend on the dogma that the world is not eternal. Whether the dogma obtain, . . . that the world is eternal, or that the world is not eternal, there still remain birth, old age, death, sorrow, lamentation, misery, grief, and despair, for the extinction of which in the present life I am prescribing.[27]

The teaching is thus a therapy for sick souls and not a complete belief-system. The Buddha is portrayed as intentionally omitting from consideration all of those questions which tend away from the provocation of enlightenment.

> Accordingly, Malunkyaputta, bear always in mind what it is that I have not elucidated, and what it is that I have elucidated. And what . . . have I not elucidated? I have not elucidated . . . that the world is eternal; I have not elucidated that the world is not eternal; . . . I have not elucidated that the saint exists after death; I have not elucidated that the saint does not exist after death. . . . And why, Malunkyaputta, have I not elucidated this? Because . . . this profits not, nor has to do with the fundamentals of religion, nor tends to aversion, absence of passion, cessation, quiescence, the supernatural faculties, supreme wisdom, and nirvana; Therefore have I not elucidated it.[28]

The episode ends with a repetition of the Four Noble Truths, that suffering arises from selfish craving.

Seekers after beliefs were frustrated in their inquiry, and thrown back upon themselves. The reply that these questions do not lead to letting go of selfish craving has the effect of raising the question, "Why do you need to know?" The questioner may then discover that what

[27] *Majjhima-Nikaya*, Sutta 63, in Warren, *Buddhism*, 120-121.
[28] *Ibid.*, 122.

was really being sought was assurances which would facilitate letting go . "I'll let go of the little self if I become one with an eternal universe, or if some purified aspect of myself turns out to survive death." The Buddhist tradition, as portrayed in the above quotations from the Pali scriptures, is aware of the subtle ways in which we hold back from genuine yieldedness.

This is especially evident in the way in which the gods are dealt with. It seems they are not denied, but are simply regarded as of no relevance to the question of enlightenment. The gods may be able to intervene in life to help the unenlightened self achieve its worldly goals, but they are of no help in reaching salvation and, in fact, are in need of liberation themselves.

> O priests, gods and men delight in existence, take pleasure in existence, rejoice in existence, so that when the doctrine for the cessation of existence is preached to them their minds do not leap toward it, are not favorably disposed toward it, do not rest in it, do not adopt it.[29]

Gods apparently have the same problem of craving that we do; perhaps from a Buddhist point of view, this would be especially true if a god became angry and vindictive toward people who did not worship him. Again, we are thrown back on ourselves; our desire for assurances and assistance is frustrated, and perhaps this will lead to the end of selfish desire. This is neither the atheism of Camus nor the theism of Luther, but what Heinrich Zimmer has called "transtheism," the belief that while the divine is real, divine aid is irrelevant to salvation. In fact, the desire for such aid is, in the view of these early Buddhist texts, a sign of the dominance of the infantile ego.[30]

The point of this exposition of early Buddhist teaching is not to convince the reader that all is mere flux or that divine aid is irrelevant to salvation, but simply to show the unique early Buddhist approach to the question of the relation of beliefs to the reversal of intention. It may well be that subsequently Buddhist teachers offered definite beliefs about an eternal essence of all things, as seems to be the case in Saraha, and beliefs about supernatural aid toward enlightenment flowing from a multitude of heavenly Buddhas also arose. These more developed beliefs are part of what differentiates Mahayana or northern Buddhism from the more reticent Hinayana forms. The Buddha is portrayed in the Pali scriptures emphasized by Hinayana as refusing to communicate to the unenlightened anything more than what will provoke enlightenment. If the self still subject to clinging hears of eternal bliss, joy, and peace, this will only feed its craving; one will then misun-

[29] *Visuddhi-Magga*, 18, in Warren, *Buddhism*, 134.
[30] Heinrich Zimmer, *Philosophies of India* (Cleveland: World, 1956), 182, 331.

derstand the joy of nirvana as the satisfaction of the little self with all of its desires, and one will grasp after "liberation" and become more tightly bound. So positive teachings about nirvana are withheld, and it is only portrayed on its negative side as extinction, the end of the present self dominated by *tanha*.

We cannot conclude that the Buddha represents an approach to letting go which is independent of any belief-system, as is the case with Camus and Heidegger. There may well be concrete beliefs that are withheld because for the unenlightened they would keep alive the craving and clinging which are the opposite of letting go. This would surely be the view of Mahayana Buddhism, which portrays the Buddha as offering more than the minimal teaching to his closest disciples. But even in this case, the Buddha's public reticence shows a subtle perception of the way in which a belief-system may constitute just one more thing to cling to, and that letting go cannot be genuine if it waits on assurances.

This awareness did not wain even within Mahayana Buddhism when it developed more explicit beliefs about supernatural aid in reaching enlightenment or about the ultimate nature of the flux of reality. For example, in a complex of Mahayana texts called the *Prajna-paramita Sutras* an attempt is made to portray the consciousness which knows enlightenment, and in these sources it is maintained that, strictly speaking, Buddhist teaching is false from the point of view of enlightenment. Buddhism in this view is merely a ferry taking lost souls from this shore of suffering to the opposite shore of enlightenment; of course, the "wisdom that has gone to the other shore" (*prajna-paramita*) does not need Buddhist beliefs anymore than travelers need the ferry when they are on the other shore. The enlightened Buddhist knows there is no river, no two shores, and no ferryboat of Buddhist teaching; there is simply nirvana.

> The Enlightened One sets forth in the Great Ferryboat (Mahayana); but there is nothing from which he sets forth. He starts from the universe; but in truth he starts from nowhere. His boat is manned with all the perfections; and is manned by no one. It will find its support on nothing whatsoever and will find its support on the state of all-knowing, which will serve it as a non-support. Moreover, no one has ever set forth in the Great Ferryboat; no one will ever set forth in it, and no one is setting forth in it now. And why is this? Because neither the one setting forth nor the goal for which he sets forth is to be found: therefore, who should be setting forth, and whither?[31]

[31] *Ashtasahasrika Prajna-paramita*, 1, in Zimmer, *India*, 485; cf. *The Perfection of Wisdom in Eight Thousand Lines and Its Verse Summary*, trans. Edward Conze (Bolinas, Ca.: Four Seasons Foundation, 1973).

Here the Buddhist seems clear that it is not belief-systems which are the essence of faith; their importance is merely that they encourage letting go.

* * * * *

The paths represented by Camus and Heidegger, on one hand, and original Buddhism, on the other, are indeed severe, and for many a much more concrete belief-system is a vital aid in religious or personal development. But the problem of diversity and mutual contradictoriness of the many belief-systems remains.

Some can accept the fact that others differ from them, and still follow their own way. This would seem, in fact, to be a sign of living in that responsive, undefensive way which is the emerging ideal of our study. But others seek to remove what they perceive as the offense of diversity. A way of doing this that is traditional within the religions based on special divine revelation, Judaism, Christianity, and Islam, is to say one's own way is divinely revealed and other belief-systems are at best human contrivances and at worst demonic inspirations intended to confuse us about the truth. This follows necessarily from the belief that God has been fully revealed in one event or scripture. This is not as arrogant as it at first sounds, since the claim is simply that God's grace has bestowed the truth on his unworthy children, not that one has been good enough or clever enough to grasp a truth hidden from others. Still, the security of this approach depends on the denial of the validity or at least the completeness of other beliefs. Needless to say, not all Jews, Christians, and Muslims take this approach.

Another way of removing the offense, much more popular among "intellectuals" in the West because it is seemingly tolerant, is to say all religions really agree in that their core is monism, the belief that in reality all seemingly separate things are one divine essence. Appearances to the contrary, this approach is often "imperialistic" in practice, simply because what all religions are said to agree on is one's own particular belief-system. This approach follows logically from the monistic picture of the world; if all reality is permeated by the divine essence, then God must be known in every belief-system under different forms, as the one pure light is colored differently by different tints of glass. For all its apparent lack of condemnation of other ways of belief, this is often worked out as an aggressive assertion of one belief against others, just as much as is the approach based on a privileged divine revelation. It is just as intolerant to insist that all religions, although they do not admit it, are really assertions of what I believe as it is to say none has any substance but the one God has revealed to me; in fact, these two statements are identical in effect. Other religions are not taken on their own terms when they are reduced to manifestations of the "perennial philosophy," and their uniqueness is considered unimportant, part of what needlessly separates believers from one another. On the contrary, to the believer the substance of faith is precisely this uniqueness and diversity. It is one thing to say that all faiths approach one truth and none possesses it and quite another to say that all belief-systems are veiled expressions of one, the monistic.

It is useful to point this out because the reversal of intention idea is commonly associated with "monistic mysticism," the belief-system which claims that all reality is in its essence the divine. Note that of the four ancient texts studied, only one or perhaps two represent this world-view. Subsequently we have encountered the idea of reversal as a spontaneous manifestation of the human ability to find success in failure, entirely apart from any religious belief at all. So mysticism can have no exclusive claim on the paradox of intention. Monism is sometimes called a perennial philosophy, its superior merit or truth being born out by its recurrence in diverse times and cultures. But theism and, for that matter, atheism and agnosticism are as surely perennial, for there is no great and ancient cultural tradition in which the personal, transcendent God is not asserted, and none in which the relevance or existence of any divine element in reality is not denied. In India, alongside Shankara's monism we find Ramanuja's theism and the ancient atheistic tradition of Samkhya; the same is true of the traditions of China and the Mediterranean.

What seems truly universal is not some particular belief-system, but the psychological discovery we have been calling the law of the reversal of effort. In diverse belief-systems, and in their absence, people transcend the limit situations through accepting them.

This is a particular application of the claim of William James that the agreement of religions is not on the level of beliefs, but on the level of action and experience.

> When we survey the whole field of religion, we find a great variety in the thoughts that have prevailed there; but the feelings on the one hand and the conduct on the other are almost always the same, for Stoic, Christian and Buddhist saints are practically indistinguishable in their lives. The theories which Religion generates, being thus variable, are secondary; and if you wish to grasp her essence, you must look to the feelings and the conduct as being the more constant elements.[32]

The belief-systems we have encountered agree in provoking the operation of reversal and in valuing the way of being we have called responsiveness or participation.

No claim is made to have discovered the "essence" of religion or

[32] James, *Varieties*, 494.

the element common to all faiths and atheism besides. All that is said is the reversal of intention is widespread as one element in religious, philosophical, and psychological paths of fulfillment, and among the texts we have studied, the only common element is this maneuver and not any particular belief about the world. The unity of the teachings of, say, Gautama, Luther, and Camus is not in their beliefs but in their effects. This approach was foreshadowed in our study of the *Gita*, in which we noticed a remarkable openness to diversity of beliefs; as long as they have the same effect, wisdom, duty and worship, the Samkhya system, belief in a personal God, and Upanishadic monism are all the same.

In one sense, two stories with the same effect are the same story. But perhaps this is to devalue the theoretical component in the texts studied and to overstress their consequences. Some may find this observation liberating because it minimizes the importance of what to them are questionable belief-systems, but others for the same reason will find it distinctly unhelpful. For most need one story to live by and not a relativism which leaves us with none. After all, for many readers what was most interesting in the study of the ancient texts was not the repetition of the simple, rather bare idea of reversal, but the teachings unique to each text which claim to initiate us into unseen realities. Just as we cannot speak "language in general" but must speak some particular language, so most people cannot practice the paradoxical way of reversal without living within and by means of one particular story. Admitting this, let the test of whether our letting go is genuine be our willingness to entertain the suspicion that other stories may have the same effect.

* * * * *

Finally, we come to the question, Is there a way of living within a belief-system that does not constitute clinging? The desire for infallible assurances as the premise of letting go compromises the yieldedness or disposability that is supposed to characterize it; thus if letting go is to be genuine yet guided by a belief-system, then one's belief must include elements of doubt and uncertainty. The foundation of the reversal of intention is the acceptance of those insecurities which are inescapable; but this has not been done as long as our belief-system is regarded as creating total security.

Let us use as an example the Pauline-Lutheran tradition because of the great emphasis placed on beliefs in popular American versions of it. One has not accepted the precariousness of the human situation simply by accepting one's sin and guilt, while believing with unhuman certainty that this problem is nothing due to divine grace; for our precariousness includes the fallibility of the very beliefs which purport to give us assurance. Thus the way of believing which is not clinging is the way which includes doubt.

An example of this way of relating to a belief-system is found in the thought of the Protestant theologian Paul Tillich. According to Tillich, every human concept of God speaks of the fullness and mystery of the infinite in terms drawn from finite human experience; but surely the divine cannot be captured and encompassed in these merely human constructs, and so every conception of God is in one sense false. "They are symbols taken from our daily experience, and not information about . . . 'God' "[33] The truth in religious symbols and myths is that they do inculcate those attitudes and postures of trust and openness which relate us to the divine, to what Tillich calls "the power of being." In this they open up levels of reality which would otherwise be hidden, in something like the way in which the Aleuts' possession of words for the different types of snow and ice make them capable of perceiving variations unknown to me. Symbols thus "participate" in what they symbolize, making it present and active. They do this without being that sacred power which they symbolize.

> The dimension of ultimate reality is the dimension of the Holy. . . . Religious symbols are symbols of the Holy. As such they participate in the holiness of the Holy. . . .
>
> But participation is not identity; they are not themselves *the* Holy. The wholly transcendent transcends every symbol of the Holy.[34]

In Tillich's view, anything can be a symbol of the sacred "ground of being" because everything manifests it and is undergirded by it; this accounts for the immense diversity of religious visions of the sacred. By this very fact, nothing exhausts the divine or reveals all of its dimensions, and this is the falseness in every religious symbol. While religious symbols relate us to the divine, they do this by pointing beyond themselves to that which transcends them. The Buddhist would say, as useful as the pointing finger is, don't mistake it for the moon.

Thus, "God is a symbol for God."[35] In this striking phrase, the first use of the term God refers to the human symbol, the picture of a supreme being, doubtless influenced by ideas of ancient Near Eastern monarchy and patriarchal family life. The second use refers to "the power of being in everything that is." The symbol relates us to the divine without informing us about it; the attitudes of trust and yieldedness which the symbol may evoke open us to hitherto unperceived

[33] Paul Tillich, *The Dynamics of Faith* (New York: Harper and Bros., 1957), 47.

[34] Paul Tillich, *Theology of Culture* (New York: Oxford University Press, 1959), 59.

[35] Tillich, *Dynamics of Faith*, 46.

currents of healing and grace, but not everything true of a Palestinian potentate or patriarch is true of God.

> That which is the true ultimate transcends the realm of finite reality infinitely. Therefore, no finite reality can express it directly and properly. Religiously speaking, God transcends his own name.[36]

That which transforms and fulfills human lives is the "God beyond God," the power of being beyond every human representation. Here Tillich invites us to live by trust in actual sacred power and not by clinging to familiar human conceptions; letting go is clearly involved in trusting that which utterly transcends our best conceptions. Those who must have certainty first before letting go will find Tillich disconcerting. Yet it is difficult to dispute that trust is not to be placed in human beliefs, but in that to which they point; what saves is the power of being and not any conception of it.

Thus Tillich says both "yes" and "no" to religious symbols and myths, accepting their effect of relating persons to the divine power while setting aside their literalness as a limitation on the divine. Religious belief-systems are to be recognized as symbolic, yet also as indispensable to religious living. Recognition of this character of religious myth and symbol gives rise to what Tillich calls "the broken myth." "A myth which is understood as a myth, but not removed or replaced, can be called a 'broken myth.' "[37] The style of faith which can live with this tension, which in one sense doubts its own beliefs, is clearly not clinging nor does it live by assurances and certainties.

> Faith is not a theoretical affirmation of something uncertain, it is the existential acceptance of something transcending ordinary experience. Faith is not an opinion but a state. It is the state of being grasped by the power of being which transcends everything that is and in which everything that is participates.[38]

Here faith is defined as trust rather than as belief; faith is not belief in some conception of God, but trust in the reality of God beyond any and every symbol for God. It is a state of relatedness and openness to the power of being, not an unhumanly certain knowledge of it. Thus faith is not *in* beliefs, but *through* them.

As a condition rather than a set of beliefs, faith is not vulnerable to that doubt which undermines every concrete belief; that is, this style of faith has already accepted the vulnerability of all human beliefs about the ultimate, and it does not rely on the literal truth of its beliefs,

[36] *Ibid.*, 44-45.
[37] *Ibid.*, 50.
[38] Tillich, *The Courage to Be*, 172-173.

but in the absence of intellectual certainty, it simply trusts in the God beyond them. Here, just as in Camus, the threat to our belief-systems is transcended by accepting that every belief is uncertain. As Luther accepted his sinfulness and trusted in God's mercy, so Tillich says we may accept our doubts about our conceptions of God and trust in God's being beyond all conception. This leads to Tillich's concept of "absolute faith."

> We have seen that he who has the courage to affirm his being in spite of fate and guilt has not removed them. He remains threatened and hit by them. But he accepts his acceptance by the power of being-itself in which he participates and which gives him the courage to take the anxieties of fate and guilt upon himself. The same is true of doubt and meaninglessness. The faith which creates the courage to take them into itself has no special content. It is simply faith, undirected, absolute.[39]

Faith which trusts in the divine while doubting the literalness of every belief has accepted the vulnerability of belief-systems and thus transcended it.

When faith is taken to mean acceptance of a belief-system, of course doubt cannot be a part of it; you either believe or you don't. But if faith is making the central concern of your life the power of being beyond our concepts, it is compatible with doubt about the specific contents of the belief which expresses it.

> If faith is understood as belief that something is true, doubt is incompatible with the act of faith. If faith is understood as being ultimately concerned, doubt is a necessary element in it.[40]

In fact, Tillich goes so far as to say,

> Serious doubt is confirmation of faith. It indicates the seriousness of the concern, its unconditional character.[41]

For if what one is committed to is really the ultimate and not some magnified image of human powers, values, or hopes, then every concept and belief must appear partial, broken, and incomplete beside it.

Tillich recognizes religious symbols have the tendency to replace that which they symbolize. The biblical name for this is idolatry, and the symbol given the unconditional status which rightly belongs only to that for which it stands is an idol. "All idolatry is nothing else than the absolutizing of symbols of the Holy, and making them identical

[39] *Ibid.*, 176-177.
[40] Tillich, *The Dynamics of Faith*, 18.
[41] *Ibid.*, 22.

with the Holy itself."[42]

> The human mind, Calvin has said, is a continuously working factory of idols. This is true of all types of faith. Every type of faith has the tendency to elevate its concrete symbols to absolute validity. The criterion of the truth of faith, therefore, is that it implies an element of self-negation.[43]

Failing to negate the concrete content of our concept of God, we may indeed be worshipping a projection of sexist, racist, or nationalist attitudes, a humanly constructed image of our own admiration of power, wealth, and "peace of mind."

From this we could suppose that the form of belief most vulnerable to captivity by secular values is "literalism," which cannot recognize the human source of its own symbols. This indeed seems to be the case in American Protestantism, in which national policy and the values of a success ethic and a consumption economy blend nicely with being "born again."

For Tillich, literalism is resistance to recognition of the symbolic character of religious language, and in taking something historical for the sacred, it is guilty of idolatry. It takes the material of religious symbols drawn from nature and culture, and reflecting in part the values of a particular time and place, in their everyday sense, as being true of the divine. In doing this it gains assurance and vigor which is impressive but temporary, being vulnerable to erosion by critical thought.

> It is afraid of every act of demythologization. It believes that the broken myth is deprived of its truth and of its convincing power. Those who live in an unbroken mythological world feel safe and certain. They resist, often fanatically, any attempt to introduce an element of uncertainty by "breaking the myth," namely by making conscious its symbolic character. Such resistance is supported by authoritarian systems, religious or political, in order to give security to the people under their control and unchallenged power to those who exercise control.[44]

In literalism, faith is defined as belief, and it functions as a security system. It is this way of relating to belief-systems which tends to generate counterfeits of letting go.

The point in rendering this sketch of part of Tillich's thought is not to recommend his language about the Holy, but to have before us an example of a way of holding beliefs which would not compromise the act of letting go. The problem of belief-systems to which both Tillich and the Buddhist *prajna-paramita* literature are sensitive is that one

[42] Tillich, *Theology of Culture*, 60.
[43] Tillich, *Dynamics of Faith*, 97.
[44] *Ibid.*, 51.

may take the means for the end; one may live at second hand, kept at a distance from the desired fulfillment by talk about it. Belief-systems are to be valued for their effect rather than for their informational content, and yet "from this side" their content is indispensable. It is important to know the difference between seeing the moon and looking at the finger pointing to it.

* * * * *

Let us say there are three ways of being a person in the world, which we might describe in these words.

> 1. Some are at home with themselves and within their world. They feel no need to prove themselves or to secure themselves through attainments. Being thus at ease within themselves, they can attain. They are naturally themselves.
> 2. Other are strangers to the way of being which would be natural to themselves, and they do not feel at home in their world. They attempt to find a role and a place for themselves through conspicuous and feverishly pursued attainment. Being unsure of themselves, they defend their brittle accomplishments with intensity. They force themselves and insist.
> 3. Lastly, some find a way of knowledge or religion based on the words of one who was at home with himself or herself and the world. They feel no need to prove themselves or to conspicuously attain, but they must defend their knowledge and cling to their belief. They are unsure of themselves, but sure of their knowledge or their leader. They are not naturally themselves, but perhaps somewhat at ease when unchallenged and in the company of their kind. They force things, but not as much as some.

Now we might refer to these in Taoist sounding terms as (1) knowing *Tao*; (2) not knowing *Tao*; and (3) instead of knowing *Tao*, or clinging to Taoist teaching. Or, so that no one feels we are posing as oriental wisemen, and so that no one feels excluded, we could call them (1) living by faith as trust in grace, without objective certainty; (2) living by works of self-reliance; and (3) living *as if* by grace, living by faith as belief.

The mark of the third way, this conditional letting go which must have assurances and clings to a belief-system taken as literally factual, is a defensiveness about one's beliefs and traditions and a denial of the validity of other ways. This is quite different from the love of one's traditions. It is as if one is willing to become dispensable oneself, provided one's beliefs are not. In contrast to this is living in and through a belief-system which is yielded toward beliefs themselves, having experienced that to which they refer; this "releasement towards beliefs" would be able to use beliefs without becoming captive to them and would have the grace to admit that letting go and its fruits are known in many places.

Strangely, the views of the theist Tillich and the atheist Heidegger are similar. Both see human life as the manifestation of being, as a property of the field of reality, as embedded within and sustained by a larger whole. Further, while only Tillich calls this larger whole "holy," both regard it with reverence and awe. And most importantly for the problem of this chapter, both cultivate a sense of the mysteriousness of being which is beyond the grasp of our best concepts and beliefs. This attitude has a high tolerance for ambiguity and indefiniteness, and a deep humility about the inability of our ideas to grasp being, and their tendency to distort its appearance. The ability to live within the ambiguous and the enigmatic, without humanly made idols, lets the mystery of being be just itself, and refuses to reduce it or to capture and domesticate it. Thus each writer urges us to see that openness to the mystery of being is more important than beliefs about it, and that clinging to beliefs is the ideological expression of willfulness which is our life-problem; just as in action, the point is not to manipulate but to respond, so in thought, the point is not to believe but to be aware.

Chapter 12

CONCLUSION: IS LETTING GO AN ACT OF WILL? THE WAY TO DO IS TO BE

> Non-willing means, therefore: willingly to renounce willing. And the term non-willing means, further, what remains absolutely outside of any kind of will.
>
> —Martin Heidegger
> *Discourse on Thinking*

> The way to use life is to do nothing through acting. The way to use life is to do everything through being.
>
> —Witter Bynner
> *The Way of Life According to Lao Tzu*

Before proceeding to the question of how one goes about letting go, it will be helpful to look back over our inquiry thus far and to restate, integrate, and amplify what has been said. The idea we have pursued is simple. There is a universal and recurrent human experience in which the blocking of some sought for attainment leads us to modify our intention, and this is found to yield an unexpected fulfillment of its own; experiences of impossibility force us to abandon our pretensions and our intensity, and in this we surprisingly achieve either what we sought or a kind of contentment that we thought could only follow the conquest of that which blocked us. In either case, we discover that the goal is reached by giving up the attempt to reach it.

Ease in conversational relations that was never found through my efforts to be clever, self-possessed, well-informed, or concerned comes when the effort is abandoned and my ineptitude and awkwardness are accepted. My painting is labored and worried, the water colors won't flow and yield the naturalness I seek to achieve, but when I decide it's only a sketch and the real painting will come tomorrow, I relax and the sought for result appears. My running time improves when I cease to feel I cannot be second; muscles tightened in opposition to my movement relax and I cease to fight my own efforts. My concentration on what I am studying actually improves when I no longer insist on perfect grades, and I do better than I expected. Those co-workers who cannot be made to approach our task in the correct and rational way so clear to me respond to my suggestions when I cease to insist and command. That thought which will not come when I write with a pen flows out on the page when I use a pencil, realizing that that which can be erased is tentative, only a trial. The carburetor which does not fit the manifold any way I force it falls into place when I quit and idly play with it this way and that. In short, when I decide that it doesn't matter and I can't succeed, success may well come, precisely because I am at peace about the outcome; the hyperintention of the desired result made its achievement impossible, and it is reached when this intensity is abandoned.

Or, if the desired outcome is not achieved, there is at least a sense of relief, of being reconciled, of returning to reality in having abandoned the pursuit of the impossible and the unreal; here that fulfillment we thought only came to those who win, comes from letting go. A kind of peace follows from accepting the soon-coming death of my father with the same calm with which he accepts it, while I thought I could only live if I could make him live. Or, I thought my discontent came from being so often unable to say the right thing, from my having been unfair and thoughtless, from failing to be a perfect friend; but when I am accepted anyway and the relationship is resumed, I find a contentment which I had sought but could not earn. Again, when I simply shelve a certain religious idea for the time being, putting off until tomorrow my decision as to its value and truth, I find the same sense of resolution that I expected could only come if I knew for certain.

In the first set of examples, I achieve the specific attainment I sought when I give up trying because the intensity of my trying prevented me. In the second set of examples, I encounter deeper levels of impossibility for which there is no remedy, for death cannot be escaped, love earned, or doubt evaded. Here I encounter the limits of human existence and not merely personally generated obstacles. But even in these instances, a sense of settlement and consolation arises which we thought could only follow if we got what we wanted, the power to command death, love, and certainty; the condition of reaching this accord was simply that we give up the attempt to reach it in the impossible way.

Of course these examples are not recipes for success, but occasional experiences from which we may extract a meaning. The point is the essence of these everyday experiences has been generalized as an approach to life as a whole. The fact that to live is, among other things, to be in jeopardy leads us into an approach to life as a whole based on willful activity. Vaguely sensing the precariousness of our lives, our self-respect, and our surety that existence is meaningful, the tempo of our action increases as we invent new forms of defense, offense, flight, and compensation. The underlying sense of vulnerability moves us to seek a self-image based on control and mastery; action becomes coercion and manipulation with an undercurrent of strange urgency, relationships come to be based on competition and defense and loneliness grows, inquiry becomes a part of the quest for power and the sense of meaningfulness diminishes. Hyperintention brings about what is feared, and we lose the life, relationship, and sense of meaning we sought to preserve; for life based on the pursuit of victory and safety is closed in and cut off, ultimately joyless, pointless, and confronted by death as defeat. Of course, this or that fear can be handled, but the lurking anxiety about our existence cannot; problems can be solved, but our precariousness cannot be escaped. Just because it is objectless, our anxiety about our vulnerability cannot be approached as a problem, and since it remains our efforts escalate. In this way, impossibility is encountered. While some redouble their efforts, and even seek to enlist magical styles of religion in the task, others act on the wisdom derived from everyday experiences of impossibility and simply let go of counter-productive effort. When there is nothing you can do, there is nothing you need do.

The goal which recedes when we seek to approach it is found close at hand when we relax. In accepting impossibility we transcend it. What was a response to particular experiences of frustration can now be generalized as a response to the impossibility of escaping threats to life, self-esteem, and meaning. Those who apply the reversal of effort to the problem of being human find release in the acceptance of insecurity as inescapable. "Crushing truths perish from being acknowledged." Since our problem is not merely "feelings of insecurity," but the actual situation of being precarious in spite of our efforts, there is nothing to do but accept this and cease demanding the impossible. If the goal cannot be achieved, the desire for it can be relinquished, and that peace which was sought through efforts after security arises in an unexpected way. Meanwhile, the cramping, exhausting, counter-productive efforts after security can be relinquished. As intensity diminishes and one opens outward, new awareness and energy arise; the energy wasted in denial is appropriated for life. This is the recurrent theme of despair and rebirth, a total reorientation to life through the experience of impossibility.

In accepting our insecurity and relinquishing pointless efforts to deny it, we have ripened and been fulfilled. A metapsychological change has arisen in which we "let go of the foolish and inordinate part of our wills." The goal of total security being impossible, the infantile demand for it must be renounced. But this need not be understood moralistically, for we did not fall into the manipulative-defensive orientation from sinfulness or out of conscious choice, but as a reflexive response to anxiety. Adding guilt to our insecurity is not much help. Of course there is real guilt in life, popularly retailed versions of psychology notwithstanding, but we are not guilty of being finite and vulnerable.

Although our precariousness and our automatic response to it are not our choice, they are our responsibility, for while the conditions of our existence are not our doing, the fulfilled development of our being is still our task. This is part of the import of the story of Adam and Eve's sin as an inherited blight on all of humanity. To reason it seems unfair to hold the descendants culpable for the ancestor's deed. Nevertheless, the metaphor of "inherited sin" does portray our actual situation as having to take responsibility for that which we did not create, as a condition of our fulfillment. The same can be said of the *anatta* doctrine or of the idea of the absurdity of existence; this may not be the situation we choose, but we do not come to ourselves until we accept it.

In letting go and accepting our insecurity we move from self-preoccupation to disposability, from hyperintention to yieldedness. According to the proponents of the ethic of reversal, this is the fulfillment of life. It amounts to a carelessness with respect to threats and therefore includes freedom in action and openness in relationships. In this sense, it is an end in itself and not a means to something else. Thus letting go is not a magical form of achieving security, for the fact of our precariousness remains. Indeed, if we deny this, if we see letting go as a way of exacting assistance or becoming invulnerable, then it is not insecurity we have accepted. But being yielded with respect to ourselves, our vulnerability can be lived out.

We might have thought that only life lived on the basis of striving and aggression produces heroes, but, in fact, acceptance has its own heroism. In his *anatta* doctrine, Gautama the Buddha expresses his acceptance of the vulnerability of the physical self; in his conviction of "original sin," Luther accepts the insecurity of the psychological self; and in his concept of "the absurd," Camus represents his acceptance of threats to the noetic self. Each accepted his nothingness and in this paradoxical way achieved a conquest.

There is, of course, another approach to the fulfillment of life which could be called the ethic of attainment in contrast to this ethic of reversal. It is a philosophical or religious refinement of the automatic willfulness generated by our precariousness. It no doubt at times leads to great good, but it is vulnerable to the upwelling awareness of our inescapable insecurity, since it is based on an optimistic view of our situation. It is strong but brittle, and after prolonged forceful resistance to adversity, it can suddenly break. It is then, and not through the acceptance of our precariousness, that genuine desperation arises. For the reversal of effort is not despairing about life, but only despairs of making it totally secure, and it is thus able to live with affirmation. But despair is deep and genuine when one has lived by the effort to attain, when one has sought meaning solely through achievement, and then impossibility is encountered, so to speak, for the first time. The weakness of the ethic of attainment is that it is based on denial of that which is disclosed about our situation by the experience of anxiety.

This is seen most clearly in those periodic social crises which have given birth to the great historical forms of the paradox of intention. The ethic of attainment as a philosophical or religious doctrine assumes a stable society supporting a learned or sanctified aristocracy which alone can fulfill the terms of the ethic. Good deeds are done, sacrifices are performed for the gods, and people manifest their powers in education, politics, and the arts. But in times of historical crisis, the confidence placed in the ethic of attainment is shaken. Since the ethic assumes a stable society with a continuous and authoritative tradition, it is vulnerable to history. In times of warfare, revolution, confrontation with other cultures, economic collapse, or rationalistic self-criticism, confidence in our ability to fulfill life wanes. This is simply due to the fact that both the cultural tradition which defined the good authoritatively and the social institutions which supported human effort are crumbling; thus one feels no longer able to know and do the good. These are the times of self-distrust and contempt for existing institutions, times of "failure of nerve," in short, times like our own.

In such periods some form of the ethic of consolation appears in response to the historical crisis and the resultant decline of the ethic of attainment. It is an ethic based on the real experience that our attempt to fulfill life through our own efforts to know and do the good leads, in fact, to failure and frustration, and it expresses itself as a criticism of the declining ethic of attainment. Historical crisis thus sensitizes certain people to the impossibility of attainment and gives rise to the idea of the reversal of effort as a way of responding to impossibility. The despair generated by disappointed optimism thus gives rise to the rebirth made possible by various forms of the ethic of consolation.

We have only to add that these insights, once they have arisen, have a life of their own; for they are relevant in all times and places and not just in times like the Hellenistic crisis or the Warring States Period, due to the universality of the experience of the limit situations of death, disappointment, suffering, guilt, and doubt.

In letting go of the effort to attain, what is abandoned is not action but a certain way of undertaking it. As life and action are inseparable, the reversal of effort does not lead to inaction but to a new kind of action. This kind of action lies between the despair of effort and the hyperintention of effort. Having accepted our vulnerability to threats, an inner stillness arises; thus it is not necessary to stop the wheel of action in order for the center to be still. Action is now free of the burden of having to render life ultimately secure and meaningful, and compulsive defense, achievement, and compensation are unnecessary.

When action is no longer a way of dealing with or denying our precariousness, we can become genuinely involved for the first time in the act itself, and the quality of the action is raised, and even its efficiency if that is appropriate. The wheel spins more truly when the center is still. Sexuality can be playful and expressive when it no longer has the burden of proving one's adequacy or of giving life a meaning. Acts of helping and caring can be genuine and neither self-righteous nor meddlesome when action is no longer an attempt to prove oneself and rearrange the world. Artistic performance or effectiveness in work are more adequate and unhampered when we are simply doing the job at hand without having to prove ourselves. All of the examples given at the beginning of this chapter might be used again here, but now not to illustrate spontaneous discoveries of the power of reversal, but to show how action is improved when it no longer must be part of the denial of our precariousness. Action which is not attached to its results, requiring of them what they cannot give, is free and flowing.

The action of those for whom activity is not a means of ultimate security includes an element of passivity, in that one yields oneself to the precariousness of life. Yet surely it is neither pure passivity nor that strident form of action which ignores and aggresses against the medium within which action occurs. It is entirely beyond the active-passive dichotomy, and terms like participation, listening, responsiveness, waiting, and attentiveness have been used to indicate action which acts with the medium. In Taoist terms, this kind of action is aware of the male and keeps to the female. Floating is a useful analogy. If undertaken as pure activity, one's stiffness and exertion lead to fatigue and, if help is too long in coming, to drowning, while if undertaken as pure passivity, the same disastrous result is reached minus the fatigue. Floating is neither merely activity nor passivity, but a state of attentiveness, responsiveness, or participation in which one acts with and not against the movement and buoyancy of the water. One is free to do this only if the attitude of trust or yieldedness has arisen.

In the ethic of reversal one has yielded up oneself, not in the sense that one wishes for annihilation, but in the sense that the insecurity of the self is accepted. From the observation that trying to achieve happiness often led to bad results, some drew the mistaken conclusion that in order to feel good we should seek to feel bad.[1] But this is to distort reversal into a technique through which goals are to be reached; this is aggressiveness and not responsiveness. The masochistic form of the ethic of reversal, which is for all we know its most widespread manifestation, is like the strident will to attain, an attempt to deny and escape our vulnerability. It is either a form of magic which seeks to coerce divine aid through the use of suffering or a stratagem which seeks escape by annihilating the self before anything painful occurs to it. The mark of the reversal ethic in its authentic form is the willingness to accept vulnerability.

In seeking to erase the self and be absorbed in the Other, masochistic reversal tries to escape the limits of the human situation. It is like the playing dead of insects, in Nietzsche's forceful terms. It is, in another metaphor, a sign of fatigue on the part of the strident, infantile ego, which seeks to return to the oceanic oneness of the first few months of life rather than to grow up. When coercive, manipulative activity fails, there is an alternative to regression to unconscious oneness, and that is the maturation of the ego in a life lived out of responsiveness. Thus when the infantile, willful ego experiences impossibility, we may renounce the ego and regress to unconsciousness and dreams of security, or we may renounce the stridency of the ego and enter upon the process of maturing. The end of the strident self need not be the end of the self; indeed, it may be its fulfillment.

If the ethic of reversal is accused of being masochistic and regressive, it is also accused of being inhumane and self-absorbed. Thus the Buddhists describe the solitary monk as a "lonely rhinoceros" intent on his own peace of mind and lacking in compassion for the suffering of those around him. It is true that many, especially ascetic practitioners of reversal, have sought invulnerability to pain and grief by practicing detachment from possessions and persons. As in the discussion of masochism, the mark of inauthenticity here is the desire to escape from vulnerability rather than to accept it. But just as yieldedness toward the self is not suicide, spiritual or physical, so yieldedness toward those we love is not withdrawal of care and affection. We found that responsiveness is neither passivity nor activity, so "releasement toward things" is neither attachment nor detachment. In the same way that responsiveness may accomplish tasks, so releasement may cherish persons. But it does so without clinging, and without asking that the other be an invulnerable, unchanging, and undying part of my security system. Releasement toward one who is loved lets that one be, accepts his or her precariousness, and does not cling to the other as a way of

[1] Hora, *Existential Metapsychiatry*, 168.

attaining security. As we pass beyond the dichotomy of active and passive, so we pass beyond that of attachment and detachment.

Every religious expression of the ethic based on letting go predicated itself on particular beliefs about the self and the world, however differently they were conceived. But surely clinging to beliefs and the assurances they give renders letting go false. Some clearly can practice reversal in the absence of any assurance that reality is supportive of the yielded self. Thus in one view, since reversal is found in diverse traditions, it cannot be dependent on any one of them; and further, it appears as a repeatedly rediscovered response to impossibility apart from any beliefs at all. Therefore, some conclude that it amounts to a psychological discovery and can be employed in life solely on these terms.

But according to others, it may not be necessary to renounce beliefs absolutely, but only to renounce clinging to them. In this view, beliefs are a means to letting go, a guide to discovering the buoyancy of the water, not an end in themselves; our trust would then be in the letting be of being, not in any particular concept of being. As we may practice yieldedness toward the self and toward others, we may be yielded about our beliefs. After all, since two stories with the same effect are in a sense the same story, the specificity of the stories cannot be as important as their effect in provoking letting go.

Looking at the great religious and philosophical expressions of the reversal idea, we notice that each claimed when we act rightly, in the mode called participation, without defensiveness or coercion, then it is not we who act, but nature, God's grace, the *Tao*, the Innate Buddha, *prakriti*, or being; something else acts, and I am to be attentive. My action thus participates in a larger vitality in which my life is embedded. While one might use such belief to practice "bad faith" and thus evade responsibility, at its best this is the belief that when we are neither passive nor stridently assertive, but attentive, then our behavior is met by a sustaining response from reality.

Our over-beliefs rush in at this point and give us assurances that all is well, our security is at hand, and we need no longer accept precariousness, but are delivered from it. But in this, belief again becomes something to which to cling. If we refuse this, we are left with this common factor in the traditional and modern expressions of the idea of reversal: life is embedded in a larger sustaining whole, and yieldedness to this, participation within it, is the fulfillment of human existence; but we should add, this does not save us from our essential vulnerability. Our trust should be in the experienced buoyancy of the water and not in any belief about why it must be so, or that no one ever drowns.

* * * * *

Now we may proceed to the problem of this chapter, which is simply, "How do I go about letting go? Is reversal itself an act of will, something I can do?" This will in turn shed light on what has emerged as our central concern, the way of being that is neither active nor passive.

Heidegger described meditative thinking as non-willing, and then went on to say that non-willing is itself an act of will for we will to cease willing. Yet, he also claimed that, viewed in another way, it is something entirely different from willing, precisely because it is cessation of the will. Clearly we are dealing with a question that does not yield readily to the assumptions of our black-and-white thinking, according to which at every moment we must be either active or passive.

It is possible to see letting go as an act of will. The psychologist Rollo May quotes a patient in the process of overcoming impotence as saying he willed to let go of his intense concern for performance.[2] Epictetus, the Stoic, sees the events of the great world as beyond the reach of our will, but claims that our desires and responses are within the power of will; thus if we will to accept whatever comes to us, we shall have peace. It might sound as if we are to willfully manage desire and response, controlling and repressing our emotional life. Yet read more sympathetically, we see that willing in Stoicism is directed at letting go of the willful demand that reality suit my desire. In any case, the peace of *ataraxia* does not arise as my attainment, but as a by-product of abandoning the effort to attain. Similarly, the preaching of the Pauline-Lutheran message characteristically calls the hearer to repent and to ask for divine forgiveness. There is a responsibility here, something to be undertaken.

But responsibility means "ability to respond," and so perhaps we should not see ourselves as the only actors, and letting go as merely a deed to be accomplished. Continuing with the example of Paul, in his letters faith itself is seen as a divine gift (I Cor. 12.9); there is literally nothing of which a person could boast in the process of salvation, for even faith is a gift and not an achievement. The Christian life should be seen as a task and a responsibility, but ultimately as God's work in the heart of the believer.

> You must work out your own salvation in fear and trembling; for it is God who works in you, inspiring both the will and the deed, for his own chosen purpose. (Phil. 2.12-13, *N.E.B.*)

Viewed from the human side, something must be done, but viewed from the divine side, God alone is the doer. The centuries-long discussion of the interrelation of divine grace and human free will in the

[2] May, *Love and Will*, 281.

genesis of faith is a reflection of the difficulty of our question. If faith itself is an act of God's grace, then letting go is not merely a deed, but the first breaking forth of that way of being we have called responsiveness or participation, which is beyond the active-passive dichotomy. This is Heidegger's second observation about what he calls non-willing, for it is not an act of will, but entirely apart from willing.

We can better approach this chapter's question if we return to Frankl's discussion of the relation of hyperintention to sleep. How do you go to sleep? Sleep will be prevented by the hyperintention to achieve it, and this makes clear that we are asking the wrong question when we ask of the reversal of intention, "How do you do it?" In an earlier chapter, Hora's example of swimming as responsiveness to the buoyancy of water was used to show that letting go is not merely passive. The lines quoted from Hora are preceded by these words.

> People who have difficulty in learning to swim, probably have in the back of their minds the wrong questions. How do you do it? What would be the right question? What is swimming? Swimming is floating.[3]

Then follows his description, previously quoted, of floating as neither willfulness nor passivity, but as attentiveness to the medium. Similarly with letting go, we should ask not "How do you go about it?" but "What is it?" The answer is responsiveness. If we hear of the reversal of effort and ask, "How do we do it?" the reply we receive is that it is not a doing, but the cessation of doing. The way you become responsive and being responsive are the same thing. In this case, the means is the end. The way to do is to be.

Now it is clear why the moralistic approach to the problem of willfulness and letting go is unhelpful. The reversal of intention should not be seen as a commandment that we could obey as an act of will, because it is not an act of will in the ordinary sense. It is participation in the reality of some particular situation.

One last aspect of the question of how reversal arises is raised by the use of techniques in both logotherapy and Zen. Few people can generate a sense of reality by thinking abstractly about "accepting death or guilt or meaninglessness." But apparently there have developed certain exercises focused on more tangible matters that can give us the experience of participation or attentiveness, the experience of being rather than doing.

Zen is rich in such exercises. In the practice of calligraphy the student inscribes a Japanese character on a very thin paper using a large brush and a watery medium. Any willful, highly controlled, studied approach will be revealed as such by the poor result; the ink will run

[3] Hora, *Existential Metapsychiatry*, 60.

and puddle, the character will appear stiff and its texture scrubbed, or the page will tear. Only spontaneity, which is careless about the result, achieves a good outcome. In the tea ceremony, elaborate preparations and procedures are studied and practiced. It would seem that the emphasis on ceremonious correctness would invite hyperintention; but when the procedure is mastered, one acts it out without acting, finding a way of being when doing becomes automatic. Now the minute particulars of taste, aroma, gesture, texture, and even sound are sensed in surprising fullness; when we cease to contrive, we are open to experience. In the practice of archery, it is evident that hyperintention can spoil the result, and so the archer is instructed to look away from the target and to realize that the target, the archer, and the arrow are, in Zen belief, already one. Hyperintention is defeated and the target is more likely to be hit. In *jujitsu* and *judo*, it is discovered that the willfulness of one's opponents can be used to defeat them, and so we learn maneuvers in which rather than meeting force with opposing force, we go with the movement of the attacker and turn that energy to our own advantage. What keeps the attackers from falling is my resistance, but when this is withdrawn, they fall through their own intensity. (In a sense, this is the way Kutuzov defeats the armies of Napoleon in Tolstoi's *War and Peace*, by constant retreat.) Finally, in flower arranging, one succeeds only if there is attentiveness to the given characteristics of the flowers; if they are "arranged," they appear contrived and unnatural, but if they are placed in a way that derives from responsiveness to their unique character, they appear at their best.

In each instance, some activity near at hand is taken as a way of discovering attentiveness; the proximate problem is, by an act of indirection, substituted for the ultimate problem. In every case, we receive tangible results, and we come to know that hyperintention spoils our action and that the reversal of intention perfects it. Whereas in other activities, "negative feedback" tells us to try harder, in these activities it means, try less, let go.

The most widespread technique of immersing the learner in the experience of participation is meditation. It is not always noticed that this, too, is an instance of indirection, of substituting a proximate problem for the ultimate one. For in meditation one does not really seek "the ultimate truth" or "knowledge of the real." The problem is much simpler, how to clear the mind. If you approach the instruction to be empty in a willful way, and fight against each instrusive thought, feeling, or image, the clutter and turmoil merely increase. Then you may discover that when intrusions are expected and accepted, a kind of peace arises which could not be achieved by will. Now the student may wonder when the great insight will arise, but it is already present as an experience.

A manual of Buddhist meditation illustrates the principle of "clear the mind by letting be" in this instruction regarding how to handle intrusions into the sought-for state of mindfulness.

> One should not allow oneself to be irritated, annoyed or discouraged by the occurrence of distracting or undesirable thoughts, but should simply *take these disturbing thoughts themselves as (temporary) objects of one's mindfulness*, making them thus a part of the practice. . . . Should feelings of irritation about one's distracted state of mind arise and persist, one may deal with them in the very same way; that is, take them as an opportunity for Contemplation of Mind Objects. . . .
>
> The same method should be applied to interruptions from outside. If there is, for instance, a disturbing noise, one may take brief notice of it as "sound;" if it was immediately followed by annoyance about the disturbance, one should register it, too, as "mind with anger." . . .
>
> In that way, disturbances of the meditative practice can be transformed into useful objects of the practice; and what appeared inimical, can be turned into a friend and teacher.[4]

This clarifies a puzzle encountered earlier regarding the nature of the state of mind sought in oriental meditation practice; in this instance, the point does not seem to be to achieve "consciousness which has no object," but consciousness that is not attached to its passing objects. Here we have in a concrete and limited experience a full recapitulation of the meaning of the paradox of intention. The goal of mindfulness that could not be forced arises when one lets be, and success in clearing the mind is achieved in spite of the apparent failure represented by intrusions, indeed, because of them. This example of mindfulness in an early phase of the course of Buddhist meditation is a tangible example of "responsiveness to whatever is real moment by moment."

The conclusion of this final inquiry in our study is that while letting go is not a willful deed in the usual sense of the term, there are both codified practices and spontaneous occasions in everyday experience through which we can be rather than do. In this time of the rush hour of the spiritual self-help manuals, it is necessary to balance this small concession to method with a reminder: the message of those texts which contained the ideas of *ataraxia*, *pistis*, *wu-wei*, and *nirvana* is that we suffer from an excess of technique.

[4] Nyanaponika Thera, *The Heart of Buddhist Meditation, a Handbook of Mental Training Based on the Buddha's Way of Mindfulness* (London: Rider, 1969), quoted in F. J. Streng, et al., *Ways of Being Religious* (Englewood Cliffs, N.J.: Prentice-Hall, 1973), 279. Emphasis occurs in original text.

Printed in Great Britain
by Amazon.co.uk, Ltd.,
Marston Gate.